The First Sultan of Zanzibar

The First Sultan of Zanzibar

Scrambling for Power and Trade
in the Nineteenth-Century
Indian Ocean

BEATRICE NICOLINI

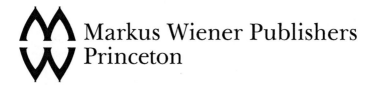 Markus Wiener Publishers
Princeton

First Markus Wiener Publishers paperback edition, 2012

Originally published in English by Brill, Leiden, The Netherlands, copyright © 2004

Copyright © 2002 for the original Italian edition (*Il Sultanato di Zanzibar nel XIX secolo: traffici commerciali e relazioni internazionali*) by L'Harmattan-Italia, Torino

This research and its publication have been made possible thanks to the financial contributions and sponsorship of the following institutions:
  The Catholic University of the Sacred Heart, Milan, Italy, within its programs of scientific research.
  The Society for Arabian Studies, The British Academy, London, which awarded the author a grant in 2003.
  The Ministry of National Heritage and Culture, Sultanate of Oman.

On the cover: This painting, privately owned by Beatrice Nicolini, was given to her by her mother, Giovanna Benedini, in hopes of inspiring her daughter's studies and writing. Portrayed in the image is a universally understood dream—the beginning of a new and a better life, in which all sorrows have been forgotten, all injustices forgiven.

For information, write to: Markus Wiener Publishers
231 Nassau Street, Princeton, NJ 08542
www.markuswiener.com

Library of Congress Cataloging-in-Publication Data
Nicolini, Beatrice.
  [Sultanato di Zanzibar nel XIX secolo. English]
  The first sultan of Zanzibar : scrambling for power and trade in the nineteenth-century Indian Ocean / Beatrice Nicolini. — 1st Markus Wiener Publishers pbk. ed.
  p. cm.
  Originally published in English: Leiden ; Boston : Brill, 2004, with title Makran, Oman and Zanzibar.
  Includes bibliographical references and indexes.
  ISBN 978-1-55876-544-3 (pbk. : alk. paper)
  1. Zanzibar—History—To 1890. 2. Zanzibar—Foreign relations. 3. Zanzibar—Commerce—History—19th century. 4. Indian Ocean—Commerce—History—19th century. I. Title.
  DT449.Z27N5313 2012
  967.8'102—dc23
                    2011026655

Markus Wiener Publishers books are printed in the United States of America on acid-free paper and meet the guidelines for permanence and durability of the Committee on Production Guidelines for Book Longevity of the Council on Library Resources.

To Cesare Nicolini, my father,
who believes in dreams coming true

CONTENTS

PART I

PART II

MAPS AND ILLUSTRATIONS

Illustrations can be found on pages 71 to 74f

1. Portrait of Saiyid bin Sultan Al Bu Sa'id, Zanzibar National Museum, Zanzibar, Tanzania. Fieldwork, 1994.

2. Omani Fort at Gwadar. Fieldwork, 1997.

3. African houses (*makuti*), Jozani Forest, Zanzibar, Tanzania. Fieldwork, 1994.

4. Map of the coasts of Oman and Baluchistan.

5. English translation of one of Napoleon's intercepted letters.

PREFACE TO THE PAPERBACK EDITION

Land and maritime realities before and after the European 'Empires' constituted crucial issues throughout the history of the Western Indian Ocean. In this study, I try to focus on more than one littoral and on more than one region, with the object of analyzing different perspectives both chronological and methodological. I am aware of the role of the Empires in these seas and on these lands, as well as of the ethnocentric views (Eurocentric included) which accompanied numerous studies for a long time, and sometimes still do. The present volume is a long, challenging 'voyage' across a vast area, with many protagonists but also with many actors with no voice. The 'voyage' could have started from Oman, which was part of a global unity[1] that long preceded the economic unification of the world starting in the sixteenth century, as well as the more recent processes of 'globalisation'.

Along the shores of the Western Indian Ocean, the myriad trade relations among the people of the Asian, Arabian, and East African coasts stretched back to time immemorial. Such connections and relationships built on trade and power were to be sought in those elements that constituted the 'equilibrium' of the Western Indian Ocean, that is, in the monsoons, in the presence of commercial thalassocracies (the 'merchant-states'), in the predominance of mercantile laws, and in the trade routes for spices, ivory, and slaves. Starting from the sixteenth century onwards, the European desire for conquest of commercial monopolies in the slave trade, and in all those endeavors essential to the creation of multiple ties, contributed to the consolidation of a 'red thread'[2] which would link three continents: Europe, Asia, and Africa.

Oman international trade activities throughout four centuries—from 1500 to the 1800s—saw numerous waves of political

---

[1] Here I'd like to stress the global dimensions but not the 'globalised' ones.

[2] This expression, more pertinent to European historiography, is here used to refer metaphorically to the red color of the Omani flag. In effect, the sovereigns of Oman, between the eighteenth and nineteenth centuries, established numerous mercantile and political-strategic concessions along the shores of the Persian/Arab Gulf and of the Western Indian Ocean.

leaders, brave seafarers, valorous merchants, and adventurers in an escalating competition between leaders and merchants from every part of Asia and Africa, as well as from Europe and the newly created United States.[3] During the period that saw the rise of European powers in the Western Indian Ocean, according to available historiography, a 'revolution' occurred from which new 'protagonists' emerged in the Asian, Arabian, and African regions. Against these backdrops, the gradual emergence of new Omani dynasties resulted from the polarization that followed the struggle against the Portuguese presence in the Persian/Arab Gulf and in the Western Indian Ocean. This struggle gave rise to gradual and discontinuous processes of unification among the Omani groups—traditionally divided and in conflict with each other—which came to the fore in the progressive affirmation of what we might define as the 'international power of the Omani Arabs' in the Persian/Arab Gulf and in the Western Indian Ocean.

The history of the international trade relations of Oman[4] has been closely connected mainly to the maritime routes across the Western Indian Ocean: sailing the Persian/Arab Gulf and the Western Indian Ocean had always depended on the winds, which occur in an annual sequence with great regularity. The 'balance' created by the monsoons[5] was achieved over a period of a year, revealing the following rhythm: from December to March, the monsoon blows from Arabia and the western coasts of India, pushing as far as Mogadishu to the northeast. The winds are light and constant, the climate hot and dry. In April, the monsoon starts to blow from the southwest, from East Africa towards the coasts of the Persian/Arab Gulf, the climate cooler but much more humid. The rains come mainly in April and May, while the driest months are November and December. Moreover, along the

---

[3] W. Gilbert, *Our Man in Zanzibar: Richard Waters, American Consul (1837-1845)*, thesis submitted to the faculty of Wesleyan University in partial fulfillment of the requirements for the Degree of Bachelor of Arts with Departmental Honors in History, Middleton, CT, April 2011. Gilbert discusses my 2004 interpretations highlighting American relations with the first sultan of Zanzibar.

[4] The word *Oman* was used by Europeans to describe all of southeastern Arabia lying to the east of the sands of the Rub'al Khali.

[5] The term derives from the Arabic *mawsin* (pl. *mawasin*) season, from the Portuguese *monção*.

East African coasts and on the islands of the Indian Ocean, the tropical climate is always tempered by sea breezes.

Since ancient times until the nineteenth century, sailing from Arabia in November in a south-southwesterly direction took thirty to forty days in ideal weather conditions, while, in December, due to the stabilization of the monsoon, the voyage took only twenty to twenty-five days. Consequently, thanks to the monsoons, the international trade relations of Oman had been historically through the sea—although we must remember that Oman trade was significant on land as well. Maritime coastal trading, as well as long distance trading, constituted the expressions of an economy that was already highly sophisticated, developed, and organized; therefore, the necessity for 'controlling' these sea trade routes prompted a crucial development: a political element.

During the sixteenth century, the Portuguese presence in the Persian/Arab Gulf did not really affect Oman trades; nevertheless, after the loss of Hormuz in 1622, the Portuguese increased their influence at Muscat while the Ya'ariba threatened the Portuguese forts along the coast of Oman, as well as the trade in pearls from Julfar and in horses from Muscat.

From the eleventh to the seventeenth century, the Ya'ariba dynasty empowered Oman foreign trade through an active naval policy against the Portuguese, combined with an expansion of their mercantile influence in sub-Saharan East Africa. During the eighteenth century, the Ya'ariba stood at the head of a flourishing mercantile 'reign' that was closely linked to the coastal cities and the principal islands of East Africa. The Ya'ariba Omani domination along East African littorals, which included Mombasa and the island of Pemba, was characteristic of quite normal changes in 'dominion' over the seas, without resulting in substantial alterations in traditional commercial organization. The presence of 'Arab' representatives was always merely so as to 'control' trade and impose taxes; this institution had its roots in the traditional Omani system of exercising power, as well as in the political agreements with local 'chiefs' and 'rulers'. In this regard, the Ya'ariba, often assisted by merchants from the coasts of western India, and defended by Asian troops, carried to the coasts of sub-Saharan East Africa the Omani power system, in which the notion of central government did not exist. After centuries of relative prosperity, the traditional thalassocratic system that had developed along the shores of the Western Indian Ocean was gradually shattered by the Europeans, who began to expand their mercantile and territorial ambitions, pursued obstinately and with determination from land (terra firma) to the seas.

The Ya'ariba society was a rich and powerful merchants and landlords society, and numerous forts were built in Oman during the Ya'ariba period. The round fort of Nizwa was started during the reign of Sultan bin Saif I (r. 1649–1680), while his son Bal'arab (r. 1688–1692) built the magnificent fort of Jabrin. Saif bin Sultan I (r. 1692–1711) was the greatest of the Ya'ariba princes and was succeeded by his eldest son Sultan bin Saif II, who in turn was succeeded as Imam in 1719 by his son Saif bin Sultan II, a boy of twelve. Unable to find any further support for his cause in Oman, he turned to Persia for help, and his country was soon invaded by a large Persian force. The Omanis suffered many defeats but were finally aided by Ahmad bin Sa'id (r. 1792–1804)—a member of the small Al Bu Sa'id group—who, at that time, was governor of the Omani town of Sohar. He succeeded in driving out the Persians and, after having overcome the Ya'ariba family and their Ghafari supporters, was elected Imam and founded the present Al Bu Sa'id dynasty.

The title of Imam gave Ahmad bin Sa'id Al Bu Sa'id a certain 'control' over Oman, and under him and his successors the country underwent expansion for more than a century. The Omanis extended their influence into the interior and into part of the present-day United Arab Emirates (U.A.E.), consisting of the future states of Abu Dhabi, Ajman, Al Fujayrah, Dubai, Ras al Khaymah, Sharjah, and Umm al Qaywayn. They also collected tributes from as far away as present-day Bahrain and Iraq. The Al Bu Sa'id conquered the Dhofar region, which is part of present-day Oman but was not historically part of the region of Oman. Although Ahmad bin Sa'id Al Bu Sa'id had succeeded in 'uniting' Oman under an Ibadi Imamate, the religious nature of his family's authority did not last long. His son, Saiyid Sa'id bin Sultan Al Bu Sa'id (r. 14 September 1806–19 October 1856), was elected to the Imamate after him, but no other family member won the official approval of the religious establishment. The Al Bu Sa'id called themselves *sultans*, a secular title having none of

the religious associations of Imam. They further distanced themselves from Ibadi traditions by moving their capital from Rustaq,
a traditional Ibadi center in the interior, to the port trading center of Muscat. The result was that the traditional conflictual relationships between the coast and the interior were reconstituted.
Starting from the eighteenth century, groups from the interior
gradually began to settle in the new coastal centers.

During the nineteenth century, the picturesque bay of the
Omani town of Muscat was a semicircle, enclosed by mountains
and overlooking rocks down to the sea on which fortifications
had been built to serve as lookouts for enemies. Surrounded by
walls and with a green valley beyond the shore, the town was a
pleasant place. The hinterland of Muscat is so mountainous that,
in the nineteenth century, it could be reached only on camel or
donkey; just outside the town the coast was mainly desert—hilly
and desolate. Water resources have always been scarce in Oman;
it is no surprise that, in 1800, the famous sweet, clean water of
Muscat was costly.[6]

A varied and vivacious world animated Muscat, thanks in part
to international trade: merchants from all over travelled there—
Arabs, Indians, Hebrews, Turks, Armenians, Africans, Persians.
The dwellings were *barasti*, huts made of rovings of palm leaves
and mud, although some were also constructed of stone and
madrepore. The Matrah market (*suq*), near Muscat, was spread
over a large area, almost entirely built upon with dwellings and
narrow and winding alleyways. Here, every kind of merchandise
could be found—silk and linen, spices, dates, coffee brought
across the desert by caravans, pearls, green and black grapes, bananas, figs, butter, fowl, goats, cattle, and even delicious mangos
imported mainly by sea. The rich Omani merchants wore long,
wide robes of extraordinarily clean, white cotton, with wide
sleeves and waists bound by belts from which emerged their
beautiful silver knives (*khanjars*) and swords. The most imposing
were the Baluch, from Baluchistan (today Pakistan/Iran): soldiers naked to the waist and armed with a knife and a double-
handed sword, sporting fierce glares and a threatening presence.

Since the end of the eighteenth century, the Al Bu Saʾid had

---

[6] P. Ward (Ed.), *Travels in Oman*, Cambridge, Cambridge University Press,
1987, p. 4.

empowered mercantile expansion towards the oceanic coasts of
Africa; thus, within the Western Indian Ocean there developed
a cultural 'ribbon' represented by continuous migratory flows.
During the nineteenth century, the 'dominions' of Muscat consisted of the island of Bahrain, the coast of Makran, some areas
along the Persian coast such as Chah Bahar, the island of Socotra,
the islands of Kuria Muria, the islands of Zanzibar and Pemba,
and adjacent ports on the East African coast from Cape Guardafui to Cabo Delgado. And it was in this very period that the presence of so many economic opportunities on the East African
littorals became a potent factor leading to the Omani Sultanate
of Zanzibar. Indeed, in 1840, Saiyid Sa'id bin Sultan Al Bu Sa'id
moved his capital from Muscat to Zanzibar, and he officially
became the first *sultan* of Zanzibar.[7]

What was described as the 'lucrative movement of goods'
traded by Oman throughout the Western Indian Ocean encom-
passed every type of merchandise and spice—for the most part
precious. To name but a few: rhubarb, borax, ginger, sesame,
ivory, tortoiseshell, rhino horn, beeswax, opium poppies, exotic
animal skins, birds of prey, diamonds, vermilion, gold, horses,
raffia, silk (which the Omanis believed to have protective powers
against disease and parasites), castor oil, tamarind, cloves, vanilla,
curry, nutmeg,[8] rubber, tropical fruit, mocha coffee (much in
fashion in Europe at the beginning of the second half of the seventeenth century), Chinese ceramics sometimes used in Oman
as precious containers for dates, musk from Tibet and China, and
enormous quantities of ambergris[9] bought on the shores of the

---

[7] The year 1840 is not the one given in all available documents and sources;
the event could have taken place at some other point between 1839 and 1842.
The discrepancy may possibly be due to the 'gaps' between official recognition
by nineteenth-century European powers and the local political realities. B.
Nicolini, *The Makran-Baluch-African Network in Zanzibar and East Africa during
the XIX century*, in S. de Silva and J.P. Angenot (Eds.), *Uncovering the History of
Africans in Asia*, Leiden, Brill Academic Publishers, 2009, pp. 81-106.

[8] The plant originally came from India, Burma, and China (in the Persian
annals it can be found under 'Chinese bark'); the Arab traders were careful not
to reveal where they obtained cinnamon.

[9] Ambergris was found floating in tropical water or could be obtained from
whales. The Arabs brought this precious product to the West and to China
where, from the ninth century, it was known as dragon's saliva; ambergris was
also an important fixing agent for the essences extracted from flowers.

island of Zanzibar or the nearby islands and considered a delicacy by the Omanis, who even put it in their sorbets!

We know that ivory was exported from the eastern coast of Africa in considerable quantities from an early date, and also rhino horn, tortoiseshell, and rocky crystal. In 1800, the principal products exported from the eastern coast of Africa and from Zanzibar included cloves, copal, ivory, hides, red pepper, sesame, copra, coconut oil, tortoiseshell, cowries, beeswax, and tallow. Imported goods included cotton, arms, powder, Venetian beads, clocks, spirits, wheaten flour, refined sugar, brass wire, glassware, chintz, and chinaware.

Major exports from Zanzibar to Oman included ivory, cloves, copal, sandalwood, coconuts, hippo teeth, cowries, rafters, rhino horn, beeswax, and ebony. The Omani seafarers from the Red Sea carried Venetian beads, coffee, aloes, and dragon's blood; those from the southern coast of Arabia sold dried fish, fish oil, ghee, and onions; and those from Oman and the Persian/ Arab Gulf brought to East Africa dates and raisins, donkeys and horses, Muscat cloths, Persian carpets and silks, nankeen, crude gunpowder, almonds, and drugs (mainly saffron and asafoetida). The Omanis also brought honey, waterjugs, ready-to-wear clothes, rosewater,[10] and gold and silver thread. The most important Arab purchase from Africa was slaves, followed by ivory tusks, cloves, coconuts, and rafters. With Europe and, beginning in 1833, with the newly created United States of America, Oman bartered coconuts, tortoiseshell, red peppers, and beeswax in exchange for hardware, cotton wool, and fabric.

The power of the Al Bu Sa'id sultans of Oman was widely known to be based on a delicate balance of forces and of ethnic and social groups that were characterized by deep differences among them. In fact, the constituents that composed the nineteenth-century Omani leadership were, and had always been, generally from three different ethnic groups: the Baluch, the Asian merchant communities, and the African regional leaders (*Mwiny Mkuu*). Within this framework, the roles played by European powers—particularly by the treaties to abolish slavery and regulate

---

[10] The famous Omani perfume, Amouage, is still today produced from Arab roses and from many of these ancient products and spices.

the arms trade that were signed between the sultans of Oman and the East India Company—were crucial to the development of the Persian/Arab Gulf and the Western Indian Ocean international networks. They contributed significantly to the gradual shifting of the Omanis from the slave trade to clove and spice cultivation—the major economic resource on the island of Zanzibar—along the coastal areas of sub-Saharan East Africa.

Cloves (*Eugenya Caryophyllata*, from the Mirtacee family; *kavafuu* in Kiswahili) had been introduced onto this tropical island at the end of the eighteenth century. Saiyid Sa'id bin Sultan Al Bu Sa'id galvanized in the Western Indian Ocean an important mercantile empire that was supported by the cultivation of cloves in Zanzibar and the Pemba islands (*Unguja*) and the expansion of the spice trade in general. The other main factors contributing to the rise of a mighty maritime trade network were the slave trade; ivory exports; and the region's association with the European powers of the nineteenth century.

Saiyid Sa'id bin Sultan Al Bu Sa'id spoke Arabic, Hindi, Persian, and Swahili; he had seen the island of Zanzibar for the first time in 1802, when he was only eleven years old—and he had remained bewitched.[11] The cultivation of cloves influenced Al Bu Sa'id's perception of Zanzibar's economic-commercial potential. Through significantly expanding this cultivation, he became the major exponent of the revaluation of the spice trade as a means of creating a power elite. This development was one of the first major thrusts in the growing importance of maritime trade. The creation of a new niche of agricultural exploitation in Zanzibar itself and in Pemba was destined to transform the islands of Zanzibar and Pemba into new centers of global mercantile interests.

---

[11] Among the numerous biographies of Saiyid Sa'id bin Sultan Al Bu Sa'id, see, for example, J.G. Lorimer, *Gazetteer of the Persian Gulf, Oman and Central Arabia*, Superintendent Government Printing, Calcutta, 1915, 2 vols., Vol. 1, pp. 440-469; R.S. Ruete, *Said Bin Sultan (1791-1856): Ruler of Oman and Zanzibar. His Place in the History of Arabia and East Africa*, London, Ouseley, 1929; R.S. Ruete, *The Al Bu Said Dynasty in Arabia and East Africa*, "Journal of the Royal Asiatic and Central Asian Society", Vol. 16, London, 1929, pp. 417-432; S.A.S. Farsi, *Seyyid Said Bin Sultan. The Joint Ruler of Oman and Zanzibar (1804-1856)*, New Delhi, Lancers Books, 1986; V. Maurizi, *History of Seyd Said, Sultan of Muscat*, London, 1819 (new ed., Cambridge, Cambridge University Press, 1984).

On 19 October 1856, Saiyid Sa'id bin Sultan Al Bu Sa'id died on a dhow[12] that was taking him from Muscat towards his favorite island, Zanzibar. His death was followed, on 5 July 1857, by that of Atkins Hamerton, the British Consul, himself in Zanzibar. The Al Bu Sa'id 'dominions' in Muscat and on Zanzibar were divided under the terms of the settlement of 13 May 1861 (with Zanzibar having to pay 40,000 Maria Theresa talers[13] to Muscat annually) and formalized by the Canning Award, confirmed by the Anglo-French Agreement of 1862. With this division, the 'possessions' were allocated to the sons of Saiyid Sa'id bin Sultan Al Bu Sa'id. Majid bin Sa'id Al Bu Sa'id (r. 1856-1870), born of an Ethiopian mother, became sultan of Zanzibar, and Thuwayni bin Sa'id Al Bu Sa'id (r. 1856-1866), born of a Georgian mother, became sultan of Muscat.

The epoch of the first sultan of Zanzibar had ended forever. Nevertheless, none of the Omani sultans really 'controlled', in the modern European sense, the East African coast from Cape Guardafui to Cabo Delgado.[14] Rather, the Western Indian Ocean endured a continuous scramble for power, as well as a series of territorial claims of control and mercantile dominance over a large—and remarkably undefined—area. Here, regional and international trade followed ancient distributions of forces and ancient routes through land as well as sea.[15] And it is precisely in these Indian Ocean routes and their profound vitality that we should search for new explanations of the past—as well as of the present.

Milan, June 2011

---

[12] *Daw* is a Swahili name, not used by the Arabs but adopted by English writers in the incorrect form 'dhow'. G.F. Hourani, *Arab Seafaring*, Princeton, Princeton University Press, 1951 (rev. ed., 1995), p. 89; D. Agius, *Classic Ships of Islam: From Mesopotamia to the Indian Ocean*, Leiden, E.J. Brill, 2008.

[13] M.R. Broome, *The 1780 Restrike Talers of Maria Theresa*, Doris Stockwell Memorial Papers, No. 1, reprinted in "Numismatic Chronicle", VII Series, Vol. XII, London, 1972, pp. 221-253; C. Semple, *A Silver Legend: The Story of the Maria Theresa Thaler*, "Barzan Studies in Arabian Culture", No. 1, Manchester, 2005.

[14] J.G. Deutsch, *The Indian Ocean and a Very Small Place in Zanzibar*, in J.G. Deutsch (Ed.), *Space on the Move. Transformations of the Indian Ocean Seascape in the Nineteenth and Twentieth Centuries*, Berlin, Verlag, 2002, pp. 61-73.

[15] The declaration of a British Protectorate over Zanzibar in 1890 translated into a bureaucratic effort to 'control' traditional maritime trade.

ACKNOWLEDGMENTS

I wish to express my gratitude to the Presidency of the Faculty of Political Science, and to the Department of Political Science of the Università Cattolica del Sacro Cuore, Milan, Italy, for having made this study possible.

For research conducted in Great Britain, I would like to thank Penelope Tuson, Director of the Middle East Research Project, The British Library, London; Prof. Anderson, Senior Lecturer in the History of Africa, School of Oriental and African Studies (SOAS), University of London; Prof. William Gervase Clarence-Smith, SOAS, University of London for his valuable advice; Timothy Collison and Janet C. Turner, staff members of The Royal Geographical Society, London; Brian Scott, Head of the Readers' Service, SOAS, University of London; Christopher Gutkind, Librarian, SOAS, University of London; the Students' Union, SOAS, University of London; and Dr. D. M. Blake, Archivist, India Office Library and Records, London.

I have had the honor of participating in the seminars of The Society for Arabian Studies of The British Academy, which have provided many interesting insights, and I wish to express my gratitude to Michael Macdonald, Venetia Porter, Derek Kennet, and Nanina Shaw Reade for the help and friendship they have extended to me during many years of work.

The staff of Exeter University has been of great help, and my special thanks go to Ruth Butler, Brian Pridham, James Onley, and Dr. Mahdi of Exeter University's Centre for Arabian Gulf Studies.

For research carried out in Zanzibar, heartfelt thanks to Prof. Abdul Sheriff; Dr. Khamis S. Khamis, Zanzibar National Archives; and Dr. Hamad H. Omar, Archives, Museums and Antiquities, Zanzibar.

For research in Oman, I am profoundly grateful to Dr. Reda M. Bhacker and Prof. Ibrahim Soghayroun, Sultan Qaboos University, Muscat, Sultanate of Oman, for having indicated new approaches. I also wish to thank H. E. Mohammed Said Khalifa Al Busaidi, former Ambassador of the Sultanate of Oman to

Italy; H. E. Yahya Abdullah Salim Al-Araimi, former Ambassador of the Sultanate of Oman to Italy; and Mrs. Wendy Savill for her unceasing assistance.

For research in Pakistan as a member of the Italian Historical, Anthropological, and Archaeological Mission in Makran and Kharan, directed by Prof. Valeria Piacentini, my mentor, my warmest thanks go to Mons. Luigi Bressan, Pro Nunzio Apostolico to Islamabad, Pakistan, in 1992. From the Sisters of St. Joseph's Convent in Quetta, Baluchistan, Pakistan, and in particular Sister Sarah Goss, I received the support and comfort of their loving care and prayers during research and fieldwork campaigns in Baluchistan. Zobaida Jalal and his family, with their affection and friendship, made it possible for me to carry out investigations in the area of Mand (Makran, Pakistan).

Prof. Bernardo Bernardi, may he rest in peace, 'forced' me to study more deeply the role of Swahili civilization. Professors Edward Alpers, Abdulaziz Lodhi, Thomas Pearson, Randall Pouwels, Patricia Risso, and Thomas Hinnenbusch—whom I met in Los Angeles, California, in 2002, during the conference on Cultural Exchange and Transformation in the Indian Ocean World—with their extraordinary ability for synthesis and their wise considerations on the current state of research into the Swahili civilization, were of great assistance in clarifying many of the more obscure aspects of this topic.

This unexpected updated and revised paperback edition honors me, and I would like to thank Markus Wiener and his staff for the collaboration and the great kindness.

As George R. R. Martin said of his own marvelous literary works, a book like this, although of quite a different nature, contains many devils, ready to leap out and bite. I, too, hope to encounter an angel.

ABBREVIATIONS

Adm.	Admiralty Records, Public Record Office, Kew
A.G.G.	Agent to the Governor General's Office, Essential Records, Baluchistan Archives
A.N.	Archives Nationales, Paris
B.L.	British Library, London
B.M. Add. Mss.	British Museum, Additional Manuscripts, London
E.I.	Encyclopedia of Islam, Leiden, 1999
F.O.	Foreign Office Records, Public Record Office, Kew
H.S.A.	Home Secretary Archives, Baluchistan Archives
I.O.R.	India Office Records, London
M.A.R.	Marine Department Records, London
P.P.	Parliamentary Papers, London
P.R.O.	Public Record Office, Kew
Z.A.	Zanzibar National Archives, Zanzibar

NOTE ON TRANSCRIPTIONS
AND TRANSLITERATIONS

Place names follow, when possible, the Geographical Atlas of the online Perry Castañeda Map Collection, University of Texas at Austin.

Names that have been anglicized by the addition of an English ending have not been written with diacritical marks (e.g., Ibadi, Omani, Baluch, Ismaili).

Names of ethnic groups and large tribes are considered collective names; therefore, only their singular forms have been used.

Common titles (e.g., Imam, Sultan) are given in their common anglicized forms with no diacritical marks.

Other titles, local place names, and personal names follow the system of transliteration of *The Encyclopaedia of Islam* (CD Rom Edition, Leiden, Brill Academic Publishers, 1999), with the following modifications: ج as 'j'; ق as 'q'.

Italicized words, other than those in Arabic and Persian, follow the spellings found in the archives, manuscripts, and documents consulted.

Swahili nouns and toponyms are here reproduced in italics following the Kamusi Project: kamusi.org.

INTRODUCTION

The methodology applied in carrying out the following study requires a few explanatory comments. The first step was essentially that of identifying the main historical and institutional themes in the light of documentation available in both western and oriental archives and collections—mainly in western languages—and through research in the field (in Asia, Arabia and Africa) with the aim of ascertaining and integrating previous bibliographical research.

Given the wide range and perspective of such an historical and historiographic approach, emphasis was placed on the re-reading and reappraisal of the principal historical-political-institutional events. In particular, those which saw the Arab Omani dynasty of the Āl Bū Sa'īdī playing a central role in regional and international interests, as well as their connections, influences and repercussions in the various areas under consideration within the wider context of the dynamics of relations with the European powers of the time.

The Omani view 'from outside' of the three terminals: Makran, Muscat and Zanzibar is, consequently, willfully a partial one in the history of the western Indian Ocean. Such themes are, however, essential when viewed against the background of Anglo-French rivalry in the Persian Gulf and Indian Ocean during the first half of the 19th century, and are central to numerous debates. The methodological perspective, therefore, whilst concerned with on 'oriental' figures and events, is still largely based on sources in western languages precisely because it concentrates on the relations between Sa'īd bin Sulṭān Āl Bū Sa'īdī, the Arab-Omani sovereign of Muscat and Zanzibar, and Europe.

The interweaving of peoples, goods and cultures gave rise, on the one hand, to numerous coastal civilisations inevitably influenced by the European presence and, on the other, to a varied series of contacts and exchanges between the peoples of these coasts and the populations of the interior of the continents examined here.

During the first half of the 19th century, the strategies followed by the European powers—and in particular the East India Company and the Anglo-Indian Government—in relation to the main ports along the shores of the Persian Gulf and the Indian Ocean inevitably led to the involvement of the local powers.

Ties had always been strong between the Arabian peninsula and the coast strip of the Makran, the latter being a centre where mercenaries were recruited to protect Arab potentates as well as offering safe shelter for these same potentates during the political-dynastic vicissitudes of the period.

Along the East African shores, movement of goods and precious spices, of ivory and, above all, of slaves destined for European and Asian markets and courts alike, were equally frequent. I have tried here to outline a scenario in which this fluid area becomes a kaleidoscopic and markedly synergic world, far more so than was theorised by writers in the last century, in which people, goods, ideas and culture circulated greatly. A world, in brief, which could already be defined in modern terms as 'global', 'globalised'.

This study, therefore, aims to evaluate the cultural synthesis of different local realities through field work and, at the same time, integrate this with the archival and bibliographical research that lies at the basis of the work itself. In this respect, the new historical perspective which tends to see, in the relations between the coasts, islands and interior of the continents no longer a state of total incommunicability, isolation and stasis but rather an intense and dynamic movements of peoples, goods and ideas—with marked effects on local societies—is also to be considered an extremely valid tool in providing a more complete and up to date interpretation of events. It is well known that studies in the history of the western Indian Ocean and of the island of Zanzibar can no longer be considered merely as hagiographic reconstructions, but must take into consideration a number of historical-political-institutional aspects. These include: the presence of different ethnic, social and religious groups together with the affirmation of Arab-Omani domination between the end of the 18th and start of the 19th century; the fundamental influence of the Indian mercantile and other Asian communities; the important presence of Arabs other than Omani, mainly from the southern regions of the peninsula, that is to say from Hadramawt, Yemen and, last but not least, the impact with the Swahili populations of the East African coast and the sub-Saharan area. All of these factors must, naturally, also be considered in relation to links with Europe.

The role played by Swahili culture in the history of the western Indian Ocean is also the object of numerous re-readings and historical reinterpretation, thanks to recent innovative theories. These, on the whole, tend to regard the true historical and linguistic position of Swahili culture in particular, and the African continent in general, within a more objective framework of influences arriving from other areas, especially Persia, Arabia and India, in which the people touching from such areas were not the only protagonists on the African stage.

An attempt to understand the idea that Europe, and Great Britain in particular, had of the first Sultan of Muscat and Zanzibar, is thus the aim of this challenge.

PART I

CHAPTER ONE

THE WESTERN INDIAN OCEAN IDYLL

Along the shores of the western Indian Ocean, relations between the people of the Asian, Arabian and East African coasts were innumerable and stretched back to time immemorial. Such links and relationships of power were to be sought in those elements which constituted the close equilibrium of the western Indian Ocean, that is, the monsoons, the presence of commercial thalassocracies, the predominance of mercantile laws, the trade routes of spices and ivory, the European desires for conquest of commercial monopolies, the slave trade . . . in brief, in all those factors essential to the creation of multiple ties, of a 'red thread'[1] which would link three continents: Europe, Asia and Africa.

During the period which saw the rise of Europe in the western Indian Ocean, a real revolution occurred from which new protagonists emerged along the Asian, Arabian and African coasts. Against this backdrop, the gradual emergence of new Arab dynasties resulted from the polarization which followed the struggle against the Portuguese presence in the western Indian Ocean. This gave rise to a gradual and discontinuous process of unification among the Arab tribes, traditionally divided and in conflict with each other, which came to the fore in the progressive affirmation of what it could be defined as the power of the Omani Arabs. Here, coastal cities made rich by trade, date growing and pearl fishing, dominated by autocratic sovereigns whose wealth also provided for great military power, confronted the interior, the hinterland of mountains and great deserts where power was decidedly uncertain and where tribes preserved a virtually absolute independence and perpetuated what it could be called a permanent 'guerrilla war'.

---

[1] This expression, more pertinent to European historiography, is here used to refer metaphorically to the red colour of the Omani flag. In effect, the sovereigns of Oman, between the 18th and 19th centuries, established numerous mercantile and political-strategic concessions along the shores of the Gulf and of the western Indian Ocean.

Two clearly distinct political realities were destined to co-exist along the coasts of southwest Asia and, in particular, in the desolate, desert region of Baluchistan, in Oman and in East Africa: the complex, multi-ethnic mercantile societies of the coasts, and the tribal, pastoral societies of the interior where, from time to time, the former succeeded in prevailing and imposing its laws.

In the ports of this maritime corridor, small city-states prospered, their gaze directed mainly seawards, while larger 'reigns' turned towards the interior and the north. The city-states jealously preserved their independence and attempts to make inroads on their commercial predominance often ended in failure for their enemies. The Arab potentates of the coasts thus created a flourishing market between the ports of south-western Asia and the Arabian, western Indian and East African coasts. And, from the 19th century on, it was the blood-red flag of the Oman that formed a tie, and not merely in the figurative sense, between the Omani enclave of the port of Gwadar in Makran-Baluchistan, the principal ports of Oman itself, the East African coasts and the island of Zanzibar through the movement of peoples, precious goods and slaves.

1.1 Makran: 'Terra Incognita'

One of the three principal terminals for this complex and interwoven system connecting merchandise, people and cultures was the coastal strip of Baluchistan: Makran.[2]

Around the 10th century we have proofs that sugar was exported from Makran to Gujarat both by land and seas routes.[3]

As information were very poor, many years later a British explorer wrote: "I'm attracted from blank spaces on maps of Central Asia; on the map of Major Oliver St. John of Persia is written 'unexplored' everywhere".[4]

Many centuries later, between the end of the 18th and the beginning of the 19th century, information regarding territories between Persia and the western borders of British India were extremely poor,

---

[2] I am deeply grateful to Prof. Valeria F. Piacentini.
[3] V.K. Jain, *Trade and Traders in Western India A.D. 1000–1300*, New Delhi, 1990, p. 103.
[4] C. Macgregor, *Wanderings in Baluchistan*, London, 1882, Introduction.

if not, in many cases, totally absent. They went back to the legendary expedition of Alexander the Great.[5] In fact, as emerges from 19th century British explorers and political agents' testimonies: "After Alexander the Great no European crossed these routes, from the frightening appearance, inhabited by hordes of looters and thieves".[6] And: "it is an extraordinary but nevertheless a true fact, that from the time of Alexander's march through *Gedrosia*, we have no record of the visit of a European to the interior of Baluchistan".[7] More than a courageous explorer tried to describe the difficult route through Baluchistan: a region with terrible roads and no supplies. Water was scarce, and even all the pains suffered in other expeditions through other Asian regions were comparable to this thankless task. The coast of southern Baluchistan was named of the *Ichthyophagoi*, fish eaters.[8]

Succeeding reports described fascinating tales of another famous European of the past: Marco Polo, who wrote about this region that he called Chesmacora and talking about it's inhabitants: "Un reame che hanno loro re, e anche sono idolatri, e di divisato linguaggio, ed é reame di molta mercatanzia e vivono di riso e di carne e di latte".[9]

Research studies carried out by the Italian Historical, Archaeological and Anthropological Research Project in Makran and Kharan, active

---

[5] D. Bivar, *Gli Achemenidi e i Macedoni: stabilità e turbolenza*, in, G. Hambly (Ed.), *Asia Centrale*, Storia Universale Feltrinelli, 16, (orig. ed.: *Fischer Weltgeschichte Zentralasien* 16, Frankfurt a.M., 1966), I, Milano, 1970, p. 30; F. Arborio Mella, *L'Impero Persiano da Ciro il Grande alla Conquista Araba*, Milano, 1979–80, p. 140; Curtius Quintus Rufus, *Alessandro Magno*, Q. Curtii, Rufi de rebus gestis Alexandri Magni libri decem, Parisiis, 1757; M. Sordi, *Alessandro Magno tra Storia e Mito*, "Ricerche dell'Istituto di Storia Antica", Milano, 1984.

[6] G.B. Eryes, *Elphinstone nel Cabul, nell'Afghanistan*, in, G.B. Sonzogno (Ed.), *Compendio di Viaggi Moderni dal 1780 ai Nostri Giorni*, Venezia, 1830, p. 115.

[7] G.N. Curzon, *Persia and the Persian Question*, London, 1892, 2 vols., vol. II, p. 254.

[8] With this term, "fish eaters", were identified in ancient times African and Asian tribes living at the extreme frontiers of the known world. *Ichthyophagoi* were considered the inhabitants of the western coast of the Red Sea and of Ethiopya. Eryes described the *Ichthyophagoi*: "the tribes showed all the misery of wild life. They dressed of fish skins; built their huts with fish bones and covered the roofs with large shells; they made fish bread and their cattle ate the same food". G.B. Eryes, *Elphinstone nel Cabul, nell'Afghanistan*, op. cit., p. 73.

[9] "A Kingdom with a king and idols, with a different language, with many goods and living of rise, meat and milk". Interesting is the theory of Malle-brun which believes that Marco Polo spoke of *Ras Makran*, promontory of Makran, as root for the term *Chesmacoran*. M. Polo, *162. Dello reame di Chesmacora*, in, *I Viaggi in Asia e in Africa nel mare delle Indie. Descritti nel sec. XIII da Marco Polo veneziano. Testo in lingua Detto il Milione*, Venezia, 1829, 2 vols., vol. I, p. 320.

in Pakistan since 1986, and directed by V.F. Piacentini, with particular reference to the studies of R. Redaelli, did identify in Makran
region a marked ethno-cultural-religious plurality.[10] Information regarding Makran, as stated above, is extremely scarce and, until the 19th
century, is based exclusively on oral tradition and the few details
provided by the occasional, audacious missionaries or no less courageous English officers sent there by the East India Company and/or
by His Majesty's Government, both concerned with the trade and
defence westwards of the colony *par excellence*, India herself.

At the start of the 19th century Makran constituted a cultural
entity quite distinct from the 'Indian' region and was seen as being
'other' also by the Persians dynasty of the Qājār: a frontier region,
its very geography inhospitable by nature and, according to tales of
the time, inhabited by warlike peoples, indomitable and famed—
from western sources—for their ferocity. Notwithstanding this, however, and thanks above all to the renewed political order of the
Qājār and their frontier feudalism, the area continued to represent
one of the main transit routes between the Iranian plateau and the
Indus valley along which most trade passed, from east to west and
north to south, by land and by sea. Moreover, given its profoundly
inhospitable geographical nature, it became the ideal refuge for rebels,
bandits, pirates and fugitives. First among these were the Arabs from
Oman, who gradually imposed their power over the main coastal
centres of the region.

Already in the 16th and 17th centuries, Baluch populations could
be found in the service of the Ya'rubī in Oman,[11] as special troops:
the officers were called *jam'dar*, and in kiswahili *jemadari* (pl. *majemadari*) ('the masters of the gate', 'head constable', transliterated var-
iously by the English sources on a phonetic basis as *jamadari* or
jemedari) and the soldiers, *sowar*. They were stationed at each of the
major ports and towns. For the Arabs of Oman these Baluch corps,
real mercenary troops, constituted their military power, the shāwkah,

---

[10] R. Readelli, *Administrative Subdivisions and Tribal Structures. The Perception of the
Territory between Tradition and Modernity*, in, V. Piacentini Fiorani, R. Redaelli (Eds.),
*Baluchistan: Terra Incognita. A new methodological approach combining archaeological, histori-
cal, anthropological and architectural studies*, Oxford, 2003, pp. 33–48.
[11] G. Rentz, heading: *Banu Kharus*, The Encyclopedia of Islam (hereafter, E.I.),
Leiden, 1999, vol. IV, p. 1084; G.R. Smith, heading: *Ya'rubī*, E.I., XI:291b, Leiden,
1999; J.C. Wilkinson, *The Imamate Tradition of Oman*, Cambridge, 1987.

an indispensable tool in the conquest and maintaining of power. It was, however, with Āl Bū Sa'īdī that the Baluch and the coastal strip of Makran became an institutional part of the Omani forces and power system.[12] And it is interesting here following the adventures and the explorations of few British agents during the first half of the 19th century through the mysterious Makran.

On 18 January 1809 Captain N.P. Grant touched at Bombay on the East India Company cruiser *Ternate* directed to the port of Gwadar, in Makran.[13] He received instructions from Brigadier General John Malcolm of exploring the western regions of Makran.[14] "The ostensible object was to purchase horses but the real purpose was to ascertain weather a European army could penetrate into India by the southern coast of Persia".[15] The mission was dangerous and Grant's time few[16] and much shortened on every alarming intelligence's report.[17] On 29 January 1809, Grant, together with Capt. David Seton of the Bombay Presidency, Resident at Muscat, and envoy in Sind, called at Gwadar, but the country appeared in conditions of such backwardness and political instability that he preferred sailing

---

[12] According to the Norwegian anthropologist Frederick Barth, it is difficult to determine precisely the origin of the Baluch presence in Oman. F. Barth, *Sohar, Culture and Society in an Omani Town*, Baltimore 1983, p. 39. Scholars are divided in their opinions. It is possible that, given the regular contacts between the two shores from earliest times on, the presence of communities which identified themselves with the Baluch culture date very far back. Miles proposed their presence already at the time of the Ya'rubī dynasty, a theory which he supported by quoting extensive Portuguese documentation. S.B. Miles, *Journey from Gwadar to Karachi*, "The Journal of the Royal Geographical Society", n. 44, 1874, p. 163. According to J.B. Kelly, *Sultanate and Imamate of Oman*, "Journal of Royal Institute of International Affairs", London, 1959, *passim*, on the contrary, it was only with Ahmad bin Sa'īd Āl Bū Sa'īdī that the recruiting of troops from among the Baluch peoples of the Makran began on a regular basis, that is to say, not before 1749.

[13] N.P. Grant, *Journal of a Route through the western parts of Makran*, "Journal of the Royal Asiatic Society", London, 1839, vol. V, art. XXII, p. 328 on.

[14] Brigadier General John Malcolm (1796–1833) appointed Envoy at the Persian court by the Count of Minto, in 1809 ordered the exploring missions of Capt. Grant and in 1810 of Lieut. Henry Pottinger. J.W. Kaye, *The Life and Correspondance of Sir John Malcolm*, London, 1856, vol. II, *passim*.

[15] N.P. Grant, *Journal of a route through the western parts of Makran*, op. cit., p. 340. (*Extract of a letter from Captain Grant to Sir Worsley, on his return from his journey through Makran*).

[16] In 1809 Grant was twenty five years old.

[17] "Native Intelligence Agents forwarded similar rumors reporting the imminence of a French foothold in Sind . . . Minto's reaction to this Intelligence was immediate". R.A. Huttenback, *British Relations with Sind, 1799–1843, An Anatomy of Imperialism*, Berkeley, Los Angeles, 1962, p. 6.

somewhere else. Therefore, they touched at Gwattar, from here
Grant's exploration was mainly conducted inside Persian Baluchistan,
in Kirman province. In ancient times part of the Khanate of Kalat,
this area was gradually conquered by Persia after the rise of the
Qājār dynasty; since this region has no natural borders, the frontiers between Makran, Kirman and Sistan in a northern position,
fluctuated during the 19th century according to the leading political-
military forces and according as well to the prevailing power of each
tribal group in the area. Thanks to Grant's report did emerge first
available information on Makran region.

In 1809 the chief of Gwattar was Mir Soban, he ruled from a
small fort surrounded by more or less 150 mud huts where mainly
fishermen lived; these people, noted Grant, exchanged their fish with
wheat coming from interior oasis as, due to the extreme scarsity of
raining water, the few wells were salted and along the Makran coast
didn't exist—and doesn't exist today—any kind of extensive cultivation. From Grant's report clearly emerged the close contacts between
the coast and the interior based on barter exchanges. The coastal
strip explored by Grant, from Jiwani, to Chahbahar and for about
40 miles in the interior was inhabited by the tribe of the Jadgal, Jat,
whose chief was Mir Soban; his residence was in Nagor, in the interior, north from Gwattar. The Jadgal, came originally from a region
close to Sind, and spoke that language, they were settled in an area
named by Grant *Bau Dashtyari*.[18] The forces of Mir Soban could
count up to 300 men of cavalry and 3,000 infantry soldiers, armed
with matchlocks and swords and: "the whole of these could only be
collected on an actual invasion of the country".[19]

The annual entries of Mir Soban amounted to about 6,000 rupees
and Grant wrote that this tribe was very powerful in Makran, so
that all tribal chiefs of the region searched for its alliance; never-

---

[18] Baho Dashtiari, from the river Dasht, is located in Persian Makran. The Jat
are of Indian origins, they were peasants in the Kachh Gondava plain; they were
conquered by the Brahui who forced them into a sort of 'feudal' relationship, they
had to following the crops in Brahui's absence times, and sending to them all the
land products; the Jat met by Grant in 1809 in western Makran were probably
escaped from Brahui domination, although their migratory movements remain still
obscure. As other tribes from Baluchistan, the Jat are characterised by endogamy,
and actually are settled in large numbers in Hyderabad. R. Hughes-Buller, *The
Gazetteer of Baluchistan, (Makran)*, Lahore, 1984, p. 94.
[19] N.P. Grant, *Journal of a route through the western parts of Makran*, op. cit., p. 329.

theless, this region was in weak hands, in a state of semi-independence where permanent villages of the interior were very few and their survive was subordinated to the presence of a fort occupied by the local chief, like Mir Soban of the Jadgal tribe in Nagor, well defended by an armed escort. A clear proof of this complex situation was that a great majority of southern Baluchistan dwellings, made of mud huts, were easily transportable, in case of unexpected danger, inside the fort.

This picture of high political instability and widespread violence described by Grant to his authorities was integrated by the description of the frequent mobility of the tribal groups settled in those territories where no irrigation systems existed and where bordering continental potentates ignored the coast, arid and desolated, with difficult sea approach, and exercising a mere nominal authority, and so that easing frequent raids and lacks of power in Makran.[20]

Grant and Seton travelled to Chahbahar along a hard route through narrow gorges and no water. On 9 February 1809, at the time of their arrival, Chahbahar was a village of about 300 huts with a mud fort built on a promontory in the eastern part of the bay, the surrounding area was desolate and poor except for some gardens watered by wells through a small river deep about 12 foot. The trade of goods between the coast and the interior of Makran was essentially on barter, and Grant witnessed an intense commercial intercourse between Chahbahar and Muscat, based mostly on ghee[21] export, and on import of cotton from Central Asia. The entries from this area, about 5,000 rupees, were initially divided between

---

[20] See P.C. Salzman., *Adaptation and Political Organization in Iranian Baluchistan*, "Ethnology", X, n. 4, 1971, pp. 433-444; P.C. Salzman, *Multi-Resource Nomadism in Iranian Baluchistan*, "Perspectives on Nomadism", Leiden, 1972; C. & S. Pastner, *Agriculture Kinship and Politics in Southern Baluchistan*, "Man", 1972; C. & S. Pastner, *Adaptation to State-Level Polities by the Southern Baluch*, "Pakistan, The Long View", Durham, 1977; S. Pastner, *Desert and Coast: Population Flux between Pastoral and Maritime Adaptations in the Old World Arid Zone*, "Nomadic People", n. 6, 1980; B. Spooner, *Politics Kinship and Ecology in Southeast Persia*, "Ethnology", VII, n. 2, 1969, pp. 139-152; U. Fabietti, *Power Relations in Southern Baluchistan: A Comparison of three Ethnographic Cases*, "Ethnology", XXXII, 1992, pp. 61-79.

[21] As clear evidence of the widespread of long-distance trade in the western Indian Ocean, at the beginning of the 14th century Ibn Battuta described a meal offered to him by the Sheikh of Mogadishu with rice steamed with ghee. Ibn Battuta, *The Travels of Ibn Battuta A.D. 1325-1354*, 2 vols., in, H.A.R. Gibb (Ed.), The Hakluyt Society Publications, II series, CXVII, Cambridge, 1959.

the local chiefs of Makran and Muscat, but the Omani Sultan took the fort by siege and, wrote Grant, governs now on the entire area. The Sultan of Muscat, at that time Sa'īd bin Sulṭān Āl Bū Sa'īdī, was nominally chief of an important commercial emporium, patrolling long-distance sea routes between Persia, Arabia, India, China and the east coast of Africa with its heart in the island of Zanzibar. On the Arabia Peninsula promontory, the town of Muscat was a rich and powerful trade market between the Gulf and the western Indian Ocean.

Seton and Grant decided to coming back to Nagor along the same road, here Mir Soban gave them letters for the chiefs of the interior, they affirmed that the two English Captains were horse merchants, and, as didn't found any horses at Nagor, they hoped in a better luck at Kasarkand. During three days march the brave explorers didn't meet any inhabited villages, the territory was too arid and stony for Baluch shepherds.

Kasarkand is located in a fertile valley, wide about 21 miles, in its centre flows a torrent and the village, with a large fort surrounded by about 500 huts, was living of considerable production of wheat, rice and dates. Sheikh Samandar was an independent chief, here Grant and Seton had to wait for the arrival of Muhammad Khan, chief of Geh, as, without his consent, they couldn't proceed toward the interior in western direction. Guided by the escort furnished by Mahomed Khan the two English, dressed as Europeans, reached Geh around the end of March. Surrounded by three torrents, Geh was rich of water, with hot springs, and was known as the second town of Makran after Kej.[22] The dominions of Geh were larger than other centres of the region, they extended from Chahbahar for a hundred miles along the coast and for eighty miles in the interior. Muhammad Khan could enrolling up to 3,500 warriors, recruited in part between minor chiefs, with whom he maintained good relationships. Grant was informed that this place was frequently object of raids by the tribes at the borders between Persia and Makran, but peace was lasting since recent years.

The march restarted towards Bampur, 14 miles between hills and desolate gorges; in these places Grant realised that a passage of an army could be easily ambushed by a small garrison.

---

[22] Kej, oasis in the valley of the Kech river, is today the centre of Turbat, provincial capital of Makran.

Once passed the sand hills, Bampur is located in a wide valley with many huts, and with a fort in its centre surrounded by walls where great production of wheat was guaranteed also for other villages. The inhabitants of Bampur were Narroi[23] and their total forces reached up to 300 well armed horsemen and 2,500 infantry forces; their principal activity was raiding and they reached Minab and Bandar Abbas. Due to the 'bad character' of the chief of Bampur on 1 April 1809 Grant had to abandon the project of travelling directly to Minab and came back to Makran. Between Geh and Jask he observed that a pile of stones defined the border between Makran and Persia. Jask, governed by Mir Haji, paid 2,500 rupees to the Imam of Muscat. Minab and Bander Abbas, reached by Grant around the end of his voyage, were as well controlled by Muscat; during the cold season Oman watched over the caravan trade of wheat coming from the interior and part of the Minab revenues were paid from Muscat to Persia.

Once completed the exploring mission, observations reported in a dispatch sent to John Malcolm confirmed the possibility of a passage for a European army through Persian Baluchistan and Makran; certainly many routes would have been very hard for an artillery's passage, but there was a chance for an infantry force, not greater than 5,000 men, which could find sufficient water and food. The total forces of Makran were estimated by Grant of about 25,000 men, although he admitted that the whole country didn't guarantee minimum environmental supplies to keeping them in a united squadron for a long time—a very keen and contemporary observation, we must say.

Moreover, Baluch were very much expert in arms: "they seldom quit their houses unarmed". Many of them were recruited by Muscat as soldiers on the dhows, sanbūq of the Omani navy, or as land troops in the desert of Oman. Local opposition could prevent but

---

[23] Visited by Henry Pottinger the succeeding year in 1810, their chief was Shah Mihrab Khan—the chief was the same but his name had been changed by Grant and Pottinger—he thought he was the brother of "Grant the European". Settled in Pottinger's Kohistan, Khorasan, which included the plateau of Sarhadd and the southern depression of Hamun-i-Mashkel, where palm dates were cultivated, the Narroi did practice the *Chupao*, raid, and spoke Persian mixed with Baluch dialect; about this frontier tribe, Pottinger gave us a wide description of their traditions and customs. H. Pottinger, *Travels Beloochistan and Sinde*, London, 1816, repr. Karachi, 1976, pp. 168–177.

not blocking the passage "except instigated by some Foreign Power";
nevertheless, concluded Grant, "no difficulty exist".[24] But soon the
hazardous and incomplete observations on the short exploration made
by Grant in south-central Asia would have cost his life. In the spring
of 1810 he was appointed as Commander of the escort to the Brigadier
General John Malcolm in his anti-French mission in Persia; once
reached the Gulf, Grant was instructed with Cornet Fotheringham,
of Madras cavalry, and two servants to exploring the routes between
the river Tigris and the dominions at the Persian frontier; close to
Kuramabad, at the borders with Turkey, he was made prisoner by
a Persian chief, whom, after a rich banquet in his tent for two days,
shot him while he was riding his horse leaving the village. It was
April 1810, Grant was 26 years old.[25] Once killed Grant, the Persian
chief kept as prisoners the other men for two more days and shot
them. On 6 May 1810 John Malcolm received a secret dispatch which
communicated that two officers of the escort were savagely killed at
the Persian border, as evidence of the essential need of geographical information as defence strategy against a European enemy. In
the past Rich, father-in-law of Sir James Mackintosh, Resident in
Baghdad, did explain to Grant that the route led to a gorge infested
by bandits and looters; moreover, the expedition carried a heavy
baggage, excessive, according to Rich. The Shah of Persia, informed
of the murder, ordered to find the guilty, blind him and cutting
his hands.

But soon a young and brave explorer was ready to challenging
the inhospitable and cruel Makran. Those 'blank spaces' in border
lands at the north-west frontier of India which obsessed Bombay,
Calcutta and Whitehall during the 19th century, pushed young ambi-
tious officers in dangerous adventures in those territories, Henry
Pottinger was one of them.

In autumn of 1809 Lieutenant Henry Pottinger (1789–1856) came
to know of a new project of exploring Baluchistan by John Malcolm
and by the Government of Bombay. But the international events,
the Spanish Revolt of 1808 and the Austrian Campaign of 1809,
brought the interests of Napoleon back to Europe. The French plans

---

[24] N.P. Grant, *Journal of a Route through the Western Parts of Makran*, op. cit., p. 340.
[25] J.W. Kaye, *The Life and Correspondance of Sir John Malcolm*, London, 1856, vol.
II, pp. 8–12.

of invasion of India by land didn't proceed due to the failure of French-Persian diplomatic relations, and due to the deep misunderstanding between French diplomacy, strongly eurocentric, and Oriental diplomacy, focused on intrigue and on personal interest. Nevertheless, the weakening of the French menace didn't prevent the Anglo-Indian Government of prosecuting explorations of those *terrae incognitae* between India and Persia, keeping in mind the possibility of a passage by a European army and considering the alarming need of geographical maps of this strategic region.

The exploration of Baluchistan by Henry Pottinger was—and is still today—considered a fundamental testimony for geographical, political, anthropological and strategic information that he reported to his political-military authorities, so much that literature on the subject defined Pottinger's route of 1810 the first real complete survey of Baluchistan made by a European in modern times.[26]

On 2 January 1810 the expedition guided by Captain Charles Christie, composed by Lieutenant Henry Pottinger, two Hindu guides, an agent of an Indian horse merchant—the cover up was once again the purchase of horses—and by a group of Afghan traders, left the Bombay Presidency, in direction of Sonmiani port, in Las Bela province.[27] On 16 January 1810 the port of Sonmiani was an important trade centre, all goods directed to Kalat and to Central Asia landed to Sonmiani; the village, few houses made of wood and clay bricks, and tamarisk huts fixed with mud, was governed by the Darogha (administrator) who had the task of collecting taxes on goods and tolls for the Jam, the chief of Las Bela, and the entries amounted

---

[26] Lieutenant Henry Pottinger was an Agent of the East India Company in the Bombay Presidency; in 1808 he was instructed by Lord Minto, Governor General of India, of an exploring mission of Sind. Between 1809 and 1810 he explored Baluchistan. He was appointed by Lord Clare, Governor General of India, to the sign of a commercial Treaty with the Amir of Sind which was signed in 1832. As Colonel, Pottinger was Resident in the region of Kutch, bordering with British India. Once survived to the First Anglo-Afghan war, in 1846 he became High Commissioner in South African territories; he was Governor at Madras, in southeastern India, and today his portrait is at Whitehall.

[27] Las means valley, plain in Jadgali dialect. In local oral legends Bela was called Kara Bela; during the 17th century the Aliani family of the Jamot tribe took the power in Las Bela exercising a semi-independence from the Khanate of Kalat. C. Masson, *Narrative of a Journey to Kalat*, London, 1843, repr. Karachi, 1976, vol. IV, p. 305; *The Imperial Gazetteer of India*, Provincial Series, Baluchistan, Lahore, 1908, p. 188.

to 50,000 rupees annually.[28] Theoretically, the Jam lineage had a vassalage relation with the Khanate of Kalat, which obliged Las Bela to hand over 50% of its fiscal revenues to Kalat, and to provide armed troops in case of threat; however, during the 19th century, the decline of Kalat authority gave a wide autonomy to the Jam, whom ceased to fulfilling his obligations. Pottinger observed the high mobility and the frequent changes in tribal alliances which never eased a real and defined control.

In the past a Jam married one of the daughters of the Nasir Khan of Kalat; since then (1794), the refusal to paying tributes to Nasir Khan successors was very frequent. The British expedition, with letters written by the Jam for the chiefs of the interior, travelled to the province of Jhalawan.

The Bizanjo tribe,[29] with 1,000 armed men, did control the hills north of Las Bela and Pottinger, offering 60 rupees, convinced them to abandoning the project of massacring the entire expedition. Rahmat Khan Bizanjo with more or less 20 armed men, his Sardar, Bahadur Khan and the Mullah led Pottinger and Christie through desolate hills and long narrow valleys within the province of Jhalawan, till Wad, a village between the mountains inhabited by the tribe of the Menghal, Brahui.

Henry Pottinger prosecuted with his group in Kalat direction, crossing the province of Sarawan, inhabited by Brahui as well; the young explorer observed that in those long valleys broken by plateau the tribal groups developed local migratory patterns mixed to nomadic environmental settlements patterns alternating plains to plateau; the camps followed the pastures migratory cycles and Henry Pottinger realised that potential projects of a creation of a territorial state with

---

[28] Jam constitutes an hereditary title of Rajiput origin, Indian, and belonging to the Sunni family of the Aliani; it belongs to a single tribal lineage and it's present today with juridical and administrative competences. P. Tate, *Kalat. A Memoir on the Country and the Family of the Ahmadzai Khans of Kalat, from a Ms. account by the Akhund Muhammad Sindik, with notes and appendices from other manuscripts as well as from printed books*, Calcutta, 1896, pp. 36–37; T. Holdich, *The Gates of India*, op. cit., pp. 138–9, 304–307.

[29] The Bizanjo were, and are still today, present also in Makran, S. Pastner affirms: "traditional ruling elite, genealogically the Bizanjo of Kolwa in eastern Makran are Brahui, but a long residence in Makran has 'baluchized' them in language and customs". S. Pastner, *Conservatism and Change in a Desert Feudalism: the Case of Southern Baluchistan*, "The Nomadic Alternative", Paris, no date, p. 249.

defined borders would have met serious, if not impossible, difficulties. And here again we cannot avoid to considering the modernity of these observations. On 9 February 1810 Pottinger and Christie reached Kalat dressed as horse merchants. Surrounded by mud walls six metres high only on three sides, Miri Kalat was the residence of Mahmud Khan, *Beglerbeg* of Baluchistan.[30]

The Khanate of Kalat, which developed around the 7th century, was a refuge for waves of invaders coming from south-western Asia, directed to India; from 10th to 15th century Kalat and the bordering provinces were subdued to foreign powers imposing tributes, often with the use of force; but it was not before the end of the 17th or the beginning of the 18th century that the Khanate succeeded in affirming its power in Baluchistan. Once subdued the sedentary agricultural tribes and enforced the tribal authority on pastoral nomadic groups, the Khanate began to developing a centralised bureaucratic apparatus through territorial expansion which included Makran.

Once left Kalat, Pottinger and Christie travelled in north-west direction and, once reached Nushki, although in contrast with instructions received, they divided themselves; here the real adventure began, because Captain Christie, on 22 March 1810, chose the northern route toward Afghanistan and Sistan,[31] while Pottinger decided to cross the desert of Makran and the Sarhadd plateau; the two travellers would have met in Persian territory.

But a sad destiny was expecting Captain Christie. On 31 October 1812 he was killed in an attack by Russian soldiers in a camp, in Persian territory, leaving only a brief summary of his exploration. Pottinger, instead, reached Kharan governed by the Sardar Abbas Khan of the Nousherwani tribe, under Mahmud Khan of Kalat till

---

[30] *Beglerbeg* was the title given by Nadir Shah of Persia, conqueror of the 18th century, to Nasir Khan; the latest owned the largest reign in the history of Baluchistan and succeeded in reaching independence from the dynasty of the Durrani Kings of Kabul, institutionalising his leadership. Around 1795 Nasir Khan's power passed to his son Mahmud, than only 14 years old, who reigned till 1816, maintaining very little of the power established by his father. The Brahui, Sunni, of linguistic Dravidian origins from southern India, married between different tribes, except for the Kambarani, the tribe of the Ahmadzai family of the Khan of Kalat. H. Pottinger, *Travels in Beloochistan and Sinde*, op. cit., pp. 26–40; *The Imperial Gazetteer of India*, op. cit., p. 134.

[31] Captain Charles Christie explored the region north of Baluchistan, and his route was followed by the Bordering Russo-Afghan Commission in 1883. T. Holdich, *The Gates of India, being an Historical Narrative*, London, I ed. 1910, repr. Quetta, 1977.

few years before his visit.[32] The Nousherwani were known as brave
warriors and in Kharan they were able to joining a force of about
600 men, favoured by the resistance and fastness of Kharan camels,
well known throughout Baluchistan.

At the beginning of the 18th century in the Makran region the
coexistence of mountainous areas, inhabited by nomadic pastoral
tribes, and of cultivable oasis populated by sedentary groups, where
villages flourished, had been organised by the Gitchki. Originating
from the valley of Gitchk, east from Panjgur, they emerged in Makran
as a political elite in close relationships with the Khanate of Kalat;
Pottinger took note that the hereditary class of the Hakim included,
beyond the Gitchki, major exponents of the following tribes:
Nousherwani, Bizanjo, Rind, Buledi, in the Buleda valley,[33] north to
the Kej oasis, and Mirwari, all ferocious warriors constituting the
political-military support to the power control in Makran. At the
beginning of the 19th century the Gitchki, through patro-client relationships, succeeded in integrating the agricultural communities, who
gave them a tenth of the land products revenues to the nomadic
pastoral tribes in exchange of military protection and defence; the
relations between these two groups were regulated on feudatory protection and economical advantages. Henry Pottinger wrote that Kej,
the main centre of Makran, was governed at that time by Hakim
Abdullah Khan, Bizanjo; he did recognise the authority of Mahmud
Khan of Kalat but refused to paying tributes, and, soon after, did
not even respect him formally.[34] At the beginning of the 18th century the Gitchki affirmed their power in Makran, but their supremacy
did not last for long time as, around 1750–90, Nasir Khan of Kalat
conquered their territories. In order to clarifying the comprehension
of the events, the fact that Nasir Khan, once in control of Makran,

---

[32] H. Pottinger, *Travels in Beloochistan and Sinde*, op. cit., p. 130.

[33] Buledi trace their origins in one ancestor, *Bu-Said*, coming from Helmand valley or from Muscat. The power of the Buledi fell in Makran around 1740, in correspondence with the rise of the Gitchki. The Buledi were Zikri, a religious sect
present in Makran since the 15th century. The Zikrism does not include the pray
in Mecca direction, but to the Koh-e-Murad, 'the Pure Light', a dark mountain
located in the vicinity of Turbat, a pilgrimage site; the Zikr is the ritual name given
to repeated songs in the name of God. S. Pastner, *Feuding with the Spirit among the
Zikri Baluch: the Saint as Champion of the Despised*, "Islam and Tribal Societies", London,
1984, p. 304.

[34] H. Pottinger, *Travels in Beloochistan and Sinde*, op. cit., p. 290 on.

prevented himself from taking in charge of its administration, but simply accepted to receiving half of the entries, is a factor of great importance.

When the Ahmadzai Khan of Kalat appeared on the scene, there were two Sardar Gitchki who administered the country: the Sardar of Panjgur, and the Sardar of Kej, the two most important oasis of Makran. The Sardar of Kej brought a controversy between brothers in front of Nasir Khan and this last deputed the district of Tump to one of them.[35] Makran was internally divided among three Sardar Gitchki: Panjgur and the valley of Gwargo, including Gitchk and Parom; Kej and the surrounding valley with Buleda; lastly, Tump and Mand, till Jiwani, a small village on the Indian Ocean, a few miles of distance from the Persian frontier.

The Khan of Kalat, on his turn, divided the country in two districts, the niabat of Kej and of Panjgur, while Tump was included in the jurisdiction of Kej. Moreover, Nasir Khan put one of his agents, Naib, resident in Kej, with the task of collecting entries of Makran.[36] After the death of Nasir Khan the country fell in a state of anarchy, with inter-tribal feuds, and the Gitchki exploited the state of weakness of the Khanate of Kalat for reconquering the power in Makran. They succeeded in escaping to Khanate taxes, both due to a situation of lack of control by the Brahui, and due to the political-territorial instability of those areas subjected to taxations.

Around the half of April the voyage of the British explorers proceeded from Kharan, through the desert, in southern districts till the oasis of Bampur, visited by Grant, and toward Persia. Shah Mirab Khan, chief of Bampur, a powerful raider, with 6,000 men, 16 wives, and 4 and a half lakh of rupees annually (one lakh = 100,000 rupees)

---

[35] A *Sanad* (decree) which describes the compromise is dated 1206 H./1791 A.D. *The Imperial Gazetteer of Baluchistan*, op. cit., p. 236 on.

[36] With regards to taxation system, before the Khanate of Kalat control, Nadir Shah wrote a *Sanad* in 1740 for the chief of Kharan; This *Sanad* authorised the successors of the Kharan chief to collecting a tax represented by 150 armed men from Kej, Tump and those areas under jurisdiction. The tax collecting systems were of two kinds: *dah-yak*, a tenth of the production and *sar-e-zarr*, a poll tax of four annas each. Both at that time and during Kalat dominion there were some categories excluded from taxation like traders and manufacturers whom were controlled by the Gitchki; They became very rich to the expenses of the peasants, reducing the total amount of the revenues due to Kalat often to insignificant sums. R. Hughes Buller, *The Gazetteer of Baluchistan, (Makran)*, op. cit., pp. 248–254.

of entries coming from his dominions and his raids, thought Pottinger
was the brother of Grant, met by him the year before.

Henry Pottinger directed himself to Khorasan and Isfahan that he
reached on 27 June 1810 and where he was joined by Captain
Christie. They communicated to Brigadier General John Malcolm,
who was in Teheran and was coming back to India, to accomplished
the exploring mission of Baluchistan.

In clear contradiction with Captain Grant reflections written the
preceding year, the report on territorial conditions, on population of
Baluchistan and the geographical map, inexistent before that time,
traced by Henry Pottinger revealed the groundlessness of British
apprehensions. The probabilities for a European army to succeeding in crossing Baluchistan were very few; the lack of water would
have stopped its march; between the Sarhadd plateau in north-west
direction and the areas belonging to the Khanate of Kalat there was
the desert. In southern direction the unbearable climate of the Makran
region would have led shortly to death a European army; lastly, the
mountain ranges which cross Baluchistan would have isolated an
army from any communication with surrounding areas.

It was crystal clear that if it seemed very difficult invading India,
it was extremely difficult penetrating into Baluchistan territories inhabited by tribes and, most of importance, exercising a political control
upon them.

With the vanishing of the French menace via land, with the exception of two short explorations made in 1828–29 by Lieutenant Brucks
from the coast west of Gwadar, and by Lieutenant Haines[37] on the
ship *Benares* in 1829, both with the scope of tracing a nautical map
of those dangerous waters for the Admiralty,[38] a new menace to
British India would have implied urgent measures for the safety of
Indian north-western borders: the Russian penetration of Central
Asia.

The historical events which led to the First Anglo-Afghan War
(1839–1842) saw Russia and Great Britain deeply involved in the
Great Game. Since Afghanistan was the centre of reciprocal political-
territorial interests of the two European Powers, Baluchistan was

---

[37] Lieutenant Haines was in service from 1820 to 1849. I.O.R. Phillimore IV,
p. 447.

[38] *Admiralty Chart*, London, 31 December, 1874, in, G.S. Ritchie, *Persian Gulf Pilot*,
London, 1898, new ed. London, 1967, p. 65 on.

obviously included in the new British strategy of creation of those 'Buffer States' to protecting Anglo-Indian borders. To this regard, during the summer of 1838 while Lieutenant Robert Leech (1813–1845)[39] was at the court of Mir Mehrab Khan of Kalat, came to know a merchant from Makran, *Hajee Abdun Nubee*, who owned a camel the Lieutenant wanted to purchasing. The manners of *Hajee* seemed to Leech much convincing, he spoke many languages, Arab, Hindi, Baluch of Makran and Pashtu, he did travel much in Arabia, in Persia and in Hindustan, and he lived for a long time in Makran. In 1824 *Hajee* was at Panjgur for six months. Lieutenant Leech decided to instructing *Hajee* of collecting information on Makran and on the surrounding territories. Leech proposed to refunding him for the trade losses during the exploration. And *Hajee* accepted; he was provided with a pass in English, with the order not to showing it to anybody except in real dangerous situations, and never showing up in the British encampment at Kalat, his mission was secret.

The skillful merchant bought pieces of cloth in Kalat with the scope of travelling in Makran as a small trader of scarves. On 2 October 1838 *Hajee* left Kalat joining the escort of *Noor Mahomed*, Khan of the Shagassi tribe directed to Kej and Panjgur with the task of collecting taxes. *Hajee* followed the route made by Pottinger toward Suhrab, from this village he travelled to Panjgur via Kharan. On his right he saw a tamarisk wood and on his left, in southern direction, he saw the desert. Kharan was a rich centre where wheat, barley and millet were cultivated. There were blacksmiths, carpenters and weavers. "*Meer Azad Khan: the Prince of blood*",[40] was the chief of Kharan and of the surrounding territories. When he came to know that troops from Kalat were coming to Panjgur for collecting tributes, he instructed 30 men armed with matchlocks for the defence of his uncle's fort, *Muheem Khan* of the Nousherwani tribe. On 25 October *Hajee* reached Panjgur, an oasis with loamy soil fertile thank to sophisticated and efficient underground irrigation systems (*qanat/kariz*).[41] The oasis of Panjgur was governed by a representative of Mehrab

---

[39] R. Leech, *Notes taken on a Tour through parts of Baluchistan in 1838 and 1839 by Hajee Abdun Nabee, of Kabul. Arranged and translated by Major Robert Leech*, "Journal of the Asiatic Society of Bengal", nn. CLIII–CLIV, London, 1844, pp. 667–707.

[40] Idem, p. 676.

[41] V. Piacentini Fiorani, R. Redaelli (Eds.), *Baluchistan: Terra Incognita*, op. cit., *passim*.

Khan of Kalat, who collected half of the entries, while the other
half went to the Gitchki. These last resembled to *Hajee* a community of Sikh, as they were the only tribe of Baluchistan who never
cut their hairs. Their chief was Mir Ahmad Gitchki, nephew of Nasir
Khan. In Makran Panjgur was called 'Paradise', but it was in permanent struggle with the Nousherwani from Kharan and from
Khoshan. The dates from Panjgur were exported in every place and
there were of 17 different types, and Pottinger offered a detailed
description. The explorer sent by Leech in Makran noted that 25
Hindu lived in Panjgur, blacksmiths, carpenters, shoemakers, gold-
smiths, hatters and weavers. The merchants of Kalat came in autumn
for purchasing dates and bringing goods from Shikarpur, while other
merchants came in summer from Gwadar and bought wool and ghee
for the Bombay market, bringing goods from Bombay like cloves,
clothes, necklace and a special ointment for sheeps. The coin used
was kashani rupee. Baluch from Panjgur didn't agree their daughters married Afghans because their heart would have broken along
the voyage and their heads would have been razed. *Hajee* travelled
in western direction, within the dominions of Azad Khan of Kharan,
toward Bampur.

As is clear, the three British explorations here briefly examined
left us significant testimonies of this little known terminal in the western Indian Ocean together with questions of great topical interest.

Crossing the coast of Makran and reaching the second terminal,
it was the Baluch who gave protection and refuge in their settled
lands, faithfulness and military service to Āl Bū Sa'īdī of Oman
when he began their rise to power in Muscat.[42]

According to Barth,[43] Baluch in Oman settled in many areas and
in separate villages, practising their customs and speaking their language, dressing their dresses, for females with very wide and flowing
sleeves and very loose bodice, in contrast to the Arabs' more close-
fitting and swung-waisted dress. The pantaloons are wide at the top
and very narrow at the calf, whereas those of the Arabs are more
straight. The embroideries of both dress and trousers are beautifully
coloured, full of sexual and cultural significances. Baluch marry in
the summer season, and Arabs avoid the summer. The Baluch groom

---

[42] J.C. Wilkinson, heading: *Muscat*, E.I., VI, p. 734.
[43] F. Barth, *Sohar*, op. cit., p. 39 on.

buys gold for his bride, while Arab groom give a bride-price to the father-in-law; Virginity for Baluch remains a private matter, while Arabs give public proofs, the Baluch nuptial hut is constructed in the bride's home, where Arabs place it in the groom's home. Baluch homes in Arabia showed a cultural vitality in colours than Arab's houses. Being Baluch is a question of geographical identity; therefore their integration in the western Indian Ocean ports and towns has been always assured and stable, due to their corporate role of defence force.

We also agree with R. Barendse that trade and tribe relationships between Swahili coast and Makran littoral during the second half of the 18th century were pre-existing to the power of the Āl Bū Sa'īdī of Oman, and highly influenced by the role of Indian—both Hindu and Muslim—merchant communities all over the regions of the western Indian Ocean, who became extremely rich and powerful.[44] The Baluch presence along the Swahili coast, apparently was closely related to their military role within the tribes of Oman, further on developing in trading in East Africa, but this is an interesting hypothesis object of further research.

From the end of the 18th century, and for all of the 19th, it was precisely these tribes of pillaging warriors who protected, hid, supported and faithfully defended the Āl Bū Sa'īdī of Oman, thanks also to the tribal structure and clan-family relationships of their society which, traditionally nomadic, could count on both 'Makran' and 'peninsular' and 'continental' solidarity. From the accounts of travellers, explorers and British officials of the time, we see emerge among others the Hot, the Rind and the Nousherwani.[45]

At the start of the 19th century, the Rind and the Nousherwani were established in the areas around the centre of Tump on the Nihing river, roughly 100 kilometres east of the town of Kej. Just outside the town there is Miri Kalat, an ancient fortress.[46] Located

[44] R. Barendse, *The Arabian Seas: The Indian Ocean World of the Seventeenth Century*, New York, 2001, *passim*.

[45] S.B. Miles, *Notes on the Tribes of 'Oman by L.C.S.B. Miles*, 27 May 1881, in, Sirhan I.S.I. Sirhan (Ed.), *Annals of Oman to 1728*, Cambridge 1984, p. 94.

[46] Miri Kalat is equivalent to the English *citadel*, a fortress inside the walls of the castle located in the highest part of the valley. Miri Kalat is a magic and mysterious place, full of energy, which inspired many myths and legends; one of them is the tragic story of two lovers Sassi and Punnu, separated by their families and condemned to loneliness and to death is still narrated among the Baluch of Makran.

on the edge of date palms green belt, the rock stands out splendid, magic and imposing; walking on stony ruins to the top, the view is breathtaking, as testimony of the glorious past of this region.[47] Palm trees are on one side of the fortress and mountains chains are on the other side.

The Hot are identified as a tribal subsection of the Rind, although some deny this origin.[48] The Rind, 'the blue-blooded' tribe of southern Baluchistan, boast of very ancient lineage. Their story is enriched with legends and heroic poems; an ancestor is supposed to have fought courageously against the terrible Afghans who wanted to invade southern Baluchistan via the Bolan pass, and many fought against the Turk and Turkmen who wanted to seize the fertile lands lying close to the Nihing valley. 'Related' to the Brahui, of Hanafi Sunni religion, and having many 'saints' and 'holy men' among their number, their reputation for courage was equalled by that for justice and respect for the principles of the Islamic law. At that time their settlement area extended along the western valley of the Nihing (in territory today divided between the Islamic Republic of Iran and Pakistan), over the plateau of Pannodi and along the Dasht as far as the Arabian Sea, the valley of the Zamuran as far as Washuk and over wide stretches of Iranian land along the coastal strip as far as Minab, if not further. The Nousherwani ('the young lions') controlled a large part of the fertile Panjgur plain and the region of Kharan further to the north. Linked to the principal centres of the Iranian plateau by natural routes, they controlled the flow of trade which passed through their territories, from time to time hosting also communities of Indians, Armenians and Ismaili.

It was these peoples, and not only these, who moved to numerous coastal territories of the western Indian Ocean, as far as the island of Zanzibar.

To this regard, it's interesting pointing out that recent genetic studies carried out in Makran by a genetist research group from the Pasteur Institute in Paris discovered that 40% of maternal gene pool is of African derivation, and only 8% paternal gene pool is of the same African origin.[49] This is a clear proof that, since ancient times,

---

[47] V.F. Piacentini, *International Indian Ocean Routes and Gwadar Kuh-batil Settlement in Makran*, "Pakistani Archaeology", 1988, pp. 304–344.

[48] R. Hughes-Buller, *The Gazetteer of Baluchistan-Makran, (Makran)* op. cit., pp. 93–94.

[49] Communication by L. Quintana-Murci, Laboratoire d'Immunogénétique Humaine, I.N.S.E.R.M., Institute Pasteur, Paris, 2003.

the presence of female slaves in tribal groups and the custom of African 'nannies' was widespread throughout southern Baluchistan tribes.

Arriving on the African island with the Arab-Omani fleets so as to fight, between the end of the 18th and the beginning of the 19th century, the Baluch settled in the coastal villages, gathered around the fortresses and in new camps such as that of Saateni, just outside the town of Zanzibar, or in the centre of the African town where the Baluch cavalry was to develop.

1.2   British descriptions of 19th Century's Muscat

What was Muscat like then? From the descriptions of travel accounts by Europeans during the 19th century, the picturesque bay of Muscat was a semicircle, enclosed by the mountains and with rocks dropping to the sea on which fortifications had been built for keeping a lookout for enemies. The town was surrounded by hills and rung round with walls and, with a green valley beyond the shore, it was a pleasant place. The hinterland of Muscat is so mountainous that, in the 19th century, it could only be reached on camel or donkey-back. Just outside the town the coast was mainly desert, hilly and desolate. Water resources have always been scarce in Oman and, in the 19th century, the price of the famous sweet, clean water of Muscat was extremely high.[50]

Descriptions of the time show a varied and vivacious world animating Muscat; merchants from all over travelled there, Arabs, Indians, Hebrews, Turks, Africans, Persians. . . . The dwellings were *barasti*, huts with roves of palm-leaves, more spacious than those on the opposite shores along the coast of Makran, and mud houses, although there were also some in stone and madrepore. The central market of Matrah, near Muscat, spread over a large area, almost entirely built upon with dwellings and narrow and winding alleyways. Here, in the 19th century, every kind of merchandise could be found, silk and linen, spices, dates, coffee brought across the desert by caravans, pearls, green and black grapes, bananas, figs, butter, fowl, goats and cattle, and even delicious mangos imported mainly by sea. The rich Omani merchants wore long, wide robes

---

[50] P. Ward (Ed.), *Travels in Oman*, Cambridge, 1987, p. 4.

of extraordinarily clean white cotton, with wide sleeves and waists
bound by belts from which emerged their beautiful silver knives, the
khanjār, and swords.

The maritime city of Muscat, thanks to its strategic position at
the entrance to the Gulf, was always held to be the best port of the
entire Arabian Peninsula. The town is surrounded by volcanic hills,
bare of any vegetation, which culminate in high mountain ranges,
the highest peak (9000 ft.) being within the Jabal al Akhdar range
where snow falls during the winter months. In the past even grapes
were grown on its slopes, from which the Portuguese, during their
presence there, made a wine called *muscatel*.

From the earliest times, the port had always been a lively and
bustling place. Its position, almost hidden among the rocks, made it
an ideal harbour for merchants, sailors, adventurers and pirates who
found their fruit and drinking water. During the 19th century it was
densely populated, a true crossroads for trade between East Africa,
the eastern shores of the Gulf and western India. It was defended
by the Marani and Jalali forts, built by the Portuguese in 1527.
Towards the end of the 18th century Muscat was described by the
English merchant and explorer Abraham Parsons as a quite cosmopolitan city, where the tolerance of the political leaders permitted flourishing trade and multi-religious, multi-ethnic coexistence.[51]
Numerous caravans arrived there daily from the interior to unload
ostrich feathers, animal horns, sheep and leather, honey and beeswax
and to bear away knives, games, spices, rice, sugar, coffee and tobacco.
The English explorer noted also that trade between Muscat and
Mocha was extremely intense; the Omani city sent 20,000 bales of
coffee to Basra, every year, destined for Constantinople. Trade towards
the interior, instead, was mainly in Persian carpets and silk, pearls,
Maria Theresa thalers and Venetian sequins (*zecchini*). He further
commented on the fact that the mangoes of Muscat were better than
the Indian fruit, and that drinking water was taken on board ships
by barges drawn by oxen as the land was too uneven for barrels to
be rolled over it. Many merchants were semi-naked and attempted
to cool themselves by the use of ingenuous fans since, as Parsons
admitted, "Muscat is the hottest place on earth".[52] Lastly, he also

---

[51] P. Ward, *Travels in Oman*, op. cit., p. 8.
[52] Ibid., p. 9.

remarked on how many of the inhabitants were ill or in need of treatment.

In the 19th century Muscat was mainly known as a fearsome den of pirates, and the British presence in the Omani port was permanent precisely from this century on. The assignment of a resident there was, however, abolished as early as 1809 due to the deleterious impact of the Muscat climate on the English. The Omani port therefore came under the jurisdiction of Bushire.

From the accounts of certain European travellers in Arabia, the most imposing were the Baluch warriors, naked to the waist and armed with a knife and a double-handed sword, with fierce glares and of threatening presence. In 1825 the permanent bodyguard of the Omani sovereign, Sa'īd bin Sulṭān Āl Bū Sa'īdī, whose income amounted to 522,000 Maria Theresa thalers,[53] of which 120,000 came from Zanzibar, consisted of 300 Baluch. At the time approximately 2,000 Baluch lived in Muscat, in the mud *barasti* outside the walls of the town. Their number was, however, forever growing. This was due both to the essentially uncertain nature of Omani power, as well as the intrinsic peculiarities of the Ibadi belief, factors which enabled the Baluch easily to insert themselves as a military force, and to the political and environmental persecution and threats under which they had always suffered in their homeland. As far as their behaviour is concerned, from a western point of view, their cynicism was such that the Baluch mercenaries often deliberately ignored local disputes, preferring to steer clear of the different political factions which contended for power in Oman and, instead, simply obey the orders of whichever Arab prince offered the highest pay.[54]

1.3 Sub-Saharan East Africa's Terminus

The other terminus of the western Indian Ocean, whose historical events were inextricably linked to those of the Asian and Arabian

---

[53] M.R. Broome, *The 1780 Restrike Talers of Maria Theresa*, Doris Stockwell Memorial Papers, no. 1, repr. in *Numismatic Chronicle*, VII series, vol. XII, London, 1972, pp. 221–253, N. Vismara, *La monetazione di Maria Teresa*, unpublished Conference at the Circolo Culturale Milanese, May, 2002; see also research made by C. Semple, The Society for Arabian Studies, London.

[54] G. Geary, *Through Asiatic Turkey*, London, 1878, cited in P. Ward (Ed.), *Travels in Oman*, op. cit., p. 41.

coasts by the power relations of the Arab of Oman with the main ports and principal mercantile centres, was Sub-Saharan East Africa. Here, again, it has to be made an essential distinction between cultural and geographical areas; according to A. O'Connor, in effect, "Eastern Africa is not a clearly defined entity".[55]

Since notable geo-morphological differences and ethnic, cultural, historical, political and social peculiarities result in numerous and often contrasting considerations concerning precise geographical definitions, is preferred here the definition of cultural synthesis which relates to the coastal strip of sub-tropical Eastern Africa, the Mrima coast, and to the Indian Ocean islands, Pate, Lamu, Pemba, Zanzibar and Mafia, where the Swahili civilization arose and developed.

Like the coasts of Makran-Baluchistan and Oman, that of Eastern Africa has always nurtured contacts with the outside world, constituting that western part of the Indian Ocean so indissolubly linked to other shores and inserted in the context of a far wider theatre. One of the natural causes for this difference consists of the wooded belt surrounding the Eastern African coast to the west. Poor and with limited rainfall, it is known in Swahili as *nyka* (wild). This impenetrable strip running from modern-day Kenya, through broken up by valleys and rivers towards the south, forms a natural barrier to contacts between the shore and the interior, as stated by N. Chittick: "it is the land, the dense forest which divides, the sea which is an open road".[56]

For centuries the East African interior was afflicted by the presence of the tse-tse fly[57] and made inhospitable by long periods of drought and malarial infection. On the contrary, the coastal area of modern-day Tanzania, with its humid and temperate climate, encouraged settlements and agricultural activities. The influence of the environmental ecosystem and the subsequent settlement patterns of

---

[55] A. O'Connor, *The Changing Geography of Eastern Africa*, in G. Chapman and K.M. Baker (Eds.), *The Changing Geography of Africa and the Middle East*, London, 1992, p. 114.

[56] The Mrima coast indicates that area within which the *mrima* dialect is spoken, that is to say from Mombasa, including Pangani, Bagamoyo and Kwale, as far as Kilwa. H.N. Chittick, *The Coast Before the Arrival of the Portuguese*, in A.B. Ogot (Ed.), *Zamani. A Survey of East African History*, Nairobi, Kenya, 1974, p. 104.

[57] The tse-tse fly of equatorial Africa transmits tripanosomiasis, a disease to which local cattle are resistant but which causes deadly epidemics among those imported from Eurasia and North Africa. J. Diamond, *Guns, Germs and Steel. The Fates of Human Societies*, New York, 1997, *passim*.

populations along the African coast on the one hand, and of the savannah of the East African interior on the other led to the development of different cultures and economies, the peoples of the coast inevitably emerging as the favoured of the two. Lying at the very edge of the monsoon area which ends at the Mozambique channel, an area of extremely unstable maritime climes, where the winds from the south-east begin to blow and favourable conditions cease, the coast of East Africa benefited from the favourable ecosystem of the Indian Ocean. Its highly important strategic position eased links between East Africa, the Red Sea, the Gulf, Arabia and Western India.

The coasts and the islands were often prone to inclusion in the world of the Indian Ocean, through which they enjoyed numerous links with overseas lands, while relations with the interior of the African continent were more sporadic, although existing, during the 18th and 19th centuries.[58] The regularity and force of the monsoons—"predictable and constant"[59]—contributed to making the African littoral a fringe of the great navigation system of the western Indian Ocean.

The astonishing balance created by the monsoons[60] was achieved over the space of a year with the following rhythm: from December to March the monsoon blows from Arabia and the western coasts of India in the north-east, pushing as far as Mogadishu. The winds are light and constant, the climate hot and dry. In April the monsoon starts to blow from the south-west,[61] from eastern Africa towards the coasts of the Persian Gulf, the climate cooler but much more humid. The rains are short, *vuli*, from November to February, and heavy, *masika*, from March to June, while the driest months are November and December. Moreover, along the East African coasts

---

[58] Lively debate continues on this topic, aimed at refuting the theories put forward by the authors of the 1975 edition of *The Cambridge History of Africa*, J.B. Webster, R. Gray, E. Alpers, to essentially anti-eurocentric ends. Among the many, see R. Pouwels, T. Pearson. See also the papers presented online to the International Conference on Cultural Exchange and Transformation in the Indian Ocean World, UCLA, Los Angeles, CA, USA, 3–4 April, 2002.

[59] C.S. Nichols, *The Swahili Coast. Politics, Diplomacy and Trade on the East African Littoral 1798–1856*, London, 1971, p. 74.

[60] The term derives from the Arabic *mawsim* (pl. *mawasim*), season, from which we also get the Portuguese *monção*.

[61] *Kaws* in Arabic, *kusi* in kiswahili.

and in the islands of the Indian Ocean, the tropical climate is always
tempered by sea breezes. Until the 19th century, sailing from Asia
and Arabia in November in a south, south-westerly direction took
thirty to forty days in ideal weather conditions while, in December,
thanks to the stabilization of the monsoon, the voyage took only
twenty to twenty-five days.[62]

This means of navigation was, moreover, assisted by the equatorial currents which push southwards, thus rendering the voyage from
the north still easier. Between March and April the north-easterly
monsoon gives way to that from the southwest and the equatorial
current strikes the coast at the latitude of Cape Delgado. Here the
winds blow towards the north and sailing from the south towards
Asia becomes just as easy and safe. Spring, therefore, was the best
season for sailing from Zanzibar. From mid-March to mid-August,
in contrast, storms are frequent and prevent navigation in the Indian
Ocean.[63] This regular alternation of currents and monsoon winds
led travellers, adventurers, merchants and explorers towards East
Africa. Over the centuries, they were all to contribute to the creation of the Swahili civilization, language and culture, a unique phenomenon in the history of the African continent. In that period,
Mogadishu, Malindi, Mombasa, Zanzibar, Kilwa and Sofala were
the most flourishing centres. The progressive homogenization between
Arab-Islamic culture and African traditions, also caused by inter-
ethnic marriages, stimulated the creation of a marked Islamic identity
along the coasts of East Africa. It is to be stressed here that although,
on the one hand, these 'city-states' along the northern African coast
often lacked points of supply in the interior, the line of longitude
along which the monsoon system moved favoured a trade network
with the Indian Ocean, thus making them economically independent
and, from time to time, cut off from the continent itself. Kilwa
exported copper, Malindi and Mombasa iron, and Mogadishu cloth.
The first mosques were built in Indian style, and copper coins were
made, clear symbols of power and political-economic supremacy.

This, in broad terms, was the maritime corridor, mainly a cultural corridor, along which the principal dynamics developed that

---

[62] See the numerous and interesting contributions in D. Parkin and R. Barnes
(Eds.), *Ships and the Development of Maritime Technology in the Indian Ocean*, London, 2002.
[63] A. Sheriff, *Slaves, Spices and Ivory in Zanzibar. Integration of an East African Commercial
Empire into the World Economy, 1770–1873*, London, 1987, p. 8.

would characterize the history of the western Indian Ocean during the first half of the 19th century.

1.4 Tribes and Trade Interfaces

The port of Gwadar in Makran, the maritime city of Muscat in Oman the island of Zanzibar in East Africa represented three important mercantile centres, three differing realities and histories which merged in the fascinating history of the eastern seas and their peoples. During the 19th century clear relationships of power existed between the Baluch of Makran, the Arabs of Oman and the Africans of Zanzibar where, according to western documents of the time; the Baluch represented military forces, the Omani were the political leaders and the Africans the slaves.

In the 19th century, the port of Gwadar was poor and backward, peopled by mercenary and unscrupulous tribes. In the same century, Muscat was characterized by a supremacy in trade and by military power, but also by ceaseless political uncertainty caused by unreliable promises and fluctuating goals. On the island of Zanzibar we can still see today the ancient marks left by the bloodiness, violence and hatred provoked by slavery, together with an underlying melancholy that pervades the history of the island where, for so long, the most prized goods were the bodies of men.

During the 19th century, interaction between these three different ethnic entities gave life to forms of conflict and to ethnic-cultural groups that emerged in the consolidation of a true thalassocracy, nominally headed by the Arabs of Oman, and the instauration of hierarchies of power.

Why, however, was it precisely the Baluch who were considered by the Omani Arabs to be the most trustworthy and safest military forces for their defence and for the numerous battles against their enemies, both at home and abroad, to the extent that they formed a military elite consisting of the bodyguard of the Sultan of Oman? It was the Portuguese who started a new phase in relations between India and East Africa. Surprise was a fundamental aspect of the Portuguese arrival on the eastern maritime scene. After centuries of prosperity, in fact, the traditional thalassocratic system that had developed along the shores of the Indian Ocean was shattered by the Europeans, who started to extend their territorial ambitions, pursued

obstinately and with determination from *terra firma*, to the seas.[64] This
spirit of conquest, animated by the fight against Islam and the conversion to Christianity of 'unbelievers,' 'bringing the light to the shad-
ows of the pagan world,' together with a desire to win the monopoly
over trade in the spices and other produce of Africa and Asia from
the Arabs and Venetian merchants, were the main reasons behind
the eastern policy of the Portuguese. This strategy foresaw a blockade of the Red Sea and the Persian Gulf by conquering the ports
of Aden and Hormuz and taking Malacca and Goa, with the aim
of controlling and running trade between India and the Far East
and, lastly, consolidating a strategic supply base in Mozambique. In
other words, the succeeding colonial power of Portugal was founded,
less on effective dominion, than on control of lines of communication and the natural monopoly of spices, thus exercising an indirect
political rule or simply commercial influence.

The longed-for riches of Africa, however, soon proved to be
ephemeral and the Portuguese policy of exploiting the Asian and
African coasts by means of tributes could not cover the costs of
maintaining their contingents and fortifications there. By the end of
the 16th century, the signs of Portuguese political and commercial
decadence in the Indian Ocean were clearly evident. High mortality rates, contraband and intrigue were not the only factors threatening Portuguese power in the ever more difficult waters of East
Africa, and these contributed to the spread of instability and poverty
in the Swahili 'city-states'. Since the political borders along the east
African coasts had not been established through any kind of agreements, it was only in 1817 that the Anglo-Portuguese Convention
defined Cape Delgado as the northernmost limit of the Portuguese
territories, while the village of Tungwe, near Cape Delgado, was
declared to be the border with the lands under Omani control.
Tungwe, however, was an important centre for the slave trade and
the Portuguese, who had built there, could clearly not agree with
such a division. It was not by chance that, for quite some time,

---

[64] See, among others, the noteworthy studies by C.R. Boxer: *Portuguese Conquest
and Commerce in Southern Asia 1500–1750*, London, 1985; *Portuguese India in the Mid-
Seventeenth Century*, Bombay, 1980 (Portuguese translation: *A Índia Portuguesa em Meados
do Séc. XVII*, Lisboa, 1982); and C.R. Boxer, *The Portuguese in the East, 1500–1800*,
in H.V. Livermore and J. Entwistle (Eds.), *Portugal and Brazil: An Introduction*, London,
1953, pp. 185–247.

Tungwe "became a bone of contention between Zanzibar and Portugal",[65] inevitably undermining relations between the Omani and the Portuguese.

Portuguese control did not have any notable influence over the south-eastern area of Africa. In the first place, there were never more than a hundred Portuguese living at Cape Delgado and serious environmental difficulties such as malarial fever and the shortage of drinking water decimated even these. For many years, a 'barrier of disease' deprived, or rather protected, Africa from European settlements. The heavy Portuguese galleons could venture into the Mozambique channel before the end of June but, after that date, were forced to sail beyond the Mozambique routes, thus making communications with the ports further north slow and problematical.

Moreover, it was mainly the coasts that were involved in this strategy for the conquest and control of the Indian sea routes. It should, however, be remembered that it was the Portuguese who imported from America manioc, pineapples, guava (*Psidium guaiava*), groundnuts and sweet potatoes, all products which undoubtedly improved the diet of the African population.

If, on the one hand, the coast and islands of East Africa were of interest to the Portuguese in the context of the *carreira da India*, with disastrous implications and consequences in terms of political and commercial stability, on the other, the Ya'rubī Omani domination which included Mombasa and the island of Pemba was characteristic of quite normal changes in dominion over the seas, without resulting in substantial alterations in commercial organization and involving little integration with local political structures. We may, therefore, agree with Miles that "the Ya'rubī were the most powerful dynasty of Oman, yet their decline was rapid, humiliating and irretrievable"[66] and with Wilkinson, who maintains that "the power of the Ya'rubī merely increased without ever being consolidated".[67] The Ya'rubī, assisted by merchants from the coasts of western India, carried to the coasts of East Africa the Omani tribal system, in which the notion of central government did not exist.

---

[65] J.M. Gray, *History of Zanzibar from the Middle Ages to 1856*, London, 1962, pp. 175–77.

[66] S.B. Miles, *The Countries and Tribes of the Persian Gulf*, 1st ed. 1919, repr. London, 1996, p. 265.

[67] J.C. Wilkinson, *Imamate Tradition of Oman*, op. cit., p. 50.

Towards the end of the 18th century, the Ya'rubī tribe stood at
the head of a flourishing mercantile reign which depended on the
coastal cities and the principal islands of East Africa. The presence
of Arab governors, often African slaves in the service of the Omani
Arabs in the dominions of the Makran coast and in East Africa, was
always merely so as to control trade and impose taxes. This institution had its roots in the tribal system of exercising power, as well
as in the political agreements with local rulers.

The rise to commercial power in the Indian Ocean of Holland
and Great Britain, together with the retaking of Muscat and Mombasa
by the Omani Arabs, where they could count on the consensus and
support of the Swahili population, marked the start of the decline
for the Portuguese empire in the East Indies.[68] Towards the end of
the 18th century, the Āl Bū Sa'īdī tribe defeated the Ya'rubī at
Muscat[69] and were destined to extend their political and commercial power also in East Africa throughout the 19th century.

Aḥmad bin Sa'īd Āl Bū Sa'īdī (1744–1783), son of a coffee merchant from Sohar, was the leader of a dynasty which linked its own
destiny to that of East Africa. In 1784 Sulṭān bin Aḥmad Āl Bū
Sa'īdī (r. 1792–1804), pretender to the 'throne' of Oman, sought
refuge in the desolate region of Makran, only a few nautical miles
from Muscat. He journeyed to *Tiz*, a fortified village, and then turned
towards Kharan where Mir Jahangir, the lead of the Nausherwani
tribe, espoused his cause. They went together to Kalat to confer
with Nasir Khan I who, having declined the Omani sovereign's
request for military assistance in re-taking Oman, offered him a
refuge for the duration of his temporary exile, the port of Gwadar,
then an insignificant village of fishermen. This was to be a short-
term concession that would cease once the struggle for power of the
claimant to the Omani throne was concluded. It is therefore held
that, towards the end of the 18th century, Nasir Khan I, Khan of
Kalat, 'granted' the port of Gwadar to Sulṭān bin Aḥmad Āl Bū
Sa'īdī in trust.[70] Kalat's later claims to Gwadar were based on the

---

[68] Although the Portuguese colonial empire was ousted by the Dutch about
halfway through the 17th century, this did not prevent a Lusitanian presence from
continuing in the trading and strategic centres of East Africa and the Indian Ocean.

[69] C.F. Beckingham, heading: *Bu Sa'id*, E.I. vol. I, p. 1281.

[70] R. Hughes-Buller, *Gazetteer of Baluchistan*, op. cit., p. 283; Miles, *The Countries
and Tribes of the Persian Gulf*, op. cit., p. 282.

fact that the grant of the *jagir* was never to be interpreted as permanent, but limited to the contingent need of Sulṭān bin Aḥmad Āl Bū Saʿīdī to seek refuge in Makran.

On the contrary, for the Omani sovereign, the grant meant naval protection of the coasts of Makran which would be guaranteed by Sulṭān bin Aḥmad Āl Bū Saʿīdī once he came to power in Oman. This, according to the Arabs, was the main reason for the trust which Nasir Khan I placed in the representative of the Āl Bū Saʿīdī.

From the reports of British officers of the time[71] we may put forward the hypothesis that the Omani occupation of the port of Gwadar could only be justified as a de facto presence, there being no coherent or true evidence or testimony as to how this occupation began or of the events which led to Oman possessing this important strategic port on the Makran coast.

Sulṭān bin Aḥmad Āl Bū Saʿīdī used his base in southern Asia to mount naval expeditions in Arabia. One of the first acts of this Arab leader was to appoint Saif bin Ali as governor of Gwadar and to order him to built a fort in the most sheltered bay of the port. This governor, in compliance with Sulṭān bin Aḥmad Āl Bū Saʿīdī's wishes, travelled with twenty men towards Chahbahar with the excuse of a fishing expedition, took it by surprise overnight, overthrowing Shafi Muhammad, a Buledi who appears to have been betrayed by an Ismaili, and annexing the land to the Omani territories. It must also be remembered that, in 1794, Sulṭān bin Aḥmad Āl Bū Saʿīdī obtained the rights to the revenue from Bandar Abbas and its domains, which then included Minab, the islands of Qishm, Hormuz and Hengam, from the Sheikh of the Beni Maʾin tribe, Mullah Husain, who owned the islands. From this moment on relations between Oman and Persia were inevitably destined to become hostile.

At the start of the 19th century the possessions of the Āl Bū Saʿīdī included the island of Bahrain, the Makran coast with its important strategic-commercial enclave of Gwadar, certain sites along the Persian coast such as Chahbahar,[72] the island of Socotra, the Kuria Muria isles, Zanzibar and nearby ports on the sub-Saharan African coast. In this way and not without numerous and cruel struggles for power,

---

[71] J.G. Lorimer, *Gazetteer of the Persian Gulf,* op. cit., pp. 601–22.

[72] With the death of Sulṭān Bin Aḥmad Āl Bū Saʿīdī, Oman lost Chahbahar in 1804, but then retook it after a short interval. In 1809 its revenue amounted to 5000 rupees a year and went in its entirety to the Sultans of Oman.

such as—among the countless acts of piracy—the two attacks on Sur
and Gwadar in 1805 by Sheikh Sultan, the leader of the Qasimi
tribe of Ras al-Khaimah and the immediate retaking of the centres
by the Omani fleet, the Āl Bū Sa'īdī achieved their greatest extent
of expansion.[73] In effect, following the affirmation of Omani rule,
Gwadar became a richer centre than the nearby harbour villages of
Pasni and Jiwani, so much so that even an American ship called
there to purchase bales of wool.

The answer lies in the creation of a terminus for a growing commercial network and in the availability and loyalty—purchased at
great price—of the Baluch troops as compared to the untrustworthiness of the Arab troops and the potential risk they could have
posed for the forces in power.

Thanks to the examination of available European sources, both
printed and manuscripts, combined to the field work, at this point
we may put forward a hypothesis in explanation of the initial query:
why was it precisely the Baluch who the Omani Arab considered
the most dependable and safest forces for their protection and for
their battles against both internal and external enemies, to the point
that they constituted a military elite, their shāwqah?

The answer lies in the creation of a terminus for a growing commercial network and in the availability and loyalty—purchased at
great price—of the Baluch troops as compared to the untrustworthiness of the Arab troops and the potential risk they could have
posed for the forces in power.

---

[73] C.E. Davies, *The Blood Arab Red Flag. An Investigation into Qasimi Piracy 1797–1820*,
Exeter, 1997.

CHAPTER TWO

THE MARITIME ROUTES TO EAST AFRICA

Through sea routes, from time immemorial, the spread of Islam through short as well as long-distance trade routes strongly influenced, and in many cases modified, East African societies.

Islam undoubtedly made a tremendous impact upon the people of East Africa and of Zanzibar. Along the centuries, due to an increasing number of merchants, travellers and immigrants coming from southern Yemen, from Hadramawt and from other non Shiite areas, a solid Sunni-Shafi community emerged.[1]

Along the littorals of East Africa the impact of Islam with pre-existing religious realities, mostly animism, was inevitably a great impact for the latter ones. During the 19th century the growing predominance of Islamic trade and exercise of power politics in East Africa led to a misconception of the delicate, as well as of the troublesome, relationships between different societies and cultures. And the process was getting deeper and deeper within both Islamic and non-Islamic societies, especially western societies. So much so that P. Chabal still thinks today about East Africans: "at the same time they (the Africans) seem locked into what outsiders all too readily tend to see as 'backward' social or psychological conventions—such as ethnicity or witchcraft".[2]

Starting from the beginning of the 19th century, the level of influence on trade routes strongly controlled by Arab and Asiatic merchants in the western Indian Ocean was high. And the reasons perhaps could be found in the endogenous characterisations of what was sadly destined to become what we tend to identify as a 'backward' reality. As is well known, Islam in East Africa—as elsewhere—was not monolithic, encompassing as it did so many regional variations and changes over times. Nevertheless, it provided a framework; and

---

[1] W. Gervase Clarence-Smith & U. Freitag (Eds.), *Hadrami Traders, Scholars and Statesmen in the Indian Ocean 1750–1960*, Leiden, 1997, *passim*.

[2] P. Chabal, *Africa: Modernity without development?*, ISIM Newsletter, n. 5, Leiden, 2000.

within this framework, Muslim merchants were more likely to empha-
sise their Muslim identity; moreover, their minority status and their
geographical isolation led to the creation of Muslim enclaves which
served as bases for extensive islamization and created an ideological
support for resistance to economic and political competition as, for
example, in Zanzibar.[3]

2.1   Indian Merchant Communities

Among the many Indian merchants trading at Muscat and in the
Gulf during the 19th century there were the Bhatta, originally from
Rajastan (from Bhatti, Subhatta, Hindu warriors of the Vaishnavit
caste). Another group of Bhatta were the Kutch, again Hindu who,
in the 17th century enjoyed great prestige at Muscat and who were
exempted from taxation by the Arabs. Together with these groups
of merchants, there were also the Khoja, who were Ismaili from
Kutch and from Kathiawar. In foreign and sea-going trade mainly
Muslim were employed (Bohra, term used in Rajasthan for a *sahukar*,
trader, usurer, and Khoja) while Jainist and Hindu (Banya and Bhatta)
were dominant in the banking and finance fields.[4]

According to F. Daftary, the Daudi Bohra, along with the Nizari
Khoja, were the earliest immigrants to East Africa.[5] The permanent
settlement of the Ismaili Bohra and Khoja in East Africa was greatly
encouraged during the early decades of the 19th century by the
Sultan of Oman. He was interested in foreign trade and managed
to extend and consolidate, benefiting from British protection, his
African dominions into a commercial empire. Sa'īd bin Sulṭān Āl
Bū Sa'īdī encouraged the immigration of Indian traders, who were
accorded religious freedom, to Zanzibar. After the Khoja, the Bohra,
coming mainly from the districts of Kutch and Kathiawar in Gujarat,
constituted the largest group of Indian immigrants in Zanzibar. The
movement to East Africa of the Indian Ismaili, engaged in trade,

---

[3] P. Risso, *Merchants and Faith. Muslim Commerce and Culture in the Indian Ocean*,
Boulder, 1995, pp. 104–105.

[4] C.R. Allen Jr., *The Indian Merchant Community of Muscat*, "Bulletin of the School
of Oriental and African Studies" (SOAS), University of London, vol. 44, n. 1, 1981,
pp. 39–53.

[5] F. Daftary, *The Ismailis: their History and Doctrines*, Cambridge, 1990, pp. 314–315.

was intensified after 1840, due to the presence of the Omani leadership. Subsequently, the Indian Ismaili moved from Zanzibar to the growing urban areas on the east coast of Africa, notably Mombasa, Tanga and Bagamoyo, where they acted as commercial agents for firm in Zanzibar or became petty merchants and shopkeepers. The Nizari Khoja had been active as traders between western India and East Africa at least since the 17th century; the early Indian Nizari immigrants came as well from Kutch, Kathiawar, Surat and Bombay, and settled on Zanzibar island. By 1820, a small community of Nizari Khoja was present in Zanzibar; their affairs were administered by two local functionaries. This traditional pattern of local organization and administration, brought over from India, was adopted also by other Nizari settlements in East Africa.

Due to naval superiority, since the 10th century, and onwards, Arab traders settled on the whole coast of western India; here, Muslim communities[6] grew and progressively included local communities either through conversion and/or intermarriages. Omani merchants became rich merchants in western India and they enjoyed high religious freedom, proved by the presence of many mosques. Piracy was widespread; and here again the presence of Baluch soldiers was justified by the Omani need to safeguarding their ships and cargoes. The participation of Indian communities to long-distance trade were initially relegated to coastal or internal trade, they were middlemen, but later on, they became deeply involved in the western Indian Ocean imports and exports business. Main imports to western India kingdoms were: silk from China, ivory from Zanzibar via Oman, then exported from India to China, fine spices and wine from the Middle East, frankincense and horses from Arabia, both imported by land—through Baluchistan—and sea, although sea route was cheaper as free from duties halts, and coral from Spain through Egypt. Western Indian exports, most of all from Gujarat, were mainly in textiles, leather goods, sugar from Makran,[7] timber, spices, stones, and slaves. These were under control of the Arabs who were primarily carriers rather than producers. Indian traders, apart from using metallic currency—gold, silver and copper—often resorted to barter.

---

[6] The Arab conquest of Sind was in 712 A.D.
[7] V.K. Jain, *Trade and Traders in Western India*, cit., p. 103.

Indian merchants were vividly described by European explorers
of the 19th century, who took note of their complexion, fairer than
that of the Arabs, their fine features, long moustaches waxed and
curled up, but no beards and a Chinese pigtail at the base of a
shaved head. Stress was also laid on the elegance and sumptuous-
ness of their attire, silk tunics with long, ruffled sleeves, a clear sign
that they were not involved in any form of manual labour.

As stated above, the role of these merchants was one of the essential and deciding factors in the extraordinary development which
occurred also on the island of Zanzibar during the 19th century,
where they were extremely active. They were called *banyan*[8] (vaniya,
in Gujurati *vaniyo*, man of the merchant caste, from the Sanskrit
vanij, merchant, later anglicized as *banyan*, a term used to indicate
Hindu as opposed to Muslim merchants). There were, moreover
'money tasters' and *sarruf* moneychangers (from whence we have the
English *shroff*) called mushrikūn by the Arabs, polytheistic but easily included in the Islamic institution of amān (protection).[9] In their
accounts and in the reports of the East India Company representatives, the English used the term *banyan* to identify both the Hindu
castes and the Indian Ismaili communities (this mix up being quite
frequent).[10] The term *banyan* identified more an occupation than a
caste, and it was interpreted in western sources as a trader; nevertheless, *banyan* tended to be viewed as a distinct ethnic group. Only
the boys went to school to becoming *banyan*, they were taught reading and writing in conventional scripts as well as special merchant
scripts which would be incomprehensible to everybody except them,
and accounts were written in deliberate obscure writing, differing for
each *banyan* family; boys were obviously taught the use of ciphers,
account-keeping and arithmetic. Outside school boys were employed
in family shop and learned the family business. Once completed the
education, they were expected to start their own business, practising

---

[8] C.H. Allen Jr., *Sayyids, Shets and Sultans: Politics and Trade in Musqat under the Al
Bu Sa'id, 1785–1914*, Ph.D. Dissertation, University of Washington, 1978, p. 128;
M.R. Bhacker, *Trade and Empire in Muscat and Zanzibar. Roots of British Domination*,
London, 1992, note 50, p. 209. For further linguistic aspects, see the notable study
by A. Lodhi, *Oriental Influences in Swahili. A Study in Language and Culture Contacts*,
Göteborg, 2000.

[9] S. Blanchy, *Karana et Banians. Les Communautés commerçantes d'origine indienne a
Madagascar*, Paris, 1995, *passim*.

[10] D. Hardiman, *Feeding the Baniya. Peasants and Usurers in Western India*, Oxford,
1996, pp. 62–91.

in distant places for some years, like, for example, in East Africa. *Banyan* business required hard work and frugal living and the habit of total secrecy in business. Credit and honour were the major values and, in case of bankruptcy, many were the cases of suicide. *Banyans* kept large sum of cash money, as reputation in paying or repaying money was judged on their solvency power. Honesty was valued as much as disposal of cash money. The families observed patriarchal principles, they ate no prohibited food and were very religious: success in business was closely related to religious merits.[11] Ostentations were much avoided except in religious celebrations and festivals and in private houses, where women wore precious jewels, gold earrings, and nose rings with pearls and rubies, necklaces and bracelets of gold and anklets of silver.[12] The wealth of a *banyan* was a meaning also of harmony and happiness within his families and in his societies.

The Omani dynasty of the Āl Bū Sa'īdī emerged at the end of the 18th century into this already fully-functioning system in the western Indian Ocean, with its wide range of links and connections and which enjoyed the mediating roles and loans of the various Indian communities present on Zanzibar and fully integrated into African reality.[13] During the 19th century, most of the tax collectors were Indian; they rented African ports to the Arabs under five-year contracts, paying annual fees.[14] The tender for the contracts, on their expiry, were renewed and assigned to the highest bidders. While land represented the main form of security for the Africans, the Arab and Asian immigrants could only depend on money and family or blood relationships. The Indian family concern, increasingly complex as the volume of their businesses increased, was therefore the economic model which enjoyed most success along the East African coasts.

---

[11] C.H. Allen, *Sayyids, Shets and Sultans*, op. cit., pp. 100–106; G.A. Akinola, *Slavery and Slave Revolts in the Sultanate of Zanzibar in the Nineteenth Century*, "Journal of the Historical Society of Nigeria", 6 June 1972, p. 118.

[12] Ibid., p. 78.

[13] W.G. Clarence-Smith, *Indian Business Communities in the Western Indian Ocean in the Nineteenth Century*, African History Seminar, SOAS, University of London, 2 December, 1987.

[14] W.G. Clarence-Smith & U. Freitag (Eds.), *Hadrami Traders, Scholars and Statesmen in the Indian Ocean*, op. cit., *passim*.

During the 19th century, the growth in the volume of trade managed by the Indian mercantile communities, with the consent of the Arabs and the military protection of the Baluch mercenaries, inevitably led to a gradual but progressive influence on the African populations. Among these the magical element, animistic rites and witchcraft, blatant symbols of the traditional system of wielding power were, at varying times, deprived of their forcefulness in the political and social fields. Entire squadrons of Baluch soldiers settled in the interior of the African continent at Tabora and at Kigoma, in the Great Lakes region. In this same century the Baluch together with the mercenaries called *shihiri*, from Hadhramawt, fought also against the Nyamwezi in the region of the Unyanyembe. Other Baluch joined the trade caravans which traded with the interior, travelling as far as the Congo.

2.2   *Why Zanzibar?*

On Zanzibar a gradual process of osmosis occurred which often linked magical practices with the precepts of the Koran, resulting in a political-social mix and management of power that reflect a multiplicity of cultural roots. This intermingling also gave impetus to commercial activity, to the point that the English explorer and adventurer, Richard Burton, defined the island of Zanzibar as: "the depot of the richest trade in Eastern Africa."[15] The vast network of international trade links run by the Indian mercantile communities was further consolidated, stretching from East Africa, Arabia, the Gulf and India as far as southeast Asia, Indonesia and even China. It was only from halfway through the 19th century that this network began to feel the effects of a European impact, the European ships before this time being inferior in both size and capital investments.

The 19th century was, therefore, an era destined to become of crucial importance in the history of East Africa, both in terms of the nature and extent of its continuity with the past and in terms of innovations and later trends: the eastern coasts of Africa were already exposed to European involvement. It was without doubt a

---

[15] R.F. Burton, *Zanzibar: City, Island and Coast*, London, 1872, 2 vols., vol. II, pp. 102–103.

period of fundamental changes in the history of Africa, changes wrought by the new interest shown by Europeans, not only in the commercial sphere, but also directed towards heavy intervention in the social and economic lives of the African peoples by means of the extension to the African continent of European international interests and power policies.

At this point, a second question arises. Why, among the numerous ports and flourishing islands, was it Zanzibar that became a focal point not only of local, but also of international events? Why, in brief, did the choice fall precisely on this island? Here, too, the answer is to be found in a tangle of interests that witnessed a growing demand for sugar cane from the Mascarene islands, and for ivory and cloves from East Africa which, in turn, led to an increasing demand for slaves for the plantations and labour for transporting merchandise. This led to great migratory movements of slaves from the interior of the African continent towards the coasts and islands.

These changes coming from the interior of sub-Saharan East Africa were, therefore, strongly felt and, in alternating phases, took preeminence over external influences, in particular those from the west. It is against this background that we may delineate the history of the East African coast, still bearing in mind the innumerable variables which intervened during the 19th century, all of which contributed to the creation of the Swahili civilization, as we have already noted, a unique phenomenon in the history of this continent.

At the start of the century the links between the East African coast and the Indian Ocean favoured ever more numerous and productive commercial contacts. The period between 1805 and 1820 is, therefore, seen by many scholars as crucial to the history of Africa.[16] In this regard, the rise of the hegemony of the Omani Āl Bū Saʿīdī tribe is emblematic.

In the early decades, the Swahili civilization came to be identified with the territory lying between the Juba river and immediately to the north of Cape Delgado. It was at the centre of this wide expanse

---

[16] See, among others, I. Wallerstein, *Africa and the World Economy*, in, J.F.A. Ajayi (Ed.), *Africa in the Nineteenth Century until the 1880s*, Unesco General History of Africa, Paris, 1989, vol. VI, p. 34; I. Hrbek, *Towards a Periodisation of African History*, in, T.O. Ranger (Ed.), *Emerging Themes of African History*, Nairobi, 1968, *passim*.

that the island of Zanzibar came to prominence, as crossroads of
trade and strategic interests for the rest of the century.

Near the coast of equatorial Africa, separated from the continent
by a mere 50 kilometres, lies the island of Zanzibar. It is the largest
coral island of East Africa and forms part of a coral reef that stretches
from the island of Pemba in the north to the island of Mafia in the
south, creating a kind of coastline detached from the continent itself.
Zanzibar is 20–30 kilometres wide and roughly 85 kilometres long.
The city of the same name lies on the western side of the island
and its port, one of the best in Africa, provided good anchorage for
deep-sea fishing vessels.

The island of Pemba (the green or the emerald island) is roughly
75 kilometres long and 20 wide, an area of approximately 984 square
kilometres, and is found 56 kilometres from Zanzibar.[17] Consisting
mainly of coralline rock, it is hillier than its sister island, Zanzibar.
Pemba was equally well-known for its cloves, still the main source
of income today. Despite the extremely heterogeneous nature of its
population, Pemba is inhabited by the homonymous Bantu tribe, the
Wapemba.[18] The largest town on the island, Wete, in the west, has
an imposing square-plan fortress built by the Portuguese which looms
over a bay of mangroves.

In the 19th century, Pemba had no harbours suitable for large
ships. With its shallow waters and dense vegetation, the island had
limited reserves of drinking water. However, since the reef protects
their coasts, Zanzibar and Pemba were the only islands of strategic
predominance thanks to two variables of fundamental importance:
the monsoons and their proximity to the African continent. One of
the reasons for their commercial success during this century was
that the islands offered better services compared to other cities of
the East African coast. The fleets of the Arab Sultan, moreover,
protected the merchants' ships, taxes were low and, not least, Zanzibar
had drinking water. The rich traffic of the western Indian Ocean
shores related to all kinds of goods and spices, principally of great
value.

---

[17] G.P.S. Freeman-Grenville, heading: *Pemba*, E.I., 1999, Leiden, VIII, p. 292a.
[18] J. Middleton, *World of the Swahili*, op. cit., *passim*.

2.3   *Magic East African Practices*

An interesting particularity of the island of Pemba was the presence there of powerful magicians, witch-doctors and magical spirits. The island was renowned as the seat of numerous individuals with para-normal powers, and tales are still told of the existence of an invisible city, *Gining'i*, in the south of the island, believed to be home to the greatest gathering of wizards and magicians.

Many residents of Zanzibar and the African coast as far as the Great Lakes, journeyed to Pemba to receive advice and treatment from these famous wizards and witch-doctors (*waganga/wachawi*). In the past, this led to a progressive concentration of the power of these charismatic figures who could provide answers, tell the future, bring the rains, heal sickness and astonish with their magic rituals, but also cast cursing spells. The victim of such a curse being made by one of Pemba's wizards was called *roga*, a category from which, however, all Asiatic people were excluded. This was due to the fact that, until the revolution of the 1960's, when numerous Asians left the island, the Indian merchant communities—both Hindu and Muslim—enjoyed not only financial but also magical powers. This did nothing to harm their pre-eminent position. In fact, some clove plantation owners of Asian descent maintained that they could control their trees from afar thanks to their magic powers. Others, instead, boasted that they could transform themselves into any animal they wished and, thus 'disguised' participate in witchcraft competitions alongside the other groups of merchants present on the island. These 'competitions' were widespread and frequent, and represented important moments of close gathering and social cohesion, apart from offering great amusement. The anthropologist N. Arnold believes that the Asian wizards were active on Pemba until the 1920's–30's.[19] From then on, they gradually gave up their magic roles, and the world of the '*wachawi gala*' saw them only as spectators. Magical practices then passed, or better, returned to the Africans.

All the inhabitants knew of the presence of a sacred fish at Chake Chake; nobody knew the precise species to which it belonged, but

---

[19] Research carried out at Pemba by Nathalie Arnold, Department of Anthropology, University of Indiana, USA. My personal thanks for the interesting information from the international forum on the Asian Diaspora in East Africa Namaskar-Africana during 2002 and 2003.

they attributed to this fish many occult powers and it was honoured with prayers and gifts. Since this mysterious creature swam in dark and muddy waters, it was believed to be an eel, probably of an aggressive nature, and moody when the gifts, especially boiled eggs, were not to its liking.[20] Numerous similarities have also been noted between the 'treatment' provided by the African witchdoctors and that of the Omani Arabs. These were clearly due to the numerous links with people from the Arabian peninsula on the African islands, which witnessed the arrival and departure of twelve Sultans over a period of roughly 133 years.

A mixture of animistic rituals and Islam was inevitable in the history of the islands of Zanzibar and Pemba. The religious leaders, mainly Ibadi or Sunni, had different roles to those of the magicians, but were, nevertheless, greatly influenced by the magical, divining, medical and astrological practices of Africa. This principally meant, both for the *wachawi* and the qādi of the Omani court, shaping reality to their own advantage with the aim of alternately defending or asserting themselves.[21] The ginn (*jinn*) or pepo, spirits, illnesses and curses existed for all, and the process of osmosis between the different communities was an ongoing one, the only difference being that while the elite of the Arabs wrote down details of their divining skills, the autochthonous peoples continued in the oral tradition of passing on knowledge, the concentration of power, as has been noted, swinging alternately between Zanzibar and Pemba.

The regular arrival of the monsoons, as we have said, enabled continuous contact to exist with India, the Red Sea and the Gulf. Its proximity to the coast provided Zanzibar with an ideal strategic position for trade between the interior and the western Indian Ocean. In the first place, it was in a central position in relation to the coast, where the forests ended and the cultivated and inhabited areas of the interior began. It also lay at the centre of the monsoon winds which made it possible to travel along the coasts from Lamu towards the Comoros for most of the year. Lastly, it was a fertile island.[22]

---

[20] F.D. Omanney, *Isle of Cloves. A view from Zanzibar*, London, 1957, pp. 193–95.

[21] L. Declich, *The Arabic manuscripts of the Zanzibar National Archives: sources for the study of popular Islam in the island during the 19th century*, International Colloquium: *Islam in East Africa: New Sources*, Rome, 2–4 December, 1999, Ed. by B. Scarcia Amoretti, Rome, 2001, pp. 47–57.

[22] J.C. Wilkinson, *Imamate Tradition of Oman*, op. cit., p. 57.

Despite the extremely heterogeneous nature of its population, the south-eastern part of Zanzibar was mainly inhabited by people of the Bantu linguistic group, known as Hadimu (Wahadimu), while to the north the Tumbatu (Watumbatu) lived. Pemba was populated by the Wapemba tribe.[23] These three groups were described by Burton in the 19th century as Sunni Muslims, although the explorer did note that "they have preserved many superstitions and idolatries which belonged to their pagan ancestors."[24] The Hadimu and Tumbatu were involved in fishing, agriculture and cattle-raising, while the Hadimu women were responsible for the entire production of rope from coconut fibre, in the villages in the south of the island. In the first decades of the century, the Hadimu and Tumbatu were moved from the most fertile areas in the west of the island by the Āl Bū Sa'īdī of Oman.[25]

2.4   *Luxury Goods*

The rich coastal trade of the western Indian Ocean involved all kinds of highly-valued merchandise and spices. Among these were rhubarb, borax, ginger, sesame, ivory, tortoise shell, rhinoceros horns, opium poppies, the skins of exotic animals, hunting falcons, diamonds, vermillion, gold, horses, raffia and, naturally, silk, which the Arab believed had special properties effective against illness and parasites. There were also castor oil, tamarind, cardamom, cumin, cubebs, cloves, vanilla, curry, cinnamon,[26] cassia, nutmeg and its derivative mace, Indian aloe and from the island of Socotra used as a perfume and soothing balm. And saffron, copal resin, rubber, tropical

---

[23] J. Middleton, *World of the Swahili*, op. cit., *passim.*

[24] R.F. Burton, *Zanzibar*, op. cit., vol. II, p. 422.

[25] Many Hadimu and Tumbatu emphasize their Shirazi, or Persian, origin. This self-identification helps them avoid pejorative labels which were due to the political persecution of the 1960's. On the other hand, the overall cover of common Shirazi ethnicity enables them to boast of a glorious, noble and ancient origin. Interview kindly permitted by A. Sheriff, Zanzibar, 19 August 1994. See also, A. Sheriff and C. Tominaga, *The Ambiguity of Shirazi Ethnicity in the History & Politics of Zanzibar*, "Christianity and Culture", 24, Sendai, 1990, pp. 1–37.

[26] A plant originating in India, Burma and China (it appears in the Persian annals with the name 'Chinese bark'). Arab traders were wary of revealing their sources of cinnamon. M.N. Pearson (Ed.), *Spices in the Indian Ocean World. An Expanding World: The European Impact on World History 1450–1800*, vol. 11, Aldershot, Hampshire, 1996.

fruits, palm leaf baskets, Mocha coffee, very fashionable in Europe from the mid-18th century on, Chinese porcelain, sometimes used as precious containers for Arabian dates,[27] musk rose water, musk from Tibet and China, enormous quantities of ambergris bought on the shores of the island of Zanzibar or neighbouring isles.[28] Ambergris floated on the surface or was obtained by whaling. The Arabs introduced this precious product to the West and China, where it was called dragon's saliva, from the 9th century onwards. It was important in fixing the instable essences extracted from flowers, and its perfume was considered a real delicacy by the Arabs who even used it in sorbets. Much confusion arose as to its origin: rumours held it to come from an underground fountain, or that is grew on the ocean floor, that it was a kind of beeswax, or even bird excrement. We know also that huge quantities of ivory were exported from the East African coasts from the earliest times, along with rhinoceros horns and tortoise shell, as well as rocky crystals.

In the 19th century, the main exports from coastal East Africa and the island of Zanzibar were: cloves, copal, ivory, leather and skins, red pepper, sesame, copra, coco oil, tortoise shell, cowry shells used as currency, beeswax, tallow and all kinds of objects. Imports consisted of cotton cloth, weapons, gunpowder, beads, watches, liquor, flour, refined sugar, cotton thread, glass goods, chintz, Chinoiserie and hunting guns. Zanzibar's main exports towards India were: ivory, cloves, copal, sandalwood, coconuts, hippopotamus teeth, cowry shells, wooden beams, rhinoceros horns, beeswax and ebony. Arab sailors from the Red Sea carried aloe and coffee, while those sailing from the southern coasts of Arabia sold dried fish, fish oil, ghee (clarified butter) and onions. Ships sailing[29] from Oman and the Persian Gulf took to Africa dates and raisins, donkeys and horses, cloth from Muscat, Persian carpets and silks, nankeen, gunpowder, almonds and spices, especially saffron and asafoetida. The Arabs traded also in

---

[27] J. Allan, *The Trade in Steel between the Indian Subcontinent and Iran*, International Conference: *Trade and Transformation in the Indian Ocean*, SOAS, University of London, 30 November 1996.

[28] L. Boulnois, *La route de la soie*, Genève, 1992, p. 205; Y. Kendaro, *A short History of ambergris by the Arabs and Chinese in the Indian Ocean*, Kinki University, Fukuoka, Japan, 1955.

[29] The famous dhows of the western Indian Ocean. See D. Agius, *In the Wake of the Dhow. The Arabian Gulf and Oman*, Reading, 2002.

honey, water-jars, pearls, indigo,[30] textiles, rose water, gold and silver thread. The most important articles bought by the Arabs in
Africa were slaves, followed by cloves, coconuts and timber.

2.5 *Europeans in Zanzibar*

Towards the end of the 18th century, the French arrived on Zanzibar,
and signed treaties and commercial agreements with the Arabs regarding the slave and ivory trades, both lucrative and flourishing activities. As the French knew the island of the western Indian Ocean
better than the English, the scarce information at the East India
Company's disposition provoked a profound change in the geographical and spatial conception of the Orient in general, and of
the Indian Ocean in particular, a conception that now went beyond
mere imagination.[31]

The 19th century accounts by European explorers of the island
of Zanzibar are interesting in that they show how entirely different
were English and French approaches. For the English explorer, the
Orient was naturally represented by India and its markets. The space
left for imagination had already been defined by territorial, political
and administrative reality and the East was identified with material

---

[30] J. Balfour-Paul, *Indigo in the Arab World*, Exeter, 1997.

[31] In 1591 the first English vessel of Edward Bonaventure visited the island of
Zanzibar. In 1601 James Lancaster (later Sir, President of the East India Company),
who had served under Sir Francis Drake, spoke of Zanzibar in relation to supplies
of wood for repairing ships, and described a small fort built by the Arabs after the
defeat of the Portuguese, with three small cannon, defended by 50 soldiers. In 1609
the ships *Union* and *Ascencion* sailed to Zanzibar. The navigator John Henderson
married a princess of the island in 1604 and their portraits are to be seen in the
National Galleries of Scotland. Alexander Hamilton visited the island in 1727;
Augustin Bissel in 1798 and Commodore Blankett in 1798–99. James Prior travelled to Kilwa and Zanzibar in September of 1811 with the frigate *Nisus* and
recorded the Arab trade with the island and Mozambique in ivory, wax and slaves,
witnessing the selling of 10,000 slaves destined for Brazil. Prior also noted that the
port of Zanzibar was not suitable for large vessels due to the presence of sand
banks. J. Prior, *Voyage on the Frigate Nisus*, London, 1819; R.F. Burton, *The Lake
Regions of Central Equatorial Africa with Notices of the Lunar Mountains and the Sources of
White Nile; being the results of Expedition undertaken under the patronage of her Majesty's
Government and the Royal Geographical Society of London, in the years 1857–1859*, n. 29,
London, 1860, pp. 604, pp. 2–6; R. Coupland, *East Africa and its Invaders*, Oxford,
1938, *passim*; C.S. Nicholls, *The Swahili Coast. Politics, Diplomacy and Trade on the East
African Littoral 1793–1815*, London, 1954, Appendix II, pp. 386–87; J.M. Gray,
History of Zanzibar from the Middle Age to 1856, London, 1962, pp. 128–132.

possession. English individualism was, therefore, closely linked to the sea, the nation being seen as the commander of a ship with the ocean around and below him, where the sovereign authority of the captain was unchallenged; a decisive concept in which the sea had to be dominated. Thus, in the immense expanses of ocean they were concerned with who the seas obeyed most frequently, and such obedience was clearly easier when the final destination was a British colony.

The French traveller, instead, tended to experience a profound sense of disorientation in the seas of the East, especially in those areas where France, her energies always divided between continental objectives and colonial maritime ambition, was not to succeed in imposing any form of sovereign presence. After the Revolution, what should have become France's 'civilizing' mission developed, in the 19th century, into a position of 'second-in-command' in the wake of British power. Such asymmetrical forces were a constant in the Indian Ocean, pointers to the divergence of British reality and French ambitions. These differences were to be seen very clearly in the reports made by explorers and political representatives of their respective Governments.

Although the island had been explored previously by officials of the East India Company at the start of the century, Zanzibar was not well known to the English. There were few nautical charts and those that existed were not very accurate. An example of the possible consequences of this lack of trustworthy topographical information is that of Commodore Blankett who, in 1798 to 1799, unaware of the opposing monsoon winds, sailed from Zanzibar for weeks along the East African coast in an attempt to reach the Red Sea so as to intercept and block the threatened French invasion of India.

At the start of the century, the East India Company in Bombay, wishing to develop political and economic links with the East African coasts, set in motion various plans for resolving this problem regarding both nautical charts of the coast and maps of the interior. They ordered systematic inspections to be made of all the coastal stretches of the routes to India, from the Arabian Peninsula to the Red Sea and the Gulf.

Fervid French consular activity in the area, which was not interrupted by Napoleon's return to Europe, hastened to compete against enemy British initiatives. What the French captain M. Dallons saw, when he explored Zanzibar in 1804 with the aim of increasing the slave trade between the mainland and the French bases on the Mascarene islands, may be read in the report he sent to the Governor General. In the first place, he stressed the serious lack of any systematic commercial relations between France and the Āl Bū Sa'īdī of Oman to whose authority the islands of the Indian Ocean were nominally subject. Dallons' *cahiers des doleances*, however, did not end here. The Captain also complained of the extreme untrustworthiness, if not total absence of any political-administrative figure through whom to carry out commercial negotiations with Zanzibar, in that the representatives of Muscat were frequently replaced, the choice for replacements not by chance usually falling on eunuchs, former slaves of the Āl Bū Sa'īdī, while civil powers were kept strictly separate from the military. This was a practice which was employed to as to prevent any possible acquisition of power and consequent autonomy on the part of the governors on the spot. Zanzibar's income, according to Dallons, amounted to 40,000 piastres a year, mainly received at the end of the north-east monsoon period, between March and April. The monies were received by the local governor who arranged for lesser sums to be passed on to Muscat on a five-yearly basis. French trade with Zanzibar was never easy, prices being fixed by the governor of the island who often subtracted 30% for himself. Moreover, the slave merchants kept back an eleven piastre tax on each slave the French bought, whereas Asian buyers paid only one piastre. A further example of the urgent need for greater intervention by France to protect its trade in the Indian Ocean may be seen in the meeting Dallons had with the governor of Zanzibar, a eunuch by the name of *Yaqut*. The French official accused the Arab representative of hindering French trade with the markets of the African coast. Up until his death in 1819, *Yaqut* effectively had total control over taxes and controlled trade and exchange between the Mrima coast and the island, accumulating immense personal wealth along the way and imposing entirely arbitrary laws and regulations.

In this respect, Dallons called for the nomination of a French Resident to head a permanent commercial representative body on Zanzibar. This request, sent to Muscat from the Île de France on the 5 Fructidor, year 12 (5th August 1804), immediately came to the notice of East India Company of Bombay's intelligence. The British response reflects the differences of approach. The French essentially concentrated on commerce and the slave trade, while the

British were interested not only in commerce but also a gradual assumption of political control. The French crisis in the Indian Ocean, together with the conclusion of the Gardane Mission in Persia,[32] led the English to occupy the 'blank spaces' left on the map of the seas. A few years later, on the 10th December 1810, two cruisers of the Bombay Marine—the *Ternate* and the *Silph*—under the commands of Captain Smee and Lieutenant Hardy, sailed from Bombay with orders to inspect the entire coast, from Cape Guardafui as far as the island of Zanzibar. The two British explorers provided a typically Eurocentric picture of local life, personalities, trade and corruption. Alongside this picture, however, we can set another, that of European competition for control and dominion over the eastern seas.

The description furnished by Smee and Hardy paint a far from attractive picture of the African coasts, mainly as a result of the hostility of their inhabitants: "from the treachery of the natives who are invariably inimical to the Europeans and their desire to plunder".[33] Smee and Hardy made gifts to the peoples encountered along the African shores of "cloths, beads, cutlery, rings and buttons to the amount of about 1000 rupees". Nevertheless, they concluded that "the inhabitants of the African interior were cruel cannibals and thieves". On the 23rd December 1810, they sent word to W.J. Hamilton, Government Secretary of the Marine Department in Bombay, that: "the whole extent of the African Coast, from Cape Guardafui to Zanzibar does not produce one good harbour, that would afford security to shipping."[34] Once in sight of Zanzibar, Smee and Hardy immediately realized that "The Island was more or less defenceless."[35] Although: "the appearance is extremely delightful . . . palms, pineapples, mangoes, many species of oranges, lemon, limes and citrons of plantains, bananas, cocoa nuts, pomegranates, pumpkins, onions, yams, brinjals, sweet potatoes, and a variety of guens, and

---

[32] V.F. Piacentini, *Aspetti originali della politica napoleonica in Persia nel quadro del duello anglo-francese*, "Storia e Politica" Milano, 1968, pp. 637–647.

[33] Smee and Hardy sent their report to Bombay; this was then sent to the Board of Control. In 1844 the report was published by the Bombay Geographical Society in its *Transactions*, thus greatly adding to knowledge of these areas. Along with topographical details, Smee and Hardy also provided information regarding politics and trade, together with a dictionary of terms in Swahili, Somali and the Galla dialect. I.O.R. L/MAR/C/586, f. 98.

[34] I.O.R. L/MAR/C/586, f. 100.

[35] J.M. Gray, *History of Zanzibar*, op. cit., pp. 1–9.

the sugar cane is extensively cultivated."[36] On the subject of imports, they reported: "cloths are imported from the Gulf of Kutch; and from Muskat, Mocha, Mukulla and Judda, Dates, Rice, Cotton cloths, Jin, Tobacco, and Copper, Ghee, Myrrh, Coffee, Gum, Frankincense, Benjamin, Elephant teeths, are brought from the country of Hurhur to Burbureca upon camels, the distance between the two places being 15 days journey."[37]

According to English accounts, the natives of Zanzibar fed on rice from India, and a kind of flour made from a plant imported by the Portuguese called *pao de farine* (in kiswahili *mahoga*), which formed the basic diet of the Africans, while not much fish was eaten, despite the abundance of fish in the waters around the island. In the city of Zanzibar, Smee and Hardy also noted that the only buildings in stone and madrepore belonged to the Omani Arab and the Indian merchants. These, the richest and most powerful men of the island, formed a small community compared to the great number of slaves, a group which accounted for roughly 5/6 of the overall population. The two explorers estimated the population to number 200,000, taking into account the temporary presence of many members of the Arab and Indian communities.[38]

At the beginning of January 1811, Smee and Hardy were met at the port of Zanzibar by a representative of the Omani sovereign, Sa'īd bin Sulṭān Āl Bū Sa'īdī.[39] This man, Yacoud or Yaqut—"a person of small stature, not very dark, (and) about thirty years of age"—was a former slave of Sa'īd bin Sulṭān Āl Bū Sa'īdī born in Asmara, who, surprised in the company of a young female slave belonging to the uncle of Sa'īd bin Sulṭān Āl Bū Sa'īdī, was castrated as punishment. Yaqut governed Zanzibar, making 15,000

[36] I.O.R. L/MAR/C/586, f. 102.

[37] I.O.R. L/MAR/C/586, Extract of Paragraph 12 of a Memoir from Ibrahim Purkar dated the 21 Sept. 1800. Marine Cruizer *Ternate*, Document 2. Translation of a paper from Ibrahim Purkar to the Honorable Jonathan Duncan, Esquire, Governor of Bombay, dated the 10 Mohurrum 1224 Hijree, 26th Feb. 1809. Marine Cruizer *Ternate*, Document 3, f. 162.

[38] G.A. Akinola, *Slavery and Slave Revolts in the Sultanate of Zanzibar in the Nineteenth Century*, "Journal of the Historical Society of Nigeria" n. 6, 1972, p. 220.

[39] *Yaqut bin Ambar Al Habashi*, was appointed governor at Zanzibar for the loyalty he showed to Sulṭān bin Ahmad Āl Bū Sa'īdī (1792–1804), and also because he owned property in Oman, which would have guaranteed his political integrity in the eyes of the Omani. R. Bhacker, *Trade and Empire In Muscat and Zanzibar*, op. cit., p. 74.

Maria Theresa thalers a year, of which only 6,000 reached Muscat.[40] He was helped by an assistant, three Arab officers who commanded a small garrison, and five hundred slaves under the orders of these officers, although the English explorers saw no evidence of any military force based on the island.

Smee and Hardy believed, moreover, that *Yaqut* did not enjoy the consensus of the local population and judged him to be 'a person warmly attached to the French interest'. This diffidence was, however, reciprocal, to the extent that *Yaqut* refused to believe that the English had taken the Île de France (Mauritius) in the summer of 1810. "This appeared an unwelcomed communication to him and we could not help noting his partiality to French by remarking previously he did not think we should succeed."[41] Confirmation of the news, in fact, only reached him halfway through the March of the following year, from a ship which arrived from Muscat.

In 1819 the representative *Yaqut* was succeeded by the Indian Topan family, given the role of Masters of Customs, or tax-collectors, by the Arabs. The Topan came from Lakhput, in the Kutch region of western India. The financing of caravans directed towards the interior to deal in slaves and the ivory trade,[42] together with unlimited credit at low interest rates, gave the Indian mercantile community immense control, also of a political nature. An example of this may be seen in the document in which Lt. Emery, on the 17th October 1824, reported that the political representative of Sa'īd bin Sulṭān Āl Bū Sa'īdī at Zanzibar, Sulayman bin Ally, was in debt to an Indian merchant to the tune of 12,000 Maria Theresa talers.[43]

In effect, about halfway through the nineteenth century, "Jairam Topan was even more powerful than the ruler himself and he had

---

[40] The Arabs imposed a tax of 5% on every article exported from Zanzibar.

[41] I.O.R. L/MAR/C/586, f. 168.

[42] The ivory from the tusks of Asian elephants, with its reddish veining, is hard and little suited to the production of precious objects since it yellows immediately and has always been inferior to that of the African elephant. There was always a great demand for African ivory in India, since Hindu women for their marriage ceremonies wore ivory bracelets from their wrists to their elbows as well as anklets. These bracelets were burnt on their death and, following the abolition of suttee, broken as a sign of mourning. A. Sheriff, *The Rise of a Commercial Empire: An Aspect of the Economic History of Zanzibar 1770–1873*, Ph.D. Thesis, University of London, 1971, pp. 118–20.

[43] Public Record Office (P.R.O.), Admiralty Records, *Journal of Lieut. Emery, who was in Mombasa from 1824 to 1826*, f. 52/3940.

a coastguard of some 150 Arabs armed with matchlocks."[44] Jairam had succeeded in uniting the trade with Arabia, Africa and India into a single economic-financial organization, firmly and capably run by himself in person.

From such testimony we may clearly identify a series of elements that enable us to interpret the Anglo-French strategy in these seas. Smee and Hardy learnt from an interpreter who spoke English that three weeks before their arrival, a French ship under the command of a certain Monsieur Dubon had reached Zanzibar. The French had taken many slaves and some Arab passengers aboard, then sailed for the Île de France. The interpreter also told them that a further three French vessels had anchored at Zanzibar to load up with slaves, but that Yaqut had sent them to Kilwa.

The appalling and humiliating sights of the slave markets in the main square of Zanzibar made a strong impression on the two Englishmen, who furnished a crude but realistic description: "The number of slaves sent annually from Zanzibar to the Île de France, Muscat and India is computed at about 10,000 of all ages and both sexes."[45] The slave market opened at three or four in the afternoon. The slaves were washed and oiled, then the sellers painted their faces with red and white stripes and sometimes they were covered in a yellow powder considered aesthetically pleasing, and given bracelets and a plain or striped cloth to wrap around their bodies. The youngest were sold first, the ages ranging from six to sixty. Buyers checked for physical imperfections, inspecting the slaves' mouths, teeth and sexual organs, and would make them run to make certain they were in good health. Children of about six were sold for four to six dollars, a girl could fetch sixty, while women with children fetched the lowest prices. When they died, their bodies were left on the beach, one of the main reasons for the spread of serious diseases.

When Smee and Hardy saw that "the French have a Factory at Zanzibar in which their flag was constantly displayed till their arrival"[46] they immediately destroyed the French flag and closed down the French trade representation. Worse still, they discovered that "they have also a Broker . . . constantly in the practice of sending Packets

---

[44] G.A. Akinola, *Slavery and Slave Revolts in the Sultanate of Zanzibar*, op. cit., p. 234.
[45] I.O.R. L/MAR/C/586, f. 170.
[46] Ibid.

from hence to Egypt, Arabia and Persia, in charge of the Muscat Arabs".[47] On the 8th September 1811, Smee and Hardy, having obtained information indispensable to the East India Company, left the island to return to the port of Bombay.

This, therefore, was Zanzibar, southernmost terminal of a powerful trade network dominated by the Omani Arabs during the first half of the 19th century, centre of the Anglo-French rivalry, than one of those numerous oriental regions which were destined to be covered by the 'British mantle' during the 19th century.

---

[47] Ibid.

CHAPTER THREE

ZANZIBAR AND SWAHILI COAST:
LAND, POWER GROUPS AND SOCIAL CLASSES

In the collective imagination, Zanzibar hangs like a splendid jewel off the African continent, a magical and exotic place of luxuriant vegetation and perfumed air, rich in spices and good water, with splendid coral beaches, crystal clear seas and sand as soft and white as talcum powder . . .

In truth, as we shall see, Zanzibar's history cannot be reduced to a mere hagiographic listing of *mirabilia*, Sultans, slaves, ivory and spices.

During the first half of the 19th century, numerous elements would lead, in a dance of polarities, to the emergence of a marked cultural, economic and political syncretism, that would often erupt into open conflict. These factors included the presence on the island of different ethnic-social and religious groups, the domination of the Omani Arab dynasty of the Āl Bū Sa'īdī, the crucial presence of Indian mercantile communities and the Asian community of Baluch mercenaries in the service of the Omani who would govern this island for roughly two centuries, the role played by other Arab communities, especially those from Yemen and other regions of the Arabian peninsula such as Hadramawt,[1] as well as the pre-colonial and colonial European and even American elements.

To understand this situation to the full, we should pause a moment to glance at the definition and composition of the Swahili civilisation, which on the island of Zanzibar had one of its principal centres of development. And here we come up against one of the greatest challenges faced in innumerable historical debates: the sheer quantity and conflicting nature of the attempts at defining the identity, origins and linguistic and cultural influences of the coastal and island

---

[1] U. Freitag & W.G. Clarence-Smith (Eds.), *Hadrami Traders, Scholars, and Statements in the Indian Ocean, 1750s–1960s*, op. cit., *passim*; L. Boxberger, *On the Edge of Empire: Hadhramawt, Emigration, and the Indian Ocean, 1880s–1930s*, SUNY Series in Near Eastern Studies, Albany, 2002.

populations of sub-Saharan East Africa and at determining how these
altered over the course of time until they finally assumed the title
of Swahili.

The currents and winds of the western Indian Ocean made possible the numerous contacts that existed with eastern Africa. Without
the monsoon winds, the African terminal would doubtless have been
excluded from the life of these seas.[2] Relations between the coast
and the interior were also important, as were their models of development and respective influences and variations. The reasons for
such relations were above all commercial, Africa providing raw materials and the other terminals importing more sophisticated articles,
thus establishing a hierarchy and ever more detailed system of rules
of exchange. The Swahili lived in the islands and along the coasts
of East Africa, urban-based merchants who dealt in long-distance
inter-continental trade.

They belonged to a sophisticated and cultivated society formed of
a single group that spoke the same, single language, a global society that represented a central rather than some form of peripheral
entity. Swahili is a Bantu language, and the term itself a Bantu word,
but it derives also from the Arabic sāhil, sawāhil, belonging to the
coasts.[3] In this respect, we can clearly see the desire of modern his-
toriographers to bring the history of the Swahili civilisation back to
Africa.

Swahili language, literature and poetry have always represented
an important source also for any attempt to understand the history
of the coast and islands of East Africa.[4] Thus, the progressive and
gradual formation of the Swahili lexicon, with which the civilisation
identifies itself, is pivotal to the history of this vast area of Africa.
It is equally important to recall that, in the past, numerous historical interpretations tended to consider the Swahili coast and its history as a kind of *tabula rasa* on which external influences played and
became interwoven. Today, instead, preference is given to re-evaluating

---

[2] See Chapter I.

[3] M. Horton and J. Middleton, *The Swahili. The Social Landscape of a Mercantile
Society*, London, 2000, pp. 8–12.

[4] R. Pouwels, *Horn and Crescent. Cultural Change and Traditional Islam in the East
African Coast A.D. 800–1900*, Cambridge, 1987; Ibid., *Eastern Africa and the Indian
Ocean to 1800, Reviewing Relations in Historical Perspective*, "International Journal of
African Historical Studies", vol. 35, nos. 2–3, 2002, pp. 385–425.

or rediscovering the importance of the autocthonous African component, seen now as the heart of Swahili civilisation which faced the external influences which came into play over the course of the centuries. The Arabic component was, obviously, considerable but its influence was nonetheless evident only in certain aspects such as jurisprudence, commerce, religion, non-African botany, measures and navigation. These linguistic contributions occurred, therefore, at a relatively late stage and related to a somewhat restricted number of subjects without influencing the original characteristics of the language. Swahili's backdrop was first and foremost the sea, the Indian Ocean, and the Swahili coast has been identified as an endless strip reaching from Ras Chiamboni, the Somali coast of Benadir, as far as Cape Delgado, roughly speaking, from Mogadishu to Mozambique.[5] We must not, however, leave the islands out of the equation as they were to play a vital role in the evolution that occurred along the coast.

3.1   Swahili Origins

The origins of the Swahili culture and civilisation have been defined in terms of five fundamental factors: 1) the nature of the coast; 2) trade between Africa, Arabia and Asia in which the Swahili played the role of merchants and intermediaries; 3) the subjection of their society to outside powers; 4) its multi-ethnic composition; 5) the developmental complexity of this African society. Interaction between these different cultures, African, Arabian and Asian, is, therefore, a key factor in understanding such complexities.

There are, of course, many works of all types and kinds on the subject, from which numerous new interpretations have emerged. Amongst these we have T. Spear who has illustrated the last fifteen years of interdisciplinary research carried out into the history of the Swahili civilisation.[6] Links between the coasts and the eastern African islands and the Arabian peninsula go back to the dawn of time. Archaeological research has revealed the existence of trade with the

---

[5] J. De Vere Allen, *Swahili Origins. Swahili Culture & the Shungwaya Phenomenon*, London, 1993.

[6] T. Spear, *Early Swahili History Reconsidered*, "International Journal of African Historical Studies", vol. 33, n. 2, 2002, pp. 257–290.

Arabian peninsula and Egypt, in mangrove wood staffs, crystal, ivory
and gold from as early as 300 B.C. Commercial links with Rome
around the first century A.D. have also been confirmed by excava-
tions that have extended the scenario outlined by C.M. Kusimba[7]
and others, reaching now to the north and east of Cape Guardafui,
in northern Somalia.

In the *Periplus Maris Erythraei*,[8] by an anonymous merchant from
Alexandria, one of the first seafaring manuals for the merchants of
the city, we read of trade being conducted in the Indian Ocean in
palm oil, tortoise shell, rhinoceros horns, cinnamon, incense, ivory
and slaves. This dates the first settlements along the East African
coasts by peoples from south-western Arabia to the first century A.D.
The *Periplus*, moreover, also provides a description of the inhabitants
of the African coast, called *Azania*, stating that they were very tall
and devoted to piracy. There are, however, many doubts as to the
authenticity of this document. Another important piece of testimony
is that provided by Ptolemy in the second century A.D., who tells
of the presence of populations going by the name of *zingi* who were
settled along the African coasts as far as the *Gulf of Barbaria*, that is
to say, south of Cape Guardafui.[9] The term, *zanj* has also been
identified as being of Persian origin, from *zangik*, meaning black.
Later Arab writings, furthermore, differentiate between the *zanj*, the
black Bantu, and other African peoples such as the Berber.[10] By the
5th–11th centuries East African connections with south-central Asia

---

[7] C.M. Kusimba, *The Rise and Fall of Swahili States*, Walnut Creek, CA, 1999.

[8] The *Periplus* is preserved in two Byzantine manuscripts, the Codex Palatinus
Gr. 398, held in Heidelberg and in the British Library, London, Add. MS. 19391.
Its precise chronological dating is still the subject of intense and lively debate. For
further information see, among others, L. Casson, *The Periplus maris Erytraei: text with
introduction, translation and commentary*, Princeton, 1989.

[9] Ptolemy (100–178 A.D. ca.), astronomer and mathematician, developed a plan-
etary system which constituted the only model for the world until the 16th century. He was most probably born in Greece, although his complete name, Claudio
Tolomeo, provides important information. Ptolemy, in fact, indicates that he was
an inhabitant of Egypt, and Claudio that he was a Roman citizen. From early
sources, moreover, we know that the astronomer spent most of his life at the
Serapeum of Canopus, near Alexandria, making those observations that would provide the foundations for his theory. Of primary importance is his work entitled
Geografia which, by applying a system of latitude and longitude, would influence car-
tographers for centuries, despite the unreliable nature of the data it contained.

[10] C.H. Becker and D.M. Dunlop, heading: *Bahr al-Zandj*, E.I., 1999.

were marked by the appearance of 'sgraffiato' pottery manufactured in Makran.[11]

Cosmas Indicopleuste, recalling Ptolemy halfway through the 6th century A.D., describes populations who he defines as the inhabitants of *Zingion*.[12]

Although the works of M. Horton have helped us to identify the development of one of the earliest coastal civilisation, Shanga,[13] dating from the 8th century A.D. on, there is still a gap in our knowledge that stretches from the 2nd to the 9th century. This is primarily due to a lack of archaeological evidence which has led to an eruption of archaeological activity that we can roughly divide into two main spheres: 1) reports on individual archaeological sites that concentrate mainly on the intrinsic relations of individual East African communities and 2) studies and research involving wider areas and aimed at revealing the existence of relations between the different Swahili families. More detailed accounts came from Arab geographers, the Arab impact with the African continent, as noted, being of enormous importance insofar as it set in motion an uninterrupted historical process of political, religious, economic and social change.

The first contacts with peoples from the Arabian peninsula started in the 8th century A.D., above all in the northern Somali area of East Africa. Arab populations were found in Mogadishu, Merca and Brava. Further to the south, the spread occurred more slowly through a gradual intensification of trade which resulted in the islands of Zanzibar and Pemba becoming the principal centres of commerce.

---

[11] Discovery by M. Horton.

[12] An Alexandrian merchant, Cosmas, nicknamed the *Indicopleuste*, in around the year 520 A.D. undertook for commercial purposes a number of lengthy voyages, especially in Arabia and East Africa. On his return to Egypt he became a hermit and compiled a series of literary works, only one of which has come down to us today, the *Topografia cristiana*. This is in twelve volumes, the last of which is only fragmentary, and is of enormous historical and cultural importance as it enables us to grasp the geographical concepts of the fifth century A.D. He imagined the earth as a great rectangle, surrounded by walls on all sides which, meeting above, formed the firmament or vault of the heavens. G.P.S. Freeman Grenville, *The East African Coast. Select Documents from the first to the earlier nineteenth century*, Oxford, 1962, pp. 5–7.

[13] Shanga, in the Lamu archipelago, is an important archaeological site. It reveals the existence of a sophisticated civilisation dated to approximately 1320 A.D. M. Horton, *Shanga: The Archaeology of a Muslim Trading Community on the Coast of East Africa*, London, 1996.

The land of the *zanj* is mentioned in the 9th century A.D. (875–885) by the Arab geographer and traveller Al Ya'qubi as a source of ambergris used for fixing perfume essences, although he does say that it is inferior in quality to that sold in the port of Aden. In the 9th century, the term applied by Abu 'Uthman 'Amru Bahr Al-Gahiz to define the inhabitants of East Africa settled along the coasts from modern-day Somalia to Mozambique is Ahl al-zang.[14] Al-Mas'udi, at the start of the 10th century (916–917) sailed among the islands of East Africa and he too tells of the land of the *zanj*.[15] Al-Mas'udi describes the inhabitants as being not particularly intelligent but good-natured and notes their trade via Arabia with India and China in ambergris, saffron, leopard skins for saddles, tortoise shells for combs and ivory. Commerce between East Africa and Arabia was also extremely lively, even though the Arab traveller described the seas of the *zanj* as being very dangerous. In the 12th century, Al-Idrisi[16] uses the Swahili term *waganga*, a witch doctor who practiced white magic.[17]

In approximately the year 1295 the first European, Marco Polo, described Mogadishu as being inhabited by Muslims involved in the ivory trade. His description of the East African coast and islands is, however, so confused that one could suppose it was based on tales told to him in China, where Africa was held to be important thanks to its ivory and other precious goods, or else in the ports of western India. In the same way he narrated the accounts of other Venetian merchants and travellers, whose journeys have been documented by

---

[14] J. Devisse, *Les Africains, la mer et les historiens*, "Cahiers d'Études Africaines", Paris, 1989, vol. 29, p. 400.

[15] Since this is to furnish a more complete picture and essentially based on western sources, the consultation of oriental sources was at one remove. Al Mas'udi, *Muruj adh-Dhahab, Muruj al-Dahab wa Ma'adin al-Jawhar, The Golden Pastures*, in, H.N. Chittick (Ed.), *The Peopling of the East African Coast*, cit., pp. 22 on; G.P.S. Freeman Grenville, *The East African Coast*, cit., pp. 14–17. See the interesting reflection on the origins and myth of the *zanj* by J. De Vere Allen, *Swahili Origins*, cit., *passim*.

[16] Al Idrisi (1099–1166 A.D.), whose full name was Abu Abdallah Muhammad Ibn Muhammad Ibn Abdallah Ibn Idris al-Qurtubi al-Hasani, was born in Ceuta, Spain, in 1099 A.D. He studied in Cordoba, travelled widely and served at the Norman court in Palermo. His death is dated, without precision, to around either 1166 or 1180 A.D.

[17] White magic is good magic *par excellence*. It takes the form of rituals, supplications, and purification rites. It is used to eliminate all forms of evil, from the evil eye to bad luck in the home, by seeking the help of the highest forces of good, be these spiritual or holy. Naturally, it functions in opposition to black magic which acts, instead, to negative ends.

finds of glass and Venetian vases along the African coasts and on the islands of the Indian Ocean.[18] In the 13th century there were roughly 37–40 cities between Mogadishu and Kilwa, the principal centres being Malindi, Zanzibar and Sofala.[19] Tales were told of the Swahili patrician residences having silver flights of stairs leading to beds of gold, the legendary gold of Sofala. In the 14th century, the famous Arab geographer and traveller Ibn Battuta (1331–32) explored the shores of modern-day Tanzania and left us a splendid description of East Africa.[20] Ibn Battuta described magnificent and sumptuous communities: "robes were placed in wooden chests of sandal and camphor"[21] and highly developed cultures such as that in Mogadishu with its Koranic school and scholars of Islamic law. Around the 15th century, Swahili civilisation also came under the influence of Indonesian elements arriving from Madagascar.[22]

Settlements held to have been Persian in the main African coastal centres were vividly described and passed down through the years in the suggestive legend of the seven Persian princes. Ali, of Abyssinian mother and Persian father named Husain, had seven brothers, chiefs of groups of warriors originally from Shiraz, hence the name Shirazi, in the Persian province of Fars. The seven princes set sail from the port of Siraf and, with their seven ships, conquered the eastern African coast as far as Mombasa. Each ship sailed into and took a

---

[18] M. Polo, *I Viaggi in Asia, in Africa, nel Mare delle Indie. Descritti nel secolo XIII da Marco Polo veneziano. Testo in lingua Detto il Milione*, 2 vols., Venezia, 1829; G.P.S. Freeman Grenville, *The East African Coast*, cit., pp. 25–26.

[19] M. Horton and J. Middleton, *The Swahili*, cit., pp. 82–83.

[20] H.A.R. Gibb (Ed.), *I. Battuta, Travels in Asia and Africa 1325–1354*, London, I ed. 1929, new ed. New Delhi, 1992; G.P.S. Freeman Grenville, *Ibn Battuta's Visit to East Africa. 1332 A.D.: A Translation*, "Uganda Journal", n. 19, 1955, pp. 1–6.

[21] G.P.S. Freeman Grenville, *The Medieval History of the Coast of Tanganyka; with special reference to recent archeological discoveries*, London, 1962, p. 194.

[22] A. Werner, *Zanzibar. The Swahili Population*, The Encyclopaedia of Islam, 4 vols., London, 1927, vol. IV, part II, pp. 1214–1217 and bibliographical notes; H.N. Chittick, *The Peopling of the East African Coast*, in, N. Chittick and R. Rotberg (Eds.), *East Africa and the Orient: cultural syntheses in pre-colonial times*, New York, London, 1975, pp. 16–43; G.P.S. Freeman Grenville, *The Medieval History of the Coast of Tanganika*, cit.; G. Mathew, *The East Coast Cultures*, in, G. Mathew, *Africa South*, no place, 2 vols., 1958; G. Shepherd, *The Making of the Swahili*, in, J. de V. Allen and T.H. Wilson (Eds.), *From Zinj to Zanzibar*, "Paideuma", n. 28, Wiesbaden, 1982; J.S. Kirkman, *The History of East Africa up to 1700*, in, J.S. Kirkman, *Prelude to East African History*, London, Nairobi, 1966; J. Middleton, *The World of the Swahili. An African Mercantile Civilization*, Yale, 1992; J. de Vere Allen, *Swahili Origins*, cit.; L. Mosca, *Il più bell'enigma del mondo: il popolamento dell'isola del Madagascar*, Napoli, 1994.

different port, and each prince founded a city, four of which have
been identified with Mombasa, the island of Pemba, the port of
Johanna in the Comoros islands and the city of Kilwa.[23] This last
was purchased in exchange for a quantity of coloured cloth sufficient
to encircle the entire island, and the Persian prince Ali married the
daughter of the island's king. This legend clearly illustrates the vast
commercial network that gave rise to trade and marriage ties between
the Persian and the African peoples. In relation to this, the exca-
vations conducted by the archaeologist N. Chittick revealed the existence of a colony of Persians from Siraf, the port of Shiraz, on the
island of Manda from the 9th–10th centuries on.[24] Furthermore, a
kufic inscription in the mosque of Kizimkazi, in the southern part
of Zanzibar, dated to the 12th century A.D. furnishes clear proof,
according to Chittick, of a Persian or Persian Gulf presence in East
Africa. Around the 13th century, with its power centred on Kilwa
where they built mosques and the first constructions in stone and
coral limestone, the Shirazi dynasty introduced copper coinage, sub-
stituting cowry shells, a further indication of the splendour of this
thalassocracy that ruled over the coasts and islands of the Indian
Ocean.

Lastly, on the islands of Zanzibar and Pemba we have the festi-
val to celebrate the Zoroastran new year, another sign of Persian
influence and called *mwaka kogwa* or *nauruzi*[25] in Kiswahili.

---

[23] According to M. Horton, the towns were: Mandakha, Shaugu, Yanbu, Mombasa,
Pemba, Kilwa, and Hanzuan. The Shirazi legend is described in the 14th century
by J. De Barros, *Cronica dos reyes de Quiloa*, transl. in G.P.S. Freeman Grenville, *The
East African Coast*, cit., 1962, p. 89. Idem, *Decadas da Asia*, Coimbra, 1930. There
are two places called Kilwa: 1) Kilwa Kisiwani which was a flourishing centre until
the 18th century and then reduced to a poverty-stricken village, and 2) Kilwa
Kivinje, 17 kilometres north of Kilwa Kisiwani which, in the 19th century, became
the most important port between Zanzibar and Mozambique. See C.S. Nicholls,
The Swahili Coast. Politics, Diplomacy and Trade on the East African Littoral 1798–1856,
London, n. 2, 1971, p. 317; A. Sheriff, *Slaves, Spices & Ivory in Zanzibar*, London,
1987, p. 46.

[24] H.N. Chittick, *The Peopling of the East African Coast*, cit.; H.N. Chittick and
R. Rotberg, *A New Look in the History of Pate*, "Journal of African History", London,
1969, vol. 10, n. 3; V. Fiorani Piacentini, *Merchants – Merchandise and Military Power
in the Persian Gulf (Suriyan – Shahriya – Siraf)*, "Memorie", Atti della Accademia
Nazionale dei Lincei, Roma, 1992, series IX, vol. III, Fasc. 2, pp. 110–184.

[25] *Mwaka* means year and *kogwa*, washed, bathed in kiswahili, the celebration still
taking place today in the area of Makunduchi, on Zanzibar. Communication from
Thomas Hinnenbush. Nauruzi means the year of Persian Zoroastran tradition. This
is not based on the lunar but the solar cycle and lasts 634 days. It is celebrated
at the spring equinox, the 21 March.

In their studies, D. Nurse and T. Spear[26] express a degree of perplexity concerning the veracity of these Persian legends harking back to a Shirazi origin. Also R. Pouwels[27] points out that the Shirazi tradition only emerged in a clear-cut form towards the 17th century, that is to say in a period in which the African coasts witnessed the presence of the Omani Arabs who put an end to the hegemony of the Swahili families. These latter, in self-defence, appealed to their Persian origins in order to assert their ethnic-social superiority over the Arab's overwhelming seizure of power. Pouwels therefore concludes that this tradition is relatively recent and does not date back to the 7th to 9th centuries when Persian merchants were, in fact, active in eastern Africa.

Commercial links with China were rendered easier by the advanced technology of Chinese shipbuilding and navigation. Tall tales were told of ships trading with the coasts of East Africa that were up to one hundred and fifty metres in length and equipped with fifty sails. Tuan Ch'eng-Shih, writing in the 9th century gave the region the name of land of the *Po-pa-li*.[28] He also wrote of a land called *Tuing-iji*, which could mean modern-day Somalia. Western sources reporting Chinese testimony speak of ivory, used to create the emperor's palanquin, and other goods such as rhinoceros horn,[29] perfumed woods, myrrh, storax gum and tortoiseshell. All these precious goods sailed to China which sent back silk, brocade, lacquer work and porcelain. It is precisely in this last commodity, porcelain, that a part of East Africa's history of outside contacts is seen to be narrated.[30]

The extraordinary extent of East Africa's maritime trade is also demonstrated by finds of Sung dynasty Chinese porcelain of the 12th century along the coast at Kilwa, and on the islands of Pate and

---

[26] D. Nurse and T. Spear, *The Swahili: Reconstructing the History and Language of an African Society 800–1500*, Philadelphia, 1985.

[27] R. Pouwels, *Horn and Crescent*, cit., *passim*; from the same author see also the paper: *Eastern Africa and the Indian Ocean to 1800, Reviewing Relations in Historical Perspective* presented at the International Conference: Cultural Exchange and Transformation in the Indian Ocean World, UCLA, Los Angeles, 5–6 April, 2002.

[28] Tuan Ch'eng Shih died in 863 A.D. He wrote a compendium which contained the very first information on East Africa. G.P.S. Freeman Grenville, *The East African Coast*, cit., p. 8.

[29] Powdered rhinoceros horn was used by the Chinese as an aphrodisiac.

[30] G.P.S. Freeman Grenville, *Zanj or Seng-Chih*, in, G.P.S. Freeman Grenville, *The Medieval History of the Coast of Tanganika*, cit., p. 35; J.J.L. Duyvendak, *China's Discovery of Africa*, London, 1949.

Mafia. Some theories, however, maintain that the Chinese were not directly involved in trade with Africa until the start of the 15th century,[31] a period in which they defined the continent as being the "barbarous distant regions hidden in an azure veil of thin vapours".[32] Nevertheless, between 1405 and 1433, seven Chinese fleets set sail under the command of the famous admiral, Chen Ho, a military leader who had been made a eunuch at the age of ten and assigned to the emperor's personal service. Chen Ho's expeditions were impressive, travelling via India to establish direct and personal commercial ties between the Ming dynasty and the Swahili families of Mogadishu, Malindi, Mombasa, Zanzibar and Kilwa. In October 1415, envoys from Malindi embarked on Chen Ho's fourth voyage and even a giraffe reached Peking, provoking such wonder as to be portrayed on silk.[33] From the second decade of the 15th century on, however, the mandarins' growing aversion to contact with barbarians from far-flung regions, and especially the excessive degree of power concentrated in the hands of admiral Chen Ho, combined to progressively reduce Chinese trade, including that with the coasts of East Africa.

Another important factor in terms of identification and differentiation, according to Middleton, is the Muslim religion, which spread through-

---

[31] During the 15th to 16th centuries, the Silk road via terra firma was replaced by the commercial maritime routes which traversed the Indian Ocean to reach China. The preference for such sea rather than land routes would result in political and social upheaval and disruption in Central Asia (one need only think of the fall of the Timurid empire and the transformation of Safavid Persia). Between 1405 and 1433 the blocking of the land routes as a result of the fall of the Moghul Empire in India and the rise of Islam, caused the Chinese emperors to send naval expeditions towards the western seas. See, in particular, M. Rossabi, *Decline of the Central Asian Caravan Trade*, in, J.D. Tracy (Ed.), *The Rise of the Merchant Empires. Long-distance Trade in the Early Modern World 1350–1750*, Cambridge, 1994 and bibliographical notes; V. Matveiev, *The Shaping of Swahili Civilization*, "Unesco Courier", Paris, 1979, pp. 66–9. For contrast, J. Shen, *New Thoughts on the Use of Chinese Documents in the Reconstruction of Early Swahili History*, "History in Africa", n. 22, 1995, pp. 349–358; Seminar: *Social Dynamics in Mughal India Sufis, Warriors, Merchants and Peasants*, organised by D.H.A. Kolff, Leiden University, The Netherlands, 8 October, 2003.

[32] P. Wheatley, *Analecta Sino Africana Recensa*, in, H.N. Chittick and R. Rotberg (Eds.), in, *East Africa and the Orient*, cit., p. 114.

[33] T. Filesi, *Le relazioni della Cina con l'Africa nel Medio Evo*, Milano, 1975, p. 57; W. Lenz, *Voyages of Admiral Zheng He before Columbus*, in, K.S. Mathew (Ed.), *Shipbuilding and Navigation in the Indian Ocean region A.D. 1400–1800*, New Delhi, 1997, pp. 147–154.

out eastern Africa around the 7th century A.D.[34] This would markedly differentiate the Swahili populations from the non-Muslim peoples of the interior. Here it is interesting to recall the hypothesis, proposed by Horton and Middleton,[35] of the existence of a coastal and insular African Islam, expressed as a separate and effective contribution to the history of the Muslim religion, rather than influenced by Arabia as other historians maintain. In support of this theory, these two scholars—one an archaeologist and the other an anthropologist—claim that the spread of Islam was never truly encouraged in Africa, a favoured territory for Arabia given the availability of slaves. In fact, once converted to Islam these could not have continued to be slaves and would have had to be included in the institution foreseen by Islamic law of amān, protection, under which non-Muslims could live peaceably alongside Muslims by paying a form of tax. A marked Muslim presence and influence did, however, remain in place by means of trade. This dated back to the Yemeni Shiite tribe of the Zaidi in the 7th century, described by Joao De Barros in the Chronicle of Kilwa, and extended to the Khariji-Ibadi of Oman towards the 9th century,[36] down to the Sunni Shafi,[37] the Koranic school followed by the majority of the Swahili and described by Ibn Battuta in the 14th century. There was also a Bantu Islam, that is to say a religious syncretism with animistic African practices which, according to the two scholars, surprisingly only began to develop after the end of the slave trade, in the second half of the 19th century. This was a process of 'arabisation without islamisation', a process which in no way conflicted with the Muslim religious presence in Africa thanks to the great flexibility resulting from its numerous and differing interpretations.

---

[34] J. Middleton, *The World of the Swahili*, cit., pp. 10–15.

[35] M. Horton and J. Middleton, *The Swahili*, cit., pp. 47–72.

[36] The Ibadi movement, a moderate Shia current of Islam named after its founder Abd Allah b. Ibad al-Murri al-Tamimi, was a branch of the Khariji—the first heterodox schismatic group of Islam in the 7th century A.D. whose radical doctrine represented a threat to the rule of the Caliphs. It spread in Oman in the 7th and 8th centuries. The Ibadi movement first arrived in East Africa in the town of Kilwa via commercial contacts between the 8th and 9th centuries. We must not forget that the Omani mercantile communities which maintained numerous trading links with eastern Africa were also profoundly influenced by both Persian and Indian culture. T. Lewicki, heading: *Al-Ibadiyya* and accompanying bibliography, E.I., op. cit., III: 648a.

The Portuguese arrived in the western Indian Ocean in 1498, initiating a project aimed at commercial control over the long-distance Asian and African maritime routes. It was the Portuguese who introduced a new phase in relations between India and East Africa and surprise was a key factor in their intervention on the scene of the oriental seas. After many centuries, in fact, the traditional thalassocratic system that had been established along the shores of the Indian Ocean was to be radically changed by the Europeans and the extending reach of their territorial ambitions, pursued as these were with such obstinacy and determination. The spirit of conquest fed by the fight against Islam, the conversion to Christianity of the infidels together with the overwhelming desire to lay their hands on Africa's gold and seize the monopoly over trade in spices and the precious goods of Africa and Asia from the Arabs and Venetians were the main factors underlying Portuguese policy in the East. Portugal's power rested more on control of communications routes and a monopoly over the spice trade than on direct domination, political power being exercised indirectly or taking the form of simple commercial influence. In 1505 the *Estado da India Oriental* was created, with its capital in Goa, India, the Viceroy, Francisco d'Almeida, enjoying arbitrary but farflung powers. The oft-sung riches of East Africa were, however, soon seen to be ephemeral and the Portuguese policy of exploiting the Asian and African coasts through the imposition of tributes did not suffice to cover the costs of maintaining contingents and fortifications there.

In 1593 Fort Jesus was built at Mombasa but, just as control over the spice trade would be wrested from their hands by the Dutch, this Portuguese stronghold was destined to be conquered in 1698 by the dynasty that preceded the Āl Bū Saʿīdī in Africa, the Yaʿrubī of Oman. This was a clamorous defeat and, although Fort Jesus returned to Portuguese possession in 1728–9, the signs of their political and commercial decline in the Indian Ocean were plain for all to see. Portuguese sources, however, which still today merit more in-depth perusal, provide numerous and interesting examples both in confirmation of and in contrast with the varying theories.

3.2 *Swahili Urban Landscape*

The cultural and artistic expressions of Swahili civilisation have always been characterised by great sophistication, its architecture displaying square-plan stone dwellings in the main cities along the coast. Its own, urban and architectural uniqueness can be perceived, unchanging in the face of a multitude of external influences. This was due to the essentially mercantile function of the Swahili people, bound by necessity to have ties with different populations and to remain as far as possible in harmony and equilibrium with them. These contacts not only favoured the newcomers but also, if not above all, the Swahilis themselves who became wealthy as a result of their lucrative trades.

The cities had always represented their bases for government, the foundations on which the social and cultural life as well as the commerce of Swahili society rested. The urban structure of Swahili towns, both along the coast and on the islands like Mombasa, Kilwa, Lamu and Zanzibar, for example, consisted of a series of central bodies branching out down long, narrow streets. The central buildings had courtyards and enclosed gardens, the building materials reflecting the kind of dwellings, in mud and straw for the less wealthy, wood and madrepore for the rich merchants. A nobleman's house covered an area of almost 250 square metres, on a single level on Zanzibar and on a number of floors at Lamu. Here the slaves lived on the ground floor, the owners on the first and their married daughters on the second or third, while the flat roofs were designed to collect rainwater. The entrance gave onto a courtyard with the owner's rooms on the opposite side so as to define clearly the different levels of purity and intimacy within the home itself. The main doors were of precious woods, decorated with floral motifs and inscriptions from the Koran. The rooms received light from the inner courtyard and no distinction was made between living room, dining-room and bedroom. Certain rooms were, however, set aside for women in labour and others for precious objects, with niches carved into the walls to hold them. Water for the bathrooms came from cisterns and the walls were high and thick to keep the rooms cool. All the roads led towards the centre indicated by the Friday mosque. These followed a rectangular plan and up to twenty could be seen at Mombasa and Lamu. More greatly influenced by Arabic style, the mosques did not have minarets and the call to prayer was made from within the building itself. There were also Koranic schools, the market place, coffee houses and the residence of the local governors. Open spaces surrounded by mangroves were used for dances, religious celebrations and political gatherings. The various quarters were strictly subdivided according to commercial activity somewhat in the manner of mediaeval cities in Europe. Food and slaves came from dwellings outside the urban centre itself and male domestic slaves slept outside the city walls. Unlike those of the Middle East and North Africa, which all had mosques, public baths and a central market, the Swahili towns did not have baths and only a few had central markets. Cemeteries were mainly found near the mosques and formed an integral part of the towns and the complete cycle of their lives, the tombs still today representing important examples of Swahili architecture.

The urban structure of the Swahili city of Zanzibar was clearly a reflection of African culture but also, at the same time, greatly influenced by its cosmopolitan trade links.

As far as relations are concerned between the Swahili families and their settlement models, ethnographical history is, sadly, still scarce although we must not forget the important contribution made in this field by J. Middleton.[38] He describes a Swahili society of middlemen, where commercial wealth is synonymous with political power. Middleton draws a clear distinction between the *washenzi* (pl. of *mshenzi*), an abused term to referring to barbarians, pagans, upcountry people, who lived in a rural context, and, according to J. Glassman,[39] the *mwungwana* (pl. *waungwana*) refined urban Muslim called by Middleton *utamaduni*, who lived in the stone towns. Most Swahili of the coast lived in rural villages, in mud and straw huts, where they worked as farmers and fishermen in a state of poverty barely above subsistence level, their hunger appeased with sorghum. The division of labour was rudimentary, as was any stratification of their society, with a counsel of elders overseeing individual villages. This was in marked contrast to the situation in the stone towns of the coasts and islands, with their complex structure, economic differentiation and various professional activities. The towns hosted numerous foreign merchants and life was extremely lively and dynamic, based on importation and exportation, money-lending (and here we see the importance of the monetary tri-partition of the western Indian Ocean, mints existing from the 9th to the 16th century that produced gold, silver and copper coins)[40] and shipbuilding and repairs. Rich Swahilis ate rice and food of a high quality and their prop-

---

[37] One of the four juridical schools of Islam.

[38] J. Middleton, *The World of the Swahili*, cit., *passim*.

[39] J. Glassman, *Feasts and Riot. Revelry, Rebellion, and Popular Consciousness on the Swahili Coast, 1856–1888*, London, 1995, Glossary, p. xv.

erty was regulated by the waqf, divided into landed property and religious wealth intended, that is, for the construction of mosques. Professional activity was extremely varied with builders and ship-wrights, woodworkers, ironsmiths and leather craftsmen, bankers, financiers and merchants all living more or less in harmony. . . . and all surrounded and protected by the stone walls put up after the Portuguese and which symbolised the exclusivity of those living within their confines, as well as the automatic exclusion and implicit dis-crimination against all those who remained outside.

3.3   Landed Property and Social Stratification

According to Swahili tradition, the subdivision and management of land was dealt with under different categories: 1) viwanda (sing. kiwanda), land for the cultivation of mangroves, for planks and poles, and rub-ber for the extraction of its resin; 2) majengo, the urban agglomerate and 3) kiambo, land for cultivation, vegetable plots, gardens and irri-gated fields.[41] Land belonging to the Swahili families, who appointed a trusted jumbe, or head farmer, was subject to the acquired rights of the families themselves which passed down through the male line. Such rights could only be denied in exceptional circumstances, and then only temporarily.

With the arrival in East Africa of the Āl Bū Sa'īdī and their polit-ical power at the start of the 19th century, we have the permanent purchase of arable land by means of enforced requisitioning by the Omani Arabs. This leads to the expropriation of land formerly owned by the Swahili. This taking of the Swahili lands was followed by conversion of their use in order to produce spices. The intensive cul-tivation of cloves, which gave a 1000% profit on production costs, resulted in the creation of an effective Omani Arab landholding aristocracy, financed by Indian merchants, which usurped the position of the Swahili landowners. On Zanzibar, the mashamba (sing. shamba),[42] from the French champ are introduced, plantations which formed a unit of measurement within the all-embracing kiambo, initially

---

[40] M. Horton and J. Middleton, The Swahili, cit., pp. 92–94.

[41] M. Horton and J. Middleton, The Swahili, cit., p. 131.

[42] S. Singer, An Investigation of Land Tenure in Zanzibar, Shamba Land, "Anthropos", n. 91, 1996 (4–6), p. 457; F. Cooper, From Slaves to Squatters: Plantation Labor and Agriculture in Zanzibar and Coastal Kenya, 1890–1925, New Haven, 1980.

concentrated around Mntoni and Kizimbani but later spreading to Bumwini, modern-day Bububu.[43] This requisitioning of tillable land and perfectioning of spice cultivation required such a massive influx of slaves that, from the 6000 per year at the start of the 18th century, figures reached 20,000 per year in the second half of the 19th. In 1811, of the 15,000 slaves who arrived on Zanzibar and Pemba, 7,000 were destined for work on the *mashamba*,[44] and in 1835 Sa'īd bin Sulṭān Āl Bū Sa'īdī possessed as many as forty-five *mashamba* on the island of Zanzibar.

The coastal Swahili economy prior to the Omani Arabs immigration was structured on the basis of three different settlement models: 1) patrician towns, 2) rural towns without slaves which lived mainly on fishing and the produce of small homesteads, and 3) areas used for pasture and inhabited by non-Swahili groups such as the Zaramo and the Mijikenda, the Oromo and the Somali. In the 18th century, these groups threatened the hegemony of the Swahili patrician families in the towns, obliging them to defend themselves with military force. Relations between the coastal Swahili communities and the East African hinterland were conducted on a personal basis, relying on use of the same language and reciprocal trust in commercial activities, the products from the interior consisting mainly of iron, salt and copper, whilst the coastal products most in demand were ivory, slaves and gold.

Due to the increasing demand for slaves by the Omani Arabs on the African islands, from the start of the 19th century caravan trade towards the interior began, with Arab representatives exercising complete control over the areas from which slaves and ivory came. It was not by chance that Tabora, a key town on the commercial route through the Unyanyembe region and lying halfway between the Great Lakes, practically became an Arab city.[45] Thus widely differing cultural identities gradually took shape between the islands and the African continent where, from the third decade of the 19th century on, the opening up of caravan routes would have the impact of a true economic and social revolution.

---

[43] A location near Mawimbini which took its name from the railway constructed there in the 1920's.

[44] M.R. Bhacker, *Trade and Empire in Muscat and Zanzibar. Roots of British Domination*, London, 1992, p. 128.

[45] A. Roberts, *Nyamwezi Trade*, in, R. Gray, D. Birmingham (Eds.), *Pre-Colonial African Trade. Essays in Central and Eastern Africa*, London, 1970, pp. 39–74.

Portrait of Sa'īd bin Sulṭān Āl Bū Sa'īdī, Zanzibar National Museum, Zanzibar, Tanzania, field work, 1994.

Omani Fort at Gwadar, field work, 1997.

African houses (*makuti*) Jozani Forest, Zanzibar, Tanzania, field work, 1994.

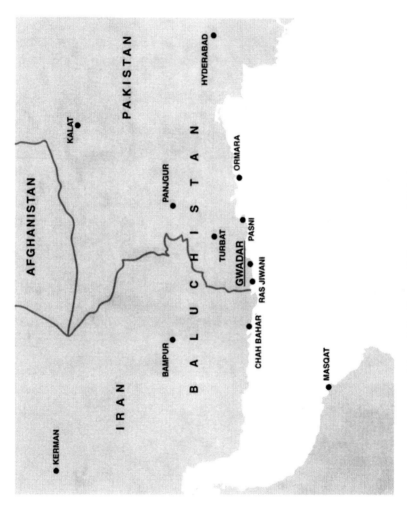

Map of the Coasts of Oman and Baluchistan.

NAPOLEON'S INTERCEPTED LETTERS

On 19 May 1798, the Army of the Orient left Toulon in France for the Egyptian campaign; the 'balance of power' established by the Anglo-Indian government was seriously threatened by the presence of Napoleon in Egypt, and, in its wider geopolitical ramifications, the crisis was destined to leave a mark on the whole succeeding history of the Middle East.

During Napoleon's expedition to Egypt, the French menace forced British policy makers to take immediate steps in order to guarantee their 'lifeline' to India. These measures were intended to address both the security of commercial maritime routes along the Persian/Arab Gulf and the East African Littoral and the British fear of a land invasion of India by a European army. The complex strategy devised by Napoleon with the object of invading British India either by land or by sea involved several regional and international actors and various potentates to whom Bonaparte dispatched emissaries and letters with a view to gaining allies and assistance in his enterprise. These included: 1) Paul I and Alexander I of Russia; 2) Fath Ali Shah Qajar of Persia, through Antoine Gardane's mission to Tehran and the Treaty of Finkenstein of 4 May 1804; 3) relationships with Turkey through Sebastiani's mission; 4) the proposal of an alliance with Tippoo Sultan of Mysore; and, more relevant to my purposes, 5) contacts with the Al Bu Sa'id of Muscat in Oman.

The facsimiles that follow are all from the same letter (to be found in the British archives)—one of the famous intercepted letters written by Napoleon to Tippoo Sultan of Mysore and to the Sheriff of Mecca with an enclosure for Sultan bin Ahmad of the Omani group of the Al Bu Sa'id (r. 1792-1804). Tippoo Sultan, the 'Tiger' of Mysore, had a relationship with the French government that was cultivated because of the latter's search for strategic alliances against the commercial and political power of the East India Company. On 25 January 1799, Napoleon's letters proposing to deliver not only Mysore but also Arabia 'from the Iron yoke of England' left Cairo. But the proposals never reached the three rulers of the 'Orient' for whom they were destined. The

Abbé Beauchamp, who was entrusted by Napoleon to deliver the precious communications, had been imprisoned by the Turks in Constantinople. Consequently, the dangerous letters fell into 'careless' hands—so careless that they were intercepted by Captain S. Wilson, the British Agent in Mocha, who translated the letters into English and transmitted them to Bombay. Jonathan Duncan, governor in council of Bombay, received the famous intercepted letters, and the atmosphere of tension and alarm immediately gave rise to political counteractions in Calcutta as well as in London.

It is interesting to note that numerous authors have quoted the text of these famous intercepted letters[1] written by Napoleon but without giving any reference to the British source: I.O.R. Marine Department Records I/I/12, *The French in India (1776-1800). Translation of a Letter from General Buonaparte to Tipoo Sultaun of Mysore written on 25th January 1799, from S. Wilson to the Fort.*

---

[1] J.G. Lorimer, *Gazetteer of the Persian Gulf, Oman and Central Arabia*, Superintendent Government Printing, Calcutta, 1915, 2 vols., Vol. 1, p. 428; R. Said Ruete, *The Al Bu Said Dynasty in Arabia and East Africa*, "Journal of the Royal Asiatic and Central Asian Society", Vol. 16, London, 1929, p. 422; R. Coupland, *East Africa and Its Invaders*, Oxford, Oxford University Press, 1938, pp. 88-89; M.V. Jackson Haight, *European Powers and South-East Africa. A Study of International Relations on the South-East Coast of Africa 1796-1856*, Imperial Studies Series, London, 1966, pp. 120-121; G. Hamilton, *Princes of Zinj. The Rulers of Zanzibar*, London, Hutchinson, 1957, pp. 29-30; S.B. Miles, *Countries and Tribes of the Persian Gulf*, London, Cass, 1966, pp. 289-290; H.C. Allen Jr., *Sayyds, Shets and Sultans: Politics and Trade in Masqat under the Al Bu Said, 1785-1914*, Ph.D. Thesis, University of Washington, 1978, p. 50; J.C. Wilkinson, *The Imamate Tradition of Oman*, Cambridge, Cambridge University Press, 1987, p. 51; M.R. Bhacker, *Trade and Empire in Muscat and Zanzibar. Roots of British Domination*, London, Routledge, 1992, p. 38; P. Risso, *Merchants and Faith. Muslim Commerce and Culture in the Indian Ocean*, Boulder, CO, Westview Press, 1995, p. 86; S.M. Al-Qasimi, *Les Relations entre l'Oman et la France (1715-1905)*, Paris, L'Harmattan, 1995, p. 67.

Translations were by him Transmitted to the
Governor in Council at Bombay. –

French Republic.

Liberty.   Equality.

Head Quarters at Cairo, 7th Pluviose
7th Year of the Republic, one and Indivisible. –

Buonaparte, Member of the National Convention,
General in Chief, to the most Magnificent Sultaun,
our greatest Friend Tippoo Saib. –

You have already been informed of
my arrival, on the borders of the Red Sea, with
an innumerable and Invincible Army, full of
the desires of delivering you from the Iron yoke
of England. –

I eagerly embrace this opportunity
of testifying to you the desire I have of being
informed by you, by the way of Muscat and
Mocha, as to your Political Situation. –

I would even wish you could send
some Intelligent Person to Suez, or Cairo, possessing

your

and in other Trades as formerly, and by the Blessing
of God, this will be daily encreasing, and the
Duties on Merchandize, and the Taxes will be
lessened. The duties on Merchandize are not
the same as they were prior to their being
raised by the Mamalukes, the Merchants
have every assistance granted them, and the
road between Suez and Cairo is open and safe,
therefore do you assure the Merchants of your
Country, that they may bring their Goods to Suez,
and sell them without dread or apprehension
and may purchase in exchange for them, such
articles as they may wish.—

         I now send you a Letter for our
Friend Teffoor bel tein, oblige me by forwarding
it to his Country.—

                A true Translation

              Signed   S. Wilson

                         Copy

your confidence, with whom I may confer.

May the Almighty increase your Power, and destroy your Enemies.

(enc.) (signed) Buonaparte

True Translation from the French.

(signed) Francis Woppers.
Translator.

Translate of a letter from General Buonaparte to the Sheriffe of Mecca, written in Arabic, without Date, and received at Jedda the 27th February 1799.

You will be fully informed by the No'queeda of this Dow, how tranquil and quiet every thing is at Cairo, and Suez, and between those places, and of the tranquillity which is established among the Inhabitants. Not a single Mammaluke oppressor remains in the country, and the Inhabitants without dread or fear, employ themselves in Manuring, Cultivating the Ground and

Copies of the above Letters were given to my Moonshee for me, by Shaik Soliman, and Mahomed Ameen, the Sheriffe's 1st Vizier and 1st Secretary.

Signed S. Wilson

A true Copy,

N B Edmonstone
&c
to the fort.

PART II

CHAPTER FOUR

THE ANGLO-FRENCH RIVALRY:
THE RISE OF ZANZIBAR (1799–1810)

Aware of the undoubtedly complex context, Europeans set out on great adventures in the western Indian Ocean.

From the end of the 18th century, and into the 19th, the eastern sea-routes formed the stage for Anglo-French rivalry, fed by crucial trade, political and diplomatic motives.

If, on the one hand, the Napoleonic wars gave the English supremacy over the seas, which led to the mantle of British Empire stretching further afield until it embraced all the seas, on the other, the connection between geostrategic factors and power politics also drew East Africa and the southern Sahara into the orbit of international politics.

Anglo-French rivalry in the Indian Ocean was fuelled by numerous factors. Amongst these, in the defensive and strategic spheres, control over the bases lying along the African coasts and on the islands, assumed enormous importance in the reciprocal exclusion resulting from commercial rivalry. Another important element was Britain's need to protect her *life-line* to India, a subject on which London became hyper-sensitive, especially following Napoleon's Egyptian expedition. Lastly, although undoubtedly not least, the rise of the Āl Bū Sa'īdī dynasty in Muscat and its subsequent transfer to the island of Zanzibar.

As regards the first factor, that is defensive and strategic aspects aimed at commercial dominance, one could postulate the hypothesis that the real overturning of the 'balance of powers' in the western Indian Ocean was also the work of a genial and forward-looking French official.

In 1735 a Navy officer, Bertrand-François Mahé de La Bourdonnais (1699–1755), was appointed Governor General of the islands Île de France and Bourbon. Of marked political-strategic ability, he immediately grasped the potential offered by establishing a French base on Île de France, the largest of the Mascarene Islands and possessed of an excellent harbour at Port Louis. He therefore decided to assign an essentially maritime role to Île de France, and a prevalently agricultural role to Bourbon. La Bourdonnais organised the cultivation of coffee and sugarcane on these two islands and built shipyards for the construction and repair of ships, guaranteeing a labour force of slaves from Mozambique and Madagascar. The French Company in India, however, no longer enjoyed the power it had once had,[1] having been overtaken by the East India Company. The French were, nevertheless, still masters of the sea and, halfway through the 18th century, the *Indiamen*, British merchant ships, were constantly threatened by French corsairs: "until the capture of Mauritius and Bourbon at the end of 1810, British shipping in the Indian Ocean was liable to capture by French vessels operating from those islands".[2]

The French traded with Zanzibar from Île de France, obtaining slaves, ivory and copper sulphate in exchange for weapons, gunpowder and Indian cloth. In 1742, they explored a group of islands which were given the name of Sechelles in 1756 by the Viscount Moreau de Séchelles, Controller General of the Finances under King Louis XV, and, afterwards, Chief of the French Navy. Already at that time, tension was running high between the British and French in the Indian Ocean, the French waiting only for orders from Europe to tear the seals from the plans for an attack on the English trading posts. However, in 1744, when the Anglo-French conflict erupted in India, La Bourdonnais received orders to maintain a defensive position and was expressly forbidden to attack any English base. The French Governor, whilst disagreeing with this stance, obeyed but reiterated his belief that maritime supremacy, based on the continued control of strategic basis in the Indian Ocean which enabled communication with France to continue, had to be maintained without being 'bogged down in eastern policy'. This provoked serious conflict with Dupleix in India, which, combined with political turmoil in Europe, led to the collapse of the 'La Bourdonnais' line. La Bourdonnais himself was discredited and, after three years in the

---

[1] Whilst this study purposefully examines matters from the English perspective, one must not forget the copious literature on the subject in French. The French Company of the East Indies was dissolved in 1769, its administration, including that of the Mascarene Islands, passing to the Crown. The Mascarene Islands, named from Pedro Mascarenhas, who visited them ca. in 1512, are including Mauritius, Réunion and Rodriguez.

[2] J.M. Gray, *History of Zanzibar*, op. cit., p. 99.

Bastille, he died a miserable death, alone and forgotten by all. The seeds of strategic and commercial insecurity, moreover, been sown widely throughout the area of British influence.

Although the volume and extent of the East India Company's trade with East Africa was only a 'mere trickle' at the start of the 19th century, the continual French raids among the islands and waters of the Indian Ocean—and, in particular, the serious commercial damage provoked by ceaseless attacks on British merchant shipping along the sea-routes for India—could no longer be tolerated. We must also remember that the coast of East Africa had now come to be part of British policy, within the wider context of extending trade links and with humanitarian and philanthropic backing. The most precious merchandise from East Africa, such as elephants tusks and gold dust exchanged for cloth, brass bracelets, glass and beads from India, had certainly helped enrich Indian merchants and guaranteeing a constant and undisturbed flow of such valuable exchanges necessarily implied the exclusion of the ever-growing French presence in eastern seas. Protection of the sea-routes to India, therefore, became a leit-motif of English policy.

Anglo-French hostilities continued intermittently in the Indian Ocean. In the 18th century, the route taken by communications and goods was: London—Marseilles—Aleppo—Basra—Surat.[3] As this was based on security in the Middle Eastern regions, English preoccupations constantly lay at the centre of the policy followed by the Court of Directors of the East India Company.[4]

Until 1820, and the introduction of steamships, the monsoon winds forced the great British merchant ships to set sail for India—or return

---

[3] H. Furber, *The Overland Route to India in the Seventeenth and Eighteenth Centuries,* "Journal of Indian History", vol. 29, London, 1951, p. 117 on.

[4] As is well known, during the first years of the 19th century, British interests in East Africa were under the nominal control of the Court of Directors of the East India Company. Political matters were, instead, the responsibility of the Board of Control. This included a committee, the Privy Council, which communicated with the Governor General of India nominated by the Cabinet, through the Secret Committee composed of three of the Company's Directors. Until 1834 the Court of Directors was divided into twelve Committees, one of which was the Committee of Secrecy. The Secret Committee maintained close contact with the Government through the Board of Control and had considerable political influence over Government decisions, although it was not always in agreement with the Board of Control. Among the many, see C.H. Philips, *The East India Company, 1784–1834,* Manchester, 1940 (repr. 1961).

to Europe—only during the winter months or the start of spring. A
hiatus of at least six-months was, therefore, necessary between voyages. Letters from the East India Company always had to leave at
the end of August or beginning of September at the very latest so
as to arrive in India before the monsoon broke. Growing French
trade and political-diplomatic contacts with sub-Saharan East Africa,
in precisely those strategic bases that were fundamental to English
shipping, resulted in an even longer time being required for communications. This caused incalculable damage to trade and had serious repercussions on both a regional and central political level. The
period of the monsoons, in effect, prevented news from arriving for
months and, consequently, any political, administrative or commercial
instructions from being communicated with any haste. The inevitable
result was that representatives of the two European powers on the
spot often obliged London and Paris to deal with questions on which
decisions had already been taken.

At this point, among the numerous defensive measures taken to
control the *life-line* with India, the East India Company in 1763
appointed a resident to Bushire[5] in the Persian Gulf, a location which
for roughly two hundred years represented the administrative centre of British interests also in East Africa. The base at Bushire, in
fact, maintained communications with the countries of the Gulf and
Arabia, referring directly to the Governor in Bombay and, though
him, to the headquarters of the Company in London. Bushire's territorial responsibility naturally also included Muscat in Oman and,
soon, the African island of Zanzibar.

During the American War of Independence (1778–83), France
sided with the thirteen American colonies and attacked the British
in India, using the Mascarene islands as its strategic support base.
Notwithstanding her victories, under the Paris Peace Treaty of 1783,[6]
France lost her territorial possessions although, in 1786, the Mascarene
islands were restored to her, islands which were destined to become
the "star and key of the Indian seas".[7] Around the end of the 18th

---

[5] The first British Resident at Bushire was Benjamin Jervis, from April 1763 to
July 1766. P. Tuson, *Zanzibar. Sources in the India Office Records. List of Political Residents
and Agents*, London, 1985.

[6] S.F. Bemis, *The Diplomacy of the American Revolution*, New York, 1935.

[7] Quoted in C. Giglio (Éd.), *Storia Universale dei Popoli e delle Civiltà* (orig. ed.:
R. Oliver and A. Attmore (Eds.), *Africa since 1800*, London, 1967), Torino, 1980,
pp. 330–332.

century, trade interests became more decisively directed towards the coasts of East Africa.

The 18th century saw the progressive decline of Kilwa in favour of Zanzibar. The shift northwards of the ivory trade, the principal centre for which was Zanzibar, was a major attraction for the Indian mercantile communities which began to supply Bombay and, soon afterwards, Europe. Zanzibar was important insofar as Indian merchants were fast making themselves indispensable for all Arab trade with East Africa. What contributed most to making Zanzibar a prestigious strategic and trading centre in the western Indian Ocean, however, was the transfer there from Muscat of court of the Āl Bū Sa'īdī.

This event also marked the arrival of international politics on the sub-Saharan African coasts, and no longer merely as the object of economic mercantile interest for the powers of the time.

There were many contributing factors which drew the attention of the Āl Bū Sa'īdī tribal leaders to the east African coasts. The commercial expansion of the port of Muscat into the regional system represented by the Indian Ocean must be recalled here: the growing trading interests of the Arabs, closely linked to those of the Indian communities[8] and the increased Western presence in the Indian Ocean.[9]

J.C. Wilkinson maintains that commercial interest in coffee from the Yemen lay behind Oman's move southwards which would soon lead it to the eastern shores of Africa.[10] The impulse was, however, without doubt also the result of an increasing demand for slaves from the French colonies. Another important factor in the move of the Omani Sultans to Africa was, according to A. Sheriff,[11] the high taxes on ivory from Mozambique imposed by the Portuguese. This resulted in the trade in elephant tusks moving from the port of Mozambique to other 'free' markets further north along the African coast. These were to replace ports under Portuguese control as centres for the collection and export of ivory and, as a result, give the Asian intermediaries a role of primary importance. From the lively debate on the historical reasons behind the move, we can clearly

---

[8] See Chapter one.
[9] M.R. Bhacker, *Trade and Empire in Muscat and Zanzibar*, op. cit., p. 26.
[10] J.C. Wilkinson, *The Imamate Tradition of Oman*, op. cit., p. 52.
[11] A. Sheriff, *Slaves, Spices & Ivory in Zanzibar*, op. cit., p. 18 on.

see a multitude of varying and apparently conflicting elements.
Amongst these, the gradual, growing and unrelenting insertion of the
East African coasts into the international policy of regional and
European powers of the period was, naturally, of significance.

4.1   Sulṭān bin Aḥmad Āl Bū Saʾīdī (1792–1804): The Father of the First Sultan of Zanzibar

Sulṭān bin Aḥmad Āl Bū Saʾīdī[12] was recognised as the prime mover
of this new policy, which would extend the economic sphere of his
family from the Persian Gulf to the waters of the western Indian
Ocean, bringing remarkable commercial expansion to their affairs.
With the aim of restoring Muscat's maritime supremacy, Sulṭān bin
Aḥmad Āl Bū Saʾīdī copied the system of taxation that the Portuguese
had introduced: a percentage on all shipping trading in the Indian
Ocean and a tax on goods transported. He did not, however, possess a fleet capable of controlling and taxing every ship in passage.
An ally was clearly needed. The new power policy set underway by
Sulṭān bin Aḥmad Āl Bū Saʾīdī, also in commercial terms, required
solid support, but this weakness was balanced out by the control he
achieved, at the end of the century, over the straits of Hormuz.
These provided access to the Persian Gulf and enabled him, by
exploiting this geo-strategic position, to impose a 'Portuguese style'
system of tolls. In his search for an ally, instead, the British started
with a handicap. They were not viewed too kindly, the Arabs recalling all too clearly their lengthy struggle to evict the Portuguese from

---

[12] It is to be noted that the term *Sultan* was not used in Muscat as a title until
the reign of Ṯc̣uwaynī bin Saʾīd bin Sulṭān Āl Bū Saʾīdī (r. 1856–68), the son of
Saʾīd bin Sulṭān Āl Bū Saʾīdī and a Georgian woman; Sulṭān bin Aḥmad is the
given name, misunderstood by the English who took Sultan to be a title. Sulṭān
bin Aḥmad Āl Bū Saʾīdī, like Saʾīd bin Sulṭān Āl Bū Saʾīdī, were called *Imaum* by
the English, that is to say 'leader', 'guide', in honour of their political prowess. The
use of the terms *Imam/Imaum* e *Sultan* in printed and manuscript documents of the
time, therefore, could be misleading. The term *Seyyid* often appears in the British
archives and is taken as meaning *Lord*, secular chief and member of the ruling
dynasty. C.H. Allen Jr., *The State of Masqat in the Gulf and East Africa. 1785–1829*,
"International Journal of Middle East Studies", Cambridge, 1982, n. 14, p. 117;
C.S. Nicholls, *The Swahili Coast*, op. cit., p. 101; G. Ligios, *Sovranità, Autorità e Potere
nella Pubblicistica Classica*, in V. Fiorani Piacentini (Ed.), *Il Pensiero Militare nel Mondo
Musulmano*, 3 vols., Roma, 1991, vol. III, pp. 95–115.

their territory, and they did not welcome British requests for concessions to build forts and trading posts at Muscat.

In 1798 Sulṭān bin Aḥmad Āl Bū Saʿīdī was still on good commercial and diplomatic terms with the French, thanks to their trade in goods and slaves in East Africa from the base on the Île de France, then governed by De Souillac. In exchange for its collaboration, France asked the Omani sovereign for the concession of the commercial port of Bandar Abbas, in the Persian Gulf, then in Omani hands. This was not denied, but Arab interests in East Africa nonetheless shifted the Omani balance in favour of France there too. Sulṭān bin Aḥmad Āl Bū Saʿīdī permitted French officers to command his soldiers, had a French personal doctor, Morier, and French captains commanded his ships.[13]

Britain was not perturbed, however, and soon found a formal means to oppose the growing French influence in the western Indian Ocean.

At that time, Sulṭān bin Aḥmad Āl Bū Saʿīdī was in contact with Tipu Sultan (1782–1799),[14] the ruler of Mysore in India and the only person to maintain a permanent embassy in Muscat. The two rulers managed important trading relations between the three ports of Mangalore, Calicut and Muscat, exchanging rice, sandalwood, pepper, cloth, cardamom and wood from India for dates, pistachios, horses, mules, copper, Chinese pottery, silk, sulphur, pearls, salt and raisins from Arabia or its extensive trading networks. In 1798, the English were at war with Tipu Sultan and his friendly relations with Sulṭān bin Aḥmad Āl Bū Saʿīdī represented an obstacle to that all-important *life-line* with British India, as well as conflicting with the interests of the East India Company. This could only alarm and provoke the 'overfearful sensitivity' of the Government of Bombay which intervened diplomatically.

The English Company decided to play the high card of Arab commercial interests in India, certain that its offers of protection and

---

[13] It is interesting to recall that, on the 3rd Novembre 1795, the Committee for the Public Health assigned a notable sum to be used to buy gifts for the *Imam* of Oman: "à la somme de 160.000 livres, un montre d'or, un kantchiar, un plateau à pied et un écritoire, une grande aigrette en diamants, rubis et émeraudes". M.A.E. Aff. Etr. Pol. Perse, vol. 8, f. 66, *Memoire de Bijoux destines par la Republique Française a etre envoyes en presents a l'Imam d'Oman et Mascate en Arabie.*

[14] I. Habib (Ed.), *Confronting Colonialism. Resistance and Modernization under Haider Ali and Tipu Sultan*, London, 2002.

logistical support to the shipping and trade of Sulṭān bin Aḥmad Āl Bū Sa'īdī in Indian ports could not be refused. In the October of the same year, a mission led by the British resident at Bushire and Muscat, *Mahdi Ali Khan* (October 1798–January 1803) succeeded in reaching an agreement, signed by Sulṭān bin Aḥmad Āl Bū Sa'īdī. This foresaw that, in exchange for trading preferences and the ceding of the commercial port of Bandar Abbas (which had been refused to the French), the Sultan would exclude the French from his lands.[15] However, as we shall see, since: "Sulṭān bin Aḥmad's relations with the British were clearly governed by economic concerns and helped cement Sultan successes, so that he received favoured treatment from the East India Company";[16] the Agreement was not enough, at least until the start of the 19th century, to prejudice relations with the French. It was in this context that the island of Zanzibar became increasingly important in the eyes of Āl Bū Sa'īdī, precisely because of the progressive and inevitable disappearance of that *favoured treatment* that the Anglo-Indian Government had conceded to the Omani Arabs.

4.2 *Napoleon and the 'intercepted letters'*

The rise of the mercantile emporium of Zanzibar coincided with a crucial period in Anglo-French rivalry which culminated in the important presence of Napoleon Bonaparte in the East.

Napoleon's expedition to Egypt was remarkable for the lucidity and clarity with which the great leader perceived local realities, thanks to information received from his well-trained consular staff, and the manner in which he made use of such information to impose his own strategy on three continents: Europe, Asia and Africa. The first European to succeed in such an aim, he moved towards his principle goal of striking Britain 'to the core' (that is to say, in India) by

---

[15] Original text in I.O.R. *Official Publications, Selections from the Records of the Bombay Government*, N. XXIV, New Series, 1856, *Treaties and Engagements. Treaty concluded between the Hon. East India Company and His Highness the Imam of Muskat under date the 12th October 1798 (VII Art.)*, p. 248 on; *East India Company's Agreement with Imam of Muscat for excluding the French from His Territories, 12th October, 1798*, repr. in: J.C. Hurewitz, *Diplomacy in the Near and Middle East. A Documentary Record*, 2 vols., Toronto, 1956, vol. I, p. 64.

[16] J.C. Wilkinson, *The Imamate Tradition of Oman*, op. cit., pp. 50–51.

means of a military expedition to Egypt, forward base for French military operations against the English, by strengthening the military presence on Île de France and Bourbon and through a complex network of contacts and alliances.

The principal elements in his project were: successive agreements with the Tsars of Russia, Paul I (1799–1801) and Alexander I (1807); an understanding with the Shah of Persia, Fath Ali Shah (1796–1834), later formalised at Finkenstein in Poland on the 4 May 1807—the Gardane mission to Persia (1807–8); an agreement with Turkey (the Sebastiani mission); an attempted alliance with Mysore in India (1798–99) and, lastly, of particular interest here, also a series of contacts with Āl Bū Sa'īdī of Muscat aimed above all at interrupting the British *life-line* to India.

Regarding this last point, the Napoleonic plan depended on French positions along the coast of sub-Saharan East Africa. This constituted a more complex version of the political line traced earlier by the first French Governor of Île de France, La Bourdonnais, who had defended and promulgated the policy at the cost of his career and life.

There is extensive literature on the subject to which we refer readers.[17] Concentrating on one or another of the many aspects of Napoleon's projects, this mass of documentation provides us with vital and well-documented information from the various archives available and furnishes a complete picture of the French plan.

---

[17] The bibliographical sequence used here is essentially geostrategic, from Persia to India and to Central Asia. C.H. Allen, *The State of Muscat in the Gulf and East Africa 1785–1829*, op. cit.; J. Malcolm, *Sketches of Persia from the Journal of a Traveller in the East*, London, 1828; J. Malcolm, *Histoire de la Perse*, Paris, 1821; J.W. Kaye, *The Life and Correspondence of Sir John Malcolm*, 2 vols., London, 1865; A. De Gardane, *Mission du Général Gardane en Perse sous le premier empire*, Paris, 1865; V. Fiorani Piacentini, *Aspetti originali della politica napoleonica in Persia nel quadro del duello anglo-francese*, op. cit.; P.M. Sykes, *A History of Persia*, 2 vols., London, 1930; P.M. Sykes, *Ten Thousand Miles in Persia*, London, 1902; H. Bellew, *From the Indus to the Tigris*, Karachi, 1977 (repr. from I° ed., 1874); D. Forrest, *Tiger of Mysore. The Life and Death of Tipu Sultan*, London, 1970; H. Furber, *The Overland Route to India in the Seventeenth and Eighteenth Centuries*, op. cit.; P. Spear, *India. A Modern History*, London, 1961; E. De Lacy, *On the Designs of Russia*, London, 1828; E. De Lacy, *On the Practicability of an Invasion of British India and the Commercial and Financial Prospects and Resources of the Empire*, London, 1829; M. Wilks, *Historical Sketches of the South India in an attempt to trace the history of Mysoor*, 3 vols., London, 1810; S.P. Hopkirk, *The Great Game. On the Secret Service in High Asia*, Oxford, 1991; H. Seton Watson, *Storia dell'Impero Russo* (orig. ed.: *The Russian Empire 1801–1917*, Oxford, 1967), Torino, 1971.

Certain documents preserved in the India Office Library and Records,[18] however shed new light on a little-known chapter in the history of the Indian Ocean's western stretches. Interesting details emerge and a new perspective is granted of the complexity and far-reaching implications of Napoleonic policy in the East in all its 'modernity'.

Though technical and military means were to prove lacking and continental contingencies would force Napoleon's attention back to the Europe chessboard, lively perspicacity, long-sightedness and a quick and certain perception of local realities in which French fortunes could be invested were never less than admirable. East Africa came into this political and strategic picture, a role which was especially closely tied to the Sulṭān bin Aḥmad Āl Bū Sa'īdī, and to two individuals in particular: Sulṭān bin Aḥmad Āl Bū Sa'īdī and Sa'īd bin Sulṭān Āl Bū Sa'īdī, his son.

Although not commanding a thorough understanding or evaluation of contemporary events in Europe and on the international scene, they were canny and wise interpreters of European rivalry and knew how to use this to their own advantage. Enjoying the constant support of their Indian financers and defended militarily by capable and courageous Baluch warriors, they found (or, better, rediscovered) a new centre of commercial and strategic power along the shores of East Africa.[19]

Napoleon's attempt to overthrow the European balance in the East was both audacious and risky: exploiting Britain's weak position in the Mediterranean, he invaded Egypt in the summer of 1798 with a force of 31,000 men. Preparations for this expedition were of an unprecedented size and nature. As we have said, Napoleon was interested in Britain's role in India and his invasion of Egypt and incursion into neighbouring Syria had incalculable consequences at the time. The appealing prospect of striking at England drove him eastwards and the idea of conquering Egypt like a latter-day Alexander must have come to his mind, fed by dreams of world power. He was obsessed with Great Britain, from its invulnerability and dominion over the seas, to its banks and credit system, and fer-

---

[18] I.O.R. *Bombay Records, Bombay Political Consultations; Residency Records; Political and Secret Deparment Records; Marine Department Records.*

[19] See below, Chapter 5.

vently desired to see this Empire collapse in ruins.[20] The French presence in Egypt was accompanied by the sending of consular embassies to the Persian court of Fath 'Ali Shah Qājār, to Tipu Sultan of Mysore, to the Sharif of Mecca and to Muscat. The French policy against the British in India thus entered into its practical phase. The strategy outlined in Paris began to take shape. In this context we find an interesting document which describes a singular event that was to have profound political repercussions and give rise to an interminable series of intrigues, suspicions and diplomatic wrangles between France, Britain and Oman.

The various stages in this mysterious and controversial episode began on the 25 January 1799.

Napoleon sent a letter from Cairo to Tipu Sultan, ruler of Mysore, as well as another communication for the Sharif of Mecca. An important detail, especially for Britain, was that these letters contained an enclosure for Sulṭān bin Aḥmad Āl Bū Sa'īdī. Napoleon's message was clear and represented a threat to the international political order established after the 1798 agreement between Great Britain and Oman, apart from being extremely dangerous for the English lifeline and for British security in India. However, the person who was to have taken the message personally to Muscat, Abbé Beauchamp (1752–1801), was diverted to Constantinople where the Turks arrested him. Thus the letters, entrusted into less than safe hands, never reached their destination.[21] Napoleon's communiqués, in fact, were

---

[20] D.G. Chandler, *Le Campagne di Napoleone* (orig ed.: *The Campaigns of Napoleon*, London, 1966), Milan, 1968, pp. 275–329. Abd Al Rahman Al-Jabarti, *Napoleon in Egypt*, (transl. by S. Moreh), London, 1995.

[21] The famous *intercepted letters* were mentioned in numerous studies, without the sources in the British archives ever being quoted. The version referred to here in the official English translation is to be found in London, in the India Office Library and Records, Marine Department Records, I/I/12, *The French in India, 1776–1800*. R. Coupland, *East Africa and its Invaders*, op. cit., pp. 88–89; J.G. Lorimer *Gazetteer of the Persian Gulf, Oman and Central Arabia*, op. cit., vol. I, Part I, p. 428; S.B. Miles, *The Countries and Tribes of the Persian Gulf*, London, 1966, pp. 289–290; R. Said Ruete, *The Al-Bu Said Dynasty in Arabia and East Africa*, "Journal of The Royal Asiatic and Central Asian Society", London, 1 July, 1929, vol. 16, part IV, p. 422; H.C. Allen Jr., *Sayyds, Shets and Sultan...*, op. cit., p. 50; M.R. Bhacker, *Trade and Empire in Muscat and Zanzibar*, op. cit., p. 38; J.C. Wilkinson, *The Imamate Tradition of Oman*, op. cit., p. 51; M.V. Jackson Haight, *European Powers and South-East Africa*, op. cit., pp. 120–121; G. Hamilton, *Princes of Zinj. The Rulers of Zanzibar*, London, 1957, pp. 29–30. For the French version of the letters and the appendix, see *Correspondance de Napoléon 1er publiée par ordre de L'Empereur Napoléon III*, vol. 5, Paris, 1860, Lettres 3900–3901, Ministére des Affaires Étrangères, Paris, in S.M. Al-Qasimi, *Les Relations entre l'Oman et la France (1715–1905)*, Paris, 1995, p. 67.

intercepted by Captain S. Wilson at Mocha in Arabia. Immediately translated they were transmitted to Jonathan Duncan, Governor of Bombay, who read them carefully. They received no less an attentive perusal in Calcutta and London.

Here follows the text addressed to Tipu Sultan of Mysore in the English version:

> French Republic Liberty Equality Head quarters at Cairo 7 Pluviose 7 year of the Republic one and indivisible. Buonaparte Member of the National Convention General in Chief to the most Magnificent Sultaun our greatest Friend Tipoo Saib. *You have already been informed of my arrival on the borders of the Red Sea with an innumerable and invincible army full of the desire of delivering you from the Iron yoke of England.* I eagerly embrace this opportunity of testifying to you the desire I have of being informed by you by the way of Muscat and Mocha as to your Political Situation. I would even wish you could send some Intelligent Person to Suez on Cairo professing your confidence with whom I may confer. May the Almighty enrose your Power and destroy your Enemy. Signed Buonaparte.[22]

Here below, instead, is the communiqué for the Sharif of Mecca:

> You will be fully informed here tranquil and quiet everything is at Cairo and Suez and between those places and of the tranquillity which is established among the inhabitants. Not a single Mamaluke oppressor remains in the Country and the inhabitants without dread of fear employ themselves in weaving cultivating the Ground and in other Trades as formerly and by the blessing of God. This will be daily increasing and the Duties on Merchandise. The duties on Merchandise are now the same as they were prior to their being raised by the Mamalukes; the Merchants have every assistance granted them and the road between Suez and Cairo is open and safe therefore do you assure the Merchants of your Country that they bring their goods to Suez and sell them without dread or apprehension and may purchase in exchange for them such articles as they may wish. I now send you a letter for our friend Tipoo Sultaun obliged may be forwarding it to his Country.[23]

---

[22] I.O.R. I/I/12, Marine Department Records. *Translation of a Letter from General Buonaparte to Tippoo Sultaun of Mysore written on 25th January 1799, from S. Wilson to the Fort,* f. 669.

[23] I.O.R. ibid., *Translate of a Letter from General Buonaparte to the Sheriff of Mecca written in arabic without date and received at Judaa the 7th February 1799, French in India, 1776–1800, from S. Wilson to the Fort,* f. 670.

These texts were followed by an 'appendix' reiterating French offers to Sulṭān bin Aḥmad Āl Bū Saʿīdī of an alliance against Great Britain. The phrase used by Napoleon in communicating with Tipu Sultan of Mysore: "You have already been informed of my arrival on the borders of the Red Sea with an innumerable and invincible army full of the desire of delivering you from the iron yoke of England" is important to our understanding of French ambitions in the Orient, and consequent Anglo-French relations, but it is above all interesting in that it provides the right key for interpreting British reactions, at this point more than justified by Napoleon's threatening proposals. The plot now thickens; Lt. Colonel M. Wilks,[24] resident of the East India Company at the court of Mysore, expressed strong doubts that this letter could have come from Cairo. In Wilks' opinion, the Napoleon's phrase "You have already been informed of my arrival on the borders of the Red Sea" suggested the existence of another letter, previous to the 25th January 1799. Moreover, the plan would have to be put into effect over a long period of time, to the extent that Napoleon expressed his desire to confer with a trusted representative of Tipu Sultan of Mysore in Cairo. Wilks concluded his reconstruction by noting that, if these letters had come to the attention of the Marques of Wellesley (1760–1842), Governor General of Bengal from 1797 to 1805, they would most certainly have been omitted from the documentation he collected together in the Seringapatam Papers. Despite Wilks' considerations, the letters (be they authentic or apocryphal) created outright panic in Bombay, Calcutta and London, which led to measures already in place being further strengthened. Other information had, in fact, already sounded the alarm.

At the end of that memorable month of January 1799, to be precise on the 29th, the British resident at Bushire had gone to Muscat, with orders to "detach the Imaum from the French".[25] At the same time, secret messages continued to arrive at Fort S. George in Bombay from Mysore, providing information on contacts between the Indian ruler and the French.[26] Tension had reached unbearable levels.

---

[24] M. Wilks, *Historical Sketches of the South India . . .*, op. cit., vol. III, p. 380.

[25] I.O.R. *Bombay Secret Letters 1798–1801, 29 Jan. 1799, Governor in Council Received. Receipts of Dispatches from the Secret Committee*, f. 672.

[26] I.O.R. *Z/P/485, Bengal Political Consultation, Index Pro Anno 1799, January 1799, General Fort St. George, From the Secretary transmits of copies of papers of Intelligence from Mysore, 18th Feb., 1799.*

Napoleon's defeat in Egypt and the killing of the 'Tiger of Mysore' in the battle against the English at Seringapatam in March 1799,[27] helped alleviate French pressure in the east, but the rivalry continued unabated. France did not intend to renounce its grandiose scheme to invade India and, whilst Great Britain enjoyed a position of uncontested power, the strategic and commercial bases in the Indian Ocean, still in French hands, along with relations with the Omani Arabs would be factors of marked political-strategic instability for the entire first decade of the 19th century. It was not by chance that Wellesley ordered his secretary to write to Duncan in Bombay, the 30 May 1799, with the dual aim of easing the tension and of alerting the Government of Bombay to the threatening reality of French plans.

> Hon.ble Sir, The late expedition under General Buonaparte into Egypt having developed the dangerous machinations of the French Directory against the English Power in India (an object which, although at first viewed as gigantic chimerical, nevertheless justly and naturally causes very sensible apprehensions at home for the safety of the Indian Empire) has called into action the most zealous and strenuous exertions to avert the blow which only a few months ago threatened its very existence. Unlikely as this event may now appear in however distant a light it may be viewed, it may be timely guarded against; and the wisdom of the British Government unquestionably be prepared to repel any such effort of our implacable enemy.[28]

On the 8 January the capable young English diplomat, Captain John Malcolm,[29] reached Muscat together with a medical officer, Archibald Hamilton Bogle; the latter took up his post as resident of the East India Company, whilst Malcolm was on an official visit. He expressed to Sulṭān bin Aḥmad Āl Bū Saʾīdī his disappointment at the close relations with France and took the opportunity to remind him that

---

[27] M.R. Bhacker, *Trade and Empire in Muscat and Zanzibar*, op. cit., pp. 38–39, and bibliographical notes.

[28] B.M. Add. Mss. 13, 703, *from J.A. Grant, Secretary to Government, to the Hon.ble Jonathan Duncan, President and Governor in Council, Bombay 30 May, 1799. Wellesley Papers, Correspondence relative to Goa, presented by the Representatives of the Marquess of Wellesley,* f. 2.

[29] Later on (1807–1808), John Malcolm, was appointed Brigadier General, he was protagonist of important political-diplomatic meetings at the Persian Court of Fath 'Ali Shah, with the object of fighting against the aims of the French mission led by General Alfred De Gardane, the French envoy in Persia. J. Malcolm, *Sketches of Persia from the Journal of a Traveller in the East*, op. cit.; A. De Gardane, *Mission du Général Gardane en Perse sous le premier empire*, op. cit., *passim*.

all of the Indian ports, from Surat to Calcutta, were in British hands. An inevitable consequence of its failure to observe the Agreements with the Anglo-Indian Government was that Muscat would be excluded *ex abrupto* from any commercial involvement in Indian markets.[30] Sulṭān bin Aḥmad Āl Bū Sa'īdī listened carefully to Malcolm's speech, assured him that his greatest desire was that of consolidating his alliance with the English and offered his full collaboration in the struggle to overcome all of Great Britain's enemies. Sulṭān bin Aḥmad Āl Bū Sa'īdī gave tangible proof of his good intentions, signing *ipso facto* the two articles which represented ratification of the 1798 Agreement. The first confirmed the Agreement, whilst the second formally recognised the presence of Bogle at Muscat.[31] By now, British friendship meant French hostility. Sulṭān bin Aḥmad Āl Bū Sa'īdī— literally blackmailed by an ever-more present and powerful Great Britain—had no way out, the choice being dictated by crude reality and events. The Omani sovereign did, however, have to consider a number of factors, including his increasing political weakness. He found himself, in fact, threatened both by enemy tribes in Arabia (the Wahhabi/Qawasim and the Joasmi pirates),[32] and by his representatives in the ports of sub-Saharan East Africa.[33] The Mazrū'ī of Mombasa, in fact, although faithful to the Ya'rubī—the previous Omani Arab dynasty—had rebelled against the arrival of the Āl Bū Sa'īdī in Muscat. The Mazrū'ī had never truly recognised the authority of Sulṭān bin Aḥmad Āl Bū Sa'īdī, and had organised numerous revolts along the east African coasts. Allied with the populations of the interior and with the inhabitants of the islands Pemba and Lamu, following a series of battles against the Muscat forces, from 1822 onwards found themselves confined to the enclave of Mombasa,

[30] S.B. Kelly, *The Countries and Tribes of the Persian Gulf*, op. cit., pp. 292–293.

[31] The Agreement was ratified by the Governor General of India the 26 April 1800. Complete text in I.O.R. *Official Publications, Selections from the Records of the Bombay Government*, n. XXIV, New Series, 1856, *Treaty 18th Jan. 1800, Capt. John Malcolm, Bahadoor, (II Art.)*, p. 151; repr. in C.U. Aitchison, *Collection of Treaties, Engagements and Sanads relating to India and Neighbouring Countries*, v ed., Dehli, 1933, vol. 11, pp. 287–88.

[32] M.R. Bhacker, *Trade and Empire in Muscat and Zanzibar*, op. cit., *passim*.

[33] Details may be found in A Sheriff, *Slaves, Spices & Ivory*, op. cit., *passim*; C.S. Nicholls, *The Swahili Coast*, op. cit., *passim*; M.R. Bhacker, *Trade and Empire in Muscat and Zanzibar*, op. cit., *passim*; R. Coupland, *East Africa and its Invaders*, op. cit., pp. 271–294; Z. Marsh and G.W. Kingsnorth, *A History of East Africa*, op. cit., pp. 32–33; J.C. Wilkinson, *The Imamate Tradition of Oman*, op. cit., *passim*.

from whence, however, they still continued to threaten the presence of the Āl Bū Saʿīdī on Zanzibar and along the eastern coasts of Africa.[34]

Sulṭān bin Aḥmad Āl Bū Saʿīdī decided to act on two fronts, and attempt to keep in with both sides. In doing so, he had to take into account a number of factors: Britain would never have sent an army to help him suppress the enemy tribes of the interior of the restless Mazrūʿī in East Africa; the presence of an English representative at Muscat; the no less important fact of the French military presence in the Mascarene Islands; lastly, whilst the Napoleonic wars had caused a drop in Franco-Omani trade, the constant diplomatic and commercial links between the Arabs and the French have continued to guarantee an income from eastern Africa of approximately 40,000 Maria Theresa thalers per annum, derived from the slave trade and commercial activities in the Indian Ocean.[35]

On the other hand, the Anglo-French rivalry in Europe had absolutely no significance whatsoever for the head of the Āl Bū Saʿīdī and meant nothing to his own personal power except in that the victor (whichever it should be) would in time return to determine the price of his fidelity. It therefore followed that, in the summer of 1802, Sulṭān bin Aḥmad Āl Bū Saʿīdī accepted the nomination of M. de Cavaignac as French representative at Muscat.[36] The situation had apparently been stabilised.

A new development in Arab politics, however, awaited the unsuspecting Cavaignac: Sulṭān bin Aḥmad Āl Bū Saʿīdī refused to allow him to disembark from his stunning, bright yellow frigate in the port of Muscat. The frustrated French commissar, after waiting for an

---

[34] See, among others, the studies on the role of the Mazrūʿī in Africa by Ibrahim Soghayroun. I. Soghayroun, *The History of the Mazrui in East Africa by Shaikh al-Amin ibn ʿAli al-Mazrui. Arab and Swahili culture in historical perspective*, unpublished paper presented at the International Colloquium: Islam in East Africa: New Sources (Archives, Manuscripts and Written Historical Sources. Oral History. Archaeology), Ed. by B. Scarcia Amoretti, Università "La Sapienza", Rome, 2–4 December, 1999, Rome, 2001.

[35] M.R. Bhacker, *Trade and Empire in Muscat and Zanzibar*, op. cit., p. 43.

[36] "*Cavaignac est nommé Commissaire des relations commerciales à Mascate... Il est arrêté que le traitement du citoyen Cavaignac est fixé à 10.000 F.*". This sum was increased, the 17 September of the same year, to 18.000 Francs per annum. M.A.E. Arch. Nat. AF IV 65, pl. 370, *Arrete Des Consuls Du 1° Messidor, 20 juin 1802*; M.A.E. Arch. Nat. AF IV 68, pl. 390, *Minute D'Arrete des Consuls de la Republique, Sur le Rapport du Ministre des Relations Exterieures, 19 août 1802*; M.A.E. Arch. Nat., AF IV 70, pl. 405, *Minute d'Arrete du Ministre des Relations Exterieures, 17 septembre 1802*.

entire month, decided to leave. At that precise moment, the stake represented by British commercial guarantees in the Indian ports was higher. Malcolm had been particularly convincing, and the Anglo-Indian Government's diplomatic advantage was immediately communicated to Bombay. The text, minus the opening preamble and closing remarks, follows here:

> In order to acquaint you of the arrival of a French Vessel here. . . . On the morning of 12 October the Sultan of Muskat arrived here and the captain of the French Vessel sent two of his officers to pay their respects to the Sultan. The Sultan on enquiring of them what the French Captain demanded, they replied it was his wish to establish a Resident and Factory in the Place. The Sultan sent two of his own people on board the Vessel to see the Captain and to acquaint him *he could not allow him to establish a Factory* as his demand was only a passport for French Vessel in and out of this Port, as formerly he had no objections and that on the morrow he should be glad to see him on shore, and to bring his papers with him . . . In the middle of the night of the 13 October the French Captain took his departure from Muskat.[37]

Sulṭān bin Aḥmad Āl Bū Sa'īdī died in November, 1804. The resulting power vacuum demanded immediate political-diplomatic intervention by the Anglo-Indian Government, which sent a diplomatic mission to Muscat.[38] The strong pressure brought to bear by Captain David Seton, British resident from 1800 to 1809, against continuing relation between the Omani Arabs and the French had, at least temporarily, a positive effect.[39] The 31 July 1806, after a series of intrigues,

---

[37] I.O.R. R/15/1/6, *Letter from the Broker at Muskat to the Lieut. Bruce, dated 28 October and received 11 December 1803, Political Residency, Bushire, Bushire Diary, 6th January 1803, 29 December, 1803,* f. 151. Italic is here added to the original text.

[38] The 16 April 1800, in line with the 1798 Agreement, Archibald Bogle, Ass. Surgeon, was nominated, who served from January to September 1800 and replaced the French doctor. From October 1800 to August 1809, Captain David Seton performed intensive tasks of diplomatic and political mediation, whilst Lt. William Watts was sent to Muscat from May to August 1808, as assistant representative. However, the English presence in Muscat was discontinuous, for economic and political reasons. These included high costs, English reluctance to be too involved in the internal affairs of Oman and the climate which was not at all favourable for a permanent European presence in the country (Bogle died in 1800, Watt in 1808, Captain Seton and Mr. Bunce in 1809). P. Tuson, *Zanzibar. Sources in the India Office Records. Administration of the Muscat and Zanzibar Agency,* op. cit., *passim.*

[39] I.O.R. R/15/1/5, *Residency Records, Political Residency Bushire, Letters Inward and Outward, 12 Dec., 1801, 14 Feb., 1803,* ff. 4–26.

conspiracies, struggles and the unscrupulous elimination of rivals,[40] Saʿīd bin Sulṭān Āl Bū Saʿīdī (b. 1791–1856), son of Sulṭān bin Aḥmad Āl Bū Saʿīdī, wrote Governor Jonathan Duncan in Bombay to inform him officially of his rise to power and to ask for official recognition by the British Government.

4.3 Saʿīd bin Sulṭān Āl Bū Saʿīdī and the British Conquest of the Île de France/Mauritius (1810)

Saʿīd bin Sulṭān Āl Bū Saʿīdī was fifteen years old; had few friends and many enemies, and the prosperity his father had created had collapsed. He soon understood the Muscat's only possible wealth was the sea itself.[41]

Revealing himself to be quite shrewd, Saʿīd bin Sulṭān Āl Bū Saʿīdī grasped the advantages for himself and his people to be obtained by expanding Muscat's commercial activities in East Africa and creating his own fleet so as to be able to control the ports of the African continent. But to rig out a fleet, in the battles against his sworn enemies in Arabia and the Persian Gulf, a firm financial bases were essential, and the necessary revenues came from Africa, not Oman. It was thus clear that the alliance between Saʿīd bin Sulṭān Āl Bū Saʿīdī and Britain, underwritten by his father, Sulṭān bin Aḥmad Āl Bū Saʿīdī, in the 1798 Agreement and ratified in 1800, was not going to produce immediate contentment. The result, at this point, was that the French began to attack Omani ships in the Indian Ocean.

---

[40] I refer here to the case of Badr bin Saif Āl Bū Saʿīdī (r. 1804–1806), an uncle who Saʿīd bin Sulṭān Āl Bū Saʿīdī killed.

[41] Various monographs exist on the life and character of this sovereign. These written sources are not always impartial, as many of the authors cited were related to the subject. They do, however, provide an interesting, not to say picturesque, picture of Saʿīd bin Sulṭān Āl Bū Saʿīdī's life. J.G. Lorimer, *Gazetteer of the Persian Gulf, Oman and Central Arabia*, op. cit., vol. 1, pp. 440–469; R.S. Ruete (descendant of Saʿīd bin Sulṭān Āl Bū Saʿīdī), *Said Bin Sultan (1791–1856). Ruler of Oman and Zanzibar. His Place in the History of Arabia and East Africa*, London, 1929; R.S. Ruete, *The Al Bu Said Dynasty in Arabia and East Africa*, op. cit., pp. 417–432; S.A.S. Farsi (Former Chief Khadi of Kenia), *Seyyid Said Bin Sultan. The Joint Ruler of Oman and Zanzibar (1804–1856)*, New Delhi, 1986; V. Maurizi (Italian doctor at the court of Muscat at the start of the 19th century), *History of Seyd Said, Sultan of Muscat*, I° ed., London, 1819, new ed., Cambridge, 1984.

After Austerlitz, Napoleon began his 'Oriental' policy in earnest, which would lead to the signing of the Finkenstein treaty with Persia— 4 May 1807—and to a new Agreement with Sa'īd bin Sulṭān Āl Bū Sa'īdī.

In June 1807 this latter sent a representative to the Île de France, *Majid bin Khalfan*, so as to restore political-diplomatic relations and, most importantly, commercial contacts. Citing his country's neutrality, Sa'īd bin Sulṭān Āl Bū Sa'īdī, permitted a French Consul to establish himself at Muscat and, the 16 June 1807, signed a treaty of 'friendship and commerce' with General René Decaen, Governor of the Île de France, in which France was accorded 'most favoured nation' privileges in the East African dominions as, commercially speaking, "the French were great favourites in Zanzibar".[42]

The long-awaited reply to Sa'īd bin Sulṭān Āl Bū Sa'īdī's letter from the Bombay Government, finally arrived in the September of the same year, 1807, after Governor Duncan had received more detailed intelligence from Captain Seton regarding the new sovereign's legitimacy and popular consensus. This was because, as Coupland said: "the shores of the Indian Ocean were one vast whispering-gallery",[43] and dangerous rumours had reached Bombay about Sa'īd bin Sulṭān Āl Bū Sa'īdī's renewed willingness in relation to French *avances*. Duncan, obliged to temper the directives arriving from London and strongly opposed to any direct involvement in the internal affairs of Oriental potentates, sent Sa'īd bin Sulṭān Āl Bū Sa'īdī the same message that Malcolm had formerly sent to the sovereign's father: such political choices would result in a far less warm welcome in Indian ports than in the past and, from then on, any French presence in the Persian Gulf would be viewed as that of an enemy and, therefore, come under attack.

The effective British naval forces, consisting of fleets of frigates and corvettes operating over forty-four million square kilometres of Indian Ocean, were by now the undisputed rulers of the waves. After Nelson's victory at Trafalgar, they faced no competition. Nonetheless, Napoleon's new scheme, based on further plans to invade British India, foresaw precisely what poor La Bourdonnais has predicted in

---

[42] The treaty was not, however, ratified by Paris. R. Coupland, *East Africa and its Invaders*, op. cit., p. 116; J.M. Gray, *History of Zanzibar*, op. cit., p. 180.

[43] R. Coupland, *East Africa and its Invaders*, op. cit., p. 112; S.B. Miles, *The Countries and Tribes of the Persian Gulf*, op. cit., pp. 310–311.

the previous century: the strengthening of the strategic base on Île de France, central to confronting English routes to the east, and as a naval counterpart to an advance by troops on land through Persia and Baluchistan,[44] with the acquiescence of Sa'īd bin Sulṭān Āl Bū Sa'īdī.

On 27 January 1807 the Governor of Île de France, Decaen, met Napoleon in Paris. Napoleon greeted him with joy, explained his plans and then sent him back to his ever-more important island with twenty vessels and four thousand, six hundred men. To these were added, in the October of the same year, a further three ships and another twelve thousand men. In the meantime, the French were providing the Arabs of Muscat with weapons and inciting acts of piracy against the British merchant ships, which reached a level that was intolerable for the East India Company.

The Government of Calcutta decided that the time had arrived to eliminate the Île de France thorn from the British side, a decision indicative of British perceptions of what was happening.

In July 1807 Lord Gilbert Minto became Governor General of India. Minto was an Age of Enlightenment man, a Whig, and had the backing of both the Tories and the Directors of the East India Company. His aim was not merely to "counter-attack Napoleon's power", but nothing less than to "destroy it".[45]

Since Minto had understood that: "the East African Scene was only part of the picture and could not be considered in isolation from the other shores of the Indian Ocean",[46] he drew up a highly detailed plan which foresaw, in the first place, an in-depth feasibility study of attacks on Île de France and Bourbon. The British navy did not have charts of the Mascarene islands, and this information was obtained from the Portuguese, faithful to their English allies at this dramatic moment and fully informed and in agreement with the plans and the British decision to occupy the French base in the western Indian Ocean. East India Company intelligence provided the information that the were roughly four thousand, five hundred white

---

[44] The Tilsit Agreements, 7 July 1807, between Napoleon and Alexander I, Tsar of Russia foresaw a daring plan for invading India by land. Nicholas Charles Oudinot, with 12,000 men and the support of the Russian army in Georgia, would have crossed the lands of south-western Asia. V. Fiorani Piacentini, *Aspetti originali della politica napoleonica in Persia nel quadro del duello anglo-francese*, op. cit., p. 639 on.

[45] R. Coupland, *East Africa and its Invaders*, op. cit., p. 126.

[46] M.V. Jackson Haight, *European Powers and South-East Africa*, op. cit., p. 161.

people and sixty thousand blacks on the Île de France, that the French Major General was M. Magallons (about 43 years old), and that, for the moment, there were no regular forces stationed on the island. As reinforcements would most probably arrive at any time, however, a surprise attack was recommended.[47]

On 16 November 1809, Vice Admiral Abermarle Bertie, sent on a mission to the Mascarene Islands by Count Caledon, Governor of the Cape, sent a copy of further interesting information to Bombay. In his report, Bertie suggested a potential willingness of the islands' inhabitants to become subjects of King George III (1760–1820), given the "rage and violence of general Decaen",[48] advancing the following considerations quoted from the original text:

> I have the honour to transmit herewith for the information of Your Lordship, Copies of my correspondence with His Excellency the Earl of Caledon, Governor of this Colony relative to the equipment and Convoy of an expedition proposed by His Excellency to be sent from hence in consequence of recent unfavourable intelligence from India. Upon the whole, I am fully of opinion that 1500 or 1800 men would be amply sufficient to occupy Bourbon. The importance of having possession of Bourbon to the Squadron as well as having a point to retire upon in case of any disaster supposing an attack being made on the Isle of France at some future period, you are too well aware of Sir, for me to point out. The Island of Bourbon has always been open to attack from a very small force the inhabitants certainly want nothing more than a fair plea to give up the island about the capture of the island there can be no doubt, and that the inhabitants, if covered (and induced from the consequences), would consider themselves *blessed in the Change*.[49]

In the spring of 1810, Minto informed Robert Towsend Farquhar (1776–1830), Commander in Chief of the troops who were to attack the Mascarene Islands, that: "it's my desire that the Isles de France and Bourbon should be subjected to the British Power".[50] In the

---

[47] B.M. Add. 13772, *Wellesley Papers*, Series 1, *5 November 1800–18, Private Secret*, ff. 7–17.

[48] P.R.O. Adm/62, *Cape of Good Hope, 1809 to 1810. Letter from La Bourbonnaise, Table Bay, 16 November, 1809, from Vice Adm. A. Bertie*, f. 32.

[49] P.R.O. Adm/62, *Cape of Good Hope, 1809 to 1810. Letter from Cape Town, 15th November, 1809 from Vice Adm. A. Bertie*; I.O.R. P/383/20, *Bombay Political Consultations, 29 Sept. to 30 Oct., 1810*, f. 4617.

[50] B.M. Add. 37292, *Wellesley Papers*, vol. XIX, *Extract of a Letter from the Right Honourable Gilbert Lord Minto, Gov. Gen. of India, to R. Farquhar, Esq., Madras, 30th April, 1810*, f. 23.

summer of 1810, without waiting for official approval from London, four thousand men left the Rodriguez isles to attack the island of Bourbon which they took on the 7 July. From Bourbon the attack began on the Île de France, which surrendered the following day. On the 18 July, Farquhar displayed a declaration in St. Denis, capital of Bourbon, which officially provided for the island to pass under the sovereignty of His Majesty, King George III at midday on the 19 of July.[51] The 28 July an identical declaration was put up in Port St. Louis, capital of the Île de France, re-christened by the British with its old Dutch name of Mauritius. Clashes between the forces of General Decaen and those under General Abercromby only ended on the 2 December 1810, with the signing of the French surrender.[52]

In British publications of the time, 1810 for sub-Saharan East Africa marked: "the end of an epoch and the beginning of a new era".[53] In 1812 Farquhar was appointed Governor and Commander-in-Chief of Mauritius. Influenced by the notable pressure of philanthropic and humanitarian movements at home in Britain, dedicated himself to fighting the slave trade which had in no way interrupted by the French or the Arabs. He drew up agreements with both Radama I, King of Madagascar, and Sa'īd bin Sulṭān Āl Bū Sa'īdī, and took care to check that they were respected.[54]

The British conquest of the two strategic islands in the western Indian Ocean was a clear strategic action which brought Sa'īd bin Sulṭān Āl Bū Sa'īdī much closer to British control. It was an important first step toward a significant shift in favour of what was to become the primary object of English policy during the 19th century in those seas: the abolition of slavery within the 'dominions' of the Arab Sultan of Oman in particular, and in the western Indian Ocean in general; and this takes us back to the history of Zanzibar.

---

[51] B.M. Add. 37292, *Wellesley Papers*, vol. XIX, *Proclamation in the Name of His Majesty George III, of the United Kingdom of Great Britain and Ireland, St. Denis, July the 18th, 1810*, f. 65.

[52] R.W. Beachey, *The Slave Trade of Eastern Africa*, op. cit., p. 41 and accompanying bibliographical note; see the detailed chapter on the conquest of Mauritius in C. Northcote Parkinson, *War in the Eastern Seas 1793–1815*, London, 1954, pp. 397–412.

[53] M.V. Jackson Haight, *European Powers and South-East Africa*, op. cit., p. 167.

[54] For biographical information on Governor Farquhar, see I.O.R. J/1/15, Marine Department Records, *Sir Robert Towsend Farquhar*, f. 216.

4.4 The Memoranda of J.S. Buckingham: A Portrait of Sa'īd bin Sulṭān Āl Bū Sa'īdī

Halfway through the 19th century, numerous merchants, officials and representatives from Asia, Europe and America were to converge on the island of Zanzibar.

The Sultan of the island, Sa'īd bin Sulṭān Āl Bū Sa'īdī, at that time had three wives, an infinite number of concubines and at least one hundred and twenty children. His wives were Azza bin Seif bin Imam Aḥmad, mother of Hilāl bin Sa'īd bin Sulṭān Āl Bū Sa'īdī, who lived in the palace at Mntoni on Zanzibar; the niece of the Shah of Persia, Fath 'Ali Shah Qājār, whom the Sultan had married in 1827 on the condition that she could spend long periods at her father's court in Teheran, from whence she no longer returned following a ferocious argument in 1832 during which Sa'īd bin Sulṭān Āl Bū Sa'īdī was even called a 'Sunni dog'. The third was Shahruzad bin Irish Mirza bin Muhammad, great granddaughter of Shah Muhammad of Persia, who Sa'īd bin Sulṭān Āl Bū Sa'īdī married in 1837. She arrived in Zanzibar with a precious dowry, a following of one hundred and fifty men and numerous horses on which to go hunting. Sharuzad had Persian baths built at Kidichi and Kizimbani, the ruins of which still today bear witness to the artistic sensitivity of this, the Sultan of Zanzibar's last wife.[55] The Sultan, himself a great sailor, possessed a fleet including the *Liverpool*, a magnificent vessel built in Bombay in 1826, with seventy-four cannon and a crew of one hundred and fifty. In 1833, in an attempt to soften British's inflexible stance in relation to the slave trade, he sent this ship as a gift to King William IV who, however, limited himself to renaming the ship *Imam*. A further eighteen ships were also at his disposal.

On 20 June 1842, James Silk Buckingham, a journalist working for the East India Company, wrote two *Memoranda* on Sa'īd bin Sulṭān Āl Bū Sa'īdī.[56]

Buckingham's description gives us a classical interpretation of the character and role of this important Arab personality, expressed in the rhetorical and Eurocentric terms of the age.

---

[55] S.A.S. Farsi, *Seyyid Said Bin Sultan. The Joint Ruler of Oman and Zanzibar*, op. cit., *passim*.

[56] F.O. 54/4, *Memoranda respecting the present Imaum of Muscat, by J.S. Buckingham, June 20th, 1842*, f. 253 on.

Buckingham met the *Imaum* on a number of occasions between 1817 and 1818 when this latter was still very young and surrounded in Arabia by seasoned enemies. Despite this, however, the British journalist immediately saw how exceptional this young prince was in his ability to grasp the hidden thoughts and intentions of those he came into contact with and, with his 'affable manners', frequently exploit such perceptions to his own advantage.

His open policy, especially in commercial affairs, was greatly appreciated by the English to whom, Buckingham concluded, he was always faithful.

Apart from his possessions in Muscat, along the Omani coasts and the Asian shores of the Makran, Buckingham notes that Sa'īd bin Sulṭān Āl Bū Sa'īdī also possessed a colony on Zanzibar with which a notable volume of trade was conducted, carrying there Indian cloth and Arab dates and returning from Africa with ivory, copal resin, gold dust and slaves.

According to this British journalist, however, the Sultan's involvement in the slave trade differed from that of the Europeans, the slaves being neither maltreated nor beaten but trained as servants, living in their masters' homes and growing up alongside their masters' children. The more intelligent among them could also hold positions of power and be made captains of his ships. The most fortunate and deserving were even entrusted with the political management of what could effectively be termed their own reigns. And it was not by mere chance, Buckingham stressed, that, apparently, Sa'īd bin Sulṭān Āl Bū Sa'īdī demonstrated no sign of prejudice in relation to the African race.

The Sultan's respect for Great Britain, he goes on to note, had been demonstrated on numerous occasions, also with the marvellous gifts he sent to all British representatives and his permitting ships of the Royal Navy and the Bombay Marine to perform the thankless task of enforcing the terms of the abolition treaties in the western Indian Ocean.

Buckingham, clearly overwhelmed and seduced by the personality and charisma of Sa'īd bin Sulṭān Āl Bū Sa'īdī, added that he felt there was no need to stress the importance of maintaining friendly relations with 'one of the principal Sovereigns of the East', especially given his role of British ally in the oriental strategic context, where British security was threatened from all sides. The importance of continuing a close friendship with the Anglo-Indian government was, therefore, quite simply a matter of stating the obvious. "Seyd Said was of a commanding figure, well made and of an engaging countenance". At the same time, Buckingham tells us, he did not boast of his power or status as prince. He never left any of his subjects or any western representatives without a personal word or encouragement, No sailor of the East India Company's navy ever suffered hunger when a guest at his court: "abundance of refreshments, food and water, sent off immediately on their arrival free of all charge".

His amazing horses, sent as gifts to the Governors of Bombay and Calcutta were, in Buckingham's opinion, further proof of this Omani sovereign's loyalty to the Anglo-Indian Government.

Buckingham, therefore, provides us with a picturesque image to be viewed against the background of 19th century British strategy. A strategy which entailed political and commercial control of the oriental dominions and earmarking of local political points of reference, and one which is still often practiced today with varying degrees of success.

4.5   David Vatrin and Vincenzo Maurizi, Two Italian Spies in the Indian Ocean?

Examination of certain documents conserved in the British archives revealed an interesting file and, from the archives of the India Office Library and Records, in particular,[57] some curious correspondence. This gives precisely documented proof of the importance which Britain accorded every 'foreign' presence that could in some way unsettle British superiority in the western waters of the Indian Ocean and emphasises, moreover, the new role played by the Mascarene islands in Britain's defensive strategy. It represents a further indication of the absolute priority of defending the *life-line* to British India, running between Arabia, East Africa and western India, where the political and commercial emergence of Zanzibar and the policy undertaken by the Omani Sultan, Sa'īd bin Sulṭān Āl Bū Sa'īdī, provided

---

[57] I.O.R. P/383/21, Bombay Records. Bombay Political Consultations. *Letters to and from J. Duncan, Esq., Governor of Bombay, 6 November to 31 December, 1810*, f. 5391–5398. B. Nicolini, *Little known aspects of the history of Muscat and Zanzibar during the first half of the nineteenth century*, Proceedings of the Seminar for Arabian Studies, vol. 27, London, 1997, pp. 193–198.

an ever more forceful impulse to the network of intercontinental maritime trade routes.[58] The shores of sub-Saharan East Africa, therefore, entered into the new international framework and would play a major role in British expansionism in the east, together with Persia, the Arabian peninsula and the two seas of the western Indian Ocean, the Persian Gulf and the Red Sea with the Arabian coastline stretching between them.

These documents help us perceive more clearly certain elements in Britain's policy towards this area which would soon form part of its empire. Great Britain and the East India Company were convinced that the local princes were unreliable, mainly concerned with preserving their own power and privileges. Both London and Bombay were fully aware of the fact that these sovereigns entirely extraneous to the events and policies of the great western powers. With this in mind, the tactic employed by the East India Company and, later, London, throughout the 19th century was that of imposing its own policy aimed at protecting regional political-strategic interests so as to maintain order and stability in the western Indian Ocean.

Thus we can see a British policy taking shape founded on very clear principles. These included non-intervention in inter-tribal and inter-ethnic conflicts and the identification and support of elites in power: this was so that these elites could continue to enjoy the personal prestige essential to maintaining their positions, accumulating wealth in order to distribute political favours to their 'faithful' followers. The result was to create and strengthen a patronage class that had the backing of the British who would ensure both internal and military order. Great Britain would thus be perceived as an essential point of reference for the continuation of power, removing the temptation of new political-commercial alliances with England's most fearful opponent, Napoleon. A final aspect of this policy was the safeguarding of this dense network of interests at the lowest cost compatible with national security and the interests of the East India Company.

Two short episodes which follow were undoubtedly marginal in respect to the great events of the time, but are, nonetheless, extremely revealing of the atmosphere, tone and policy of Great Britain in

---

[58] From British records, Sa'īd bin Sulṭān Āl Bū Sa'īdī had long been convinced that the East India Company was a 'big, fat lady'.

relation to its European adversaries present in the Indian Ocean. The presence of an Italian in these waters had marked political significance in the context of Anglo-French rivalry.

Vincenzo Maurizi (nicknamed *Shaikh Mansur*), originally from Rome, was a doctor at the court of Sa'īd bin Sulṭān Āl Bū Sa'īdī who appointed him commander of artillery in the struggle against the enemy tribes of the Omani interior, but from 1809 onwards, Vincenzo Maurizi's position at the Omani court was in serious danger. An English officer denounced him to Sa'īd bin Sulṭān Āl Bū Sa'īdī in person, accusing him of being a spy in Napoleon's pay.

This affair still today is full of gaps and imprecisions, but it would appear that Maurizi had left Italy, his homeland, precisely as a result of his Francophile sympathies that had been the cause of furious arguments with his family. He travelled to Greece where he expressed his discontent to representatives of the Ottoman Turkish powers. Since the Ottoman Empire was then allied to Napoleon, it is very likely that the Italian doctor had performed acts of espionage before arriving in Constantinople. From then on, Maurizi was considered by the English to be a secret agent of the French Government, destined for the strategic English base at Mocha, in Arabia. He stayed in Arabia for roughly one year and, in 1810, travelled to Baghdad and Persia. Following Napoleon's defeat in Egypt, he returned to Muscat.

When accused by the English of being a French spy, Maurizi cited in his defence two English experts on Persian military institutions, who had the precise task of ascertaining his *bona fides*. One of these was Sir Gore Ouseley (1770–1844), the other Mr. Henry Lindsay, later Major General, Sir Lindsay-Bethune (1787–1851). According to R. Bidwell,[59] if Maurizi had really been a spy for the French, it would have been extremely difficult, if not impossible to have invoked such prestigious men in his defence. The Italian doctor, however, was able enough to avoid the most obvious consequence of such serious accusations, that is to say, his own death.

Suspicions concerning loyalty to the British lion continued unabated and, the following year, certain secret documents reappeared from which an important and worrying connection could be seen with

---

[59] R. Bidwell, *Bibliographical Notes on European Accounts of Muscat, 1500–1900*, "Arabian Studies", London, vol. 4, 1978, pp. 123–160.

another Italian also suspected of espionage at the Omani court.[60] These revealed the suggestion of a real link between two characters whose lives were connected by English suspicions. The fact that these papers outlining *also* Maurizi's case were found in a collection of letters relating to suspect movements of another Italian spy in the Indian Ocean, is both intriguing and extremely complex.

The 16 September 1810, the British Resident at Bushire, William Bruce, wrote to the Governor of Bombay to inform him of the presence of a suspicious element by the name of Vincenzo Maurizi who 'claimed to be a doctor'. Bruce advised the English agents in Muscat to pay close attention to Maurizi's activities, naturally without being noticed:

> At present there is a suspicious person here by name Vincent Maurizi, who passes himself out for an Italian doctor ... he has been here for some time and came from Muscat in May, and remained only a short time, proceeding again to Bussora from whence he returned in an Arab ship in July and has since then been living in Muscat ... As soon as he was suspected he was a Secret Agent, was requested to keep a watch over his actions, without at the same time giving him any cause to suppose he had received any account about him.[61]

Let us now, however, move on to the second character in this obscure and complex affair of Italian spies in the service of the French in the eastern seas.

An episode which occurred towards the end of 1810, which we could call the Vatrin affair, was indicative of the tension and preoccupation caused by Napoleon's activities in the East. This episode, as we have said, was marginal but typical of the almost obsessive attention paid by Britain to any movement which could threaten their aims of establishing order and stability both in the region and, by extension, in the international context. The Vatrin affair came to light when the two French bases in the Indian Ocean of Mauritius and Bourbon had already fallen firmly under British sovereignty. Set against the general background, it took on particular relevance within the context of Britain's 'overfearfulness' of a possible French invasion

---

[60] I.O.R. P/383/21, Bombay Records. Bombay Political Consultations. *Letters to and from J. Duncan, Esq., Governor of Bombay, 6 November to 31 December, 1810*, ibid.

[61] I.O.R., P/383/21, *From Hon.ble Company's Broker at Muscat to the Hon.ble Jonathan Duncan Esquire, Governor of Bombay, 16 September, 1810*, ff. 5349–50.

of India, and revealed the rapidity with which western methods of seizing and legitimising power functioned and interacted in the region.

At the end of 1810 it was clear that the East India Company's strategic and commercial interests were not entirely safe. French vessels have carried on the slave trade and a running battle all along the coasts and throughout the islands of East Africa. Nor had the taking of Bourbon and the Île de France/Mauritius put an end to such activity, constantly encouraged by what the English officials saw as a marked political fickleness—not to say, untrustworthiness—on the part of Sa'īd bin Sulṭān Āl Bū Sa'īdī. In tune with what the British saw as opportunism, in the autumn of 1810 this sovereign repeatedly requested military assistance from the British to defend himself against French corsairs.[62] The ever-watchful eyes of the British espionage network in the Indian Ocean continued its policing tasks, including that of controlling the movement of spies between East Africa and Arabia. During an exchange of prisoners between Britain and France after the French defeat in the Mascarene islands, a packet of secret letters came into Sa'īd bin Sulṭān Āl Bū Sa'īdī's possession. He immediately handed them over to the British, taking this ideal opportunity to demonstrate his 'loyalty' to the Government of His Majesty, George III (r. 1760–1820) in exchange for political and military aid.

In one of these letters, the representative of the Company in Muscat informed Jonathan Duncan, Governor of Bombay, of the following:

> The letter from this man in the French Character, which has fallen into the hands of Syyeed Saeed, has been enclosed by His Highness in a Communication by himself, and is forwarded by the present Packet from Bussora under charge of a Captain Clements, by whom it will be delivered. . . . Hon.ble Sir, an Indian who came here on the port of the French two years ago, returned to Egypt, and gives out that he is the bearer of French Dispatches, which he wishes to convey to the Mauritius this same person has mentioned to His Highness, that a French Frigate may now be expected at Muscat, but the truth, or otherwise of this report, is yet to be known.[63]

---

[62] I.O.R. P/383/20, *From Mons. Bruix, French Chief at Surat, to F. Warden, Chief Secr. to Gov., Bombay Castle, 5 October, 1810*, f. 5240.

[63] I.O.R. P/383/21, *Translate of a Letter from the Hon.ble Company's Broker at Muscat to the Hon.ble Jonathan Duncan Esquire, Governor of Bombay, dated 19 October and received the 5th November 1810*, ff. 5387–88.

It is obvious that an exchange of secret French despatches had been discovered but, as the British official noted, the whole truth was yet to revealed.

The incompleteness of this information was a source of great anxiety for the officials of the East India Company. This alarming communiqué was, however, followed by another letter from a certain Lt. Colonel David Vatrin (or Vatrèn) to the Governor of the Île de France, René Decaen. With this, the content of the mysterious package that had fallen into Sa'īd bin Sulṭān Āl Bū Sa'īdī's hands, began to emerge:

> You have expressed the desire to obtain possession of such of the despatches of the French as might be in the possession of their Agent destined for the Mauritius. The Frenchmen above noticed some time ago, apply to me for the Vessel to convey to the Mauritius, but I decline on account of our existing close, and intimate connection, for our friends, and enemies are reciprocal, and whatever may be injurious to the British Government, must be detrimental to me. *Muscat intercepted French Paper.* Is a sort of Paper in Italian addressed to the Officer of the Great Nation, requesting them to respect Shaikh Ahmed, a person much in the interests, and who had been of great service to the underwritten in his wants. It is dated Muskat 14 September 1810 and signed *Lieutenant Colonel David Vatrèn.* On the envelope it is marked in arabick (sic) to be shown to any Frenchman. Is a Letter in very bad French . . . to General Decaen, dated Moka, 10 April, 1810 . . . a *David Vatrin,* who gave himself out, as being of French extraction, and had arrived way of Constantinople bringing letters for M. Decaen General of the Isle of France, and that he had his expenses deprived. The writer complains of his poverty, mentions that his brother, who had formally been at the Mauritius, was gone to Zanzibar in hopes of forcing a passage to that island in order to receive the balance of the account due for five years, that he trusts M. Decaen would order payment of the balance on the freight of the French House.[64]

From a study of sources available it becomes clear that David Vatrin could not, in effect, represent any kind of threat whatsoever to the British plans against France in the Indian Ocean. He was described as a man of average heights, an naturalised Frenchman but originally an Italian engineer. In 1797, Vatrin had served in an infantry regiment of the French army with the rank of Lt. Colonel, fighting

---

[64] I.O.R. P/383/21, *Translate of a Letter from the Imaum of Muscat to the Hon.ble Jonathan Duncan Esquire, Governor of Bombay, without date and received the 5th November 1810,* ff. 5393–98. Italics are here reproduced as in the original manuscript.

to conquer Naples which, from 1806 to 1808, was governed by Napoleon's brother, Giuseppe Bonaparte (1768–1844).[65]

In 1798 he was sent to Greece and Albania with the Seven Islands expedition, but was unfortunately wound and arrested in battle. Vatrin suffered greatly and numerous attempts were made to convert him to Islam. As he refused to do so, he remained as a slave in Albania, forced to chop wood with others for five long and painful years. In December 1809 this Italian adventurer was handed over to the Serbs by a merchant from Santorini, but he was soon imprisoned by the Turks and sent to Constantinople. Once freed, the unhappy Vatrin succeeded in some unknown way to reach Cairo, the Arabian peninsula, Mocha and the port of Muscat, where he placed himself at the service of the French Government in its struggle against British India. He had fled to the east, like so many supporters of Bonaparte, in search of better luck, his lost brother and a little wealth.

At this point, the Governor of Bombay, Jonathan Duncan, could make a connection between this information and a previous report from the assistant to the British mission at Mocha in Arabia, John Benzoni.

The pieces of the mosaic seemed to be falling into place for the Anglo-Indian administration:

> *A French Emissary named Vatren, Italian,* Engineer and Chief of Brigate in the French Service, is a man of middle size he left Cairo early in January, for Jedda, and India, saying he had a brother in some places in the East *and the attack on the Isles of Bourbon and France may be connected with this man's mission.*[66]

David Vatrin would, in fact, turn out to be one of many suspects in a period during which the Napoleonic threat led to an important turning point in political-diplomatic relations between Britain and her dominions in the western Indian Ocean.

What emerged from this twisted story was a factor of notable significance for the Governor of Bombay: proof of the loyalty shown

---

[65] P. Colletta, *Storia del Reame di Napoli*, Milano, 1989. See A.M. Rao, *Le strutture militari nel Regno di Napoli* and J. Davis, *L'Italia nella diplomazia delle grandi potenze*, Istituto per la Storia del Risorgimento Italiano, LVIII Congress, Milano, 2–5 October, 1996.

[66] I.O.R. P/383/21, *Translate of a Letter from John Benzoni Esq., Assistant to the British Mission in Arabia to General René Decaen, Governor of Île de France, Mocha, 23 August, 1810*, f. 5986. Italics is here reproduced as in the original text.

to Britain by Sa'īd bin Sulṭān Āl Bū Sa'īdī. Even more important in the eyes of the English Governor was the act by which this loyalty was made manifest, the delivery of the suspicious letters into British hands by Arabs of whose trustworthiness they had not been certain. This in a situation in which any and all information arriving from 'oriental' allies regarding the enemy was of vital significance.

In the autumn of 1810, this Omani Arab 'loyalty' to Great Britain was confirmed by the letter sent by the Secretary to the Governor of Bombay, R.J. Goodwin, to the English Resident in Muscat. Goodwin received the praises of the Anglo-Indian Government for having discovered the package of letters addressed by Vatrin to the Government of the Île de France and having prevented the possibly catastrophic consequences that could have arisen should the papers have ended up in less discerning hands. The text of this letter includes the following:

> I am directed by the Hon.ble the Gov. in Council to acknowledge the receipt of your letter and to express the great satisfaction at your successful interposition in intercepting the correspondence between Mr. Vatrin and the Government of the French Island.[67]

Also of interest in this same letter is a brief reference to the Arab request for planks of wood, denied by the English in order to prevent the pirates who infested the Gulf from building ships and other vessels. Here we may clearly see how even the smallest detail was of the essence in the struggle to assert their supremacy over the Persian Gulf and the western sector of the Indian Ocean.

On the 9 November 1810, therefore, Duncan decided to write to the Omani sovereign to compliment him on his extraordinary demonstration of loyalty, defining this as being 'almost like that a western ruler'. He wrote thus:

> I have had the pleasure to receive your Highness's letter, together with the Papers therein referred to, being the Documents seized in the possession of Mr. Vatren who, as now appears instead of being an accredited Agent of the French Government, is nothing more than a mere *Political Swindler*, still however I cannot but view your ready compliance with regard to the Seizure of this Papers, a *strong indication of your Highness attachment to the English cause, and of your desire to cultivate in the*

---

[67] I.O.R. P/383/21, *Translate of a Letter from R.J. Goodwin to the Company's Broker at Muscat, dated 25 October, 1810*, ff. 5819–20.

true spirit of harmony, the ties of cordiality and friendship that have so long sub-sisted between the two States. For the rest, I request your Highness will continue to afford me the pleasure of frequently hearing of your welfare, in which I cannot be otherwise than take active interest, as well as in the prosperity of your Highness Administration.[68]

Thus Governor Duncan dismissed David Vatrin as a mere political fraudster, a swindler, whose actions could in no way represent a threat to the complex diplomatic network which the Governor of Bombay and his representatives near to Sa'īd bin Sulṭān Āl Bū Sa'īdī had woven in the waters of the Persian Gulf. In short, David Vatrin was not a spy.

The documentation quoted here evokes the tones and atmosphere of the time, studded with anxiety, intrigues, suspicion and the more or less threatening presence of spies and secret packages of letters.

The elements which emerge from such documents induce us to formulate further hypotheses. We are immediately impelled to ask ourselves why documents were found precisely in the collection of *Muscat intercepted French Papers,* mainly related to David Vatrin, concerning Maurizi, the personal physician of Sa'īd bin Sulṭān Āl Bū Sa'īdī. And what really could have been the link between this Italian doctor and David Vatrin? Maurizi was trusted by the Omani sovereign, commanded his artillery, lived at the Āl Bū Sa'īdī court in Muscat and had unlimited access to information. The accusations made against Maurizi put his very life at risk, but he apparently was in no way connected to the sad tale of hapless Vatrin, a simple adventurer driven by a lack of money towards serving the French in the wide expanses of the Indian Ocean.

Is it, however, possible that these two characters did in fact come into contact in services performed for the French Government in the Mascarene islands, thus explaining the documents which link them? If we consider their respective feelings of resentment and their positions, at least during a certain period, then these would undoubtedly argue in favour of their working together against Britain. The subsequent discovery that British suspicions regarding both Italians were, to differing degrees, groundless leads us to think that they were caught up in a British defensive strategy that left nothing to chance

---

[68] I.O.R. P/383/21, *Copy of a Letter from the Hon.ble Jonathan Duncan Esq., Governor of Bombay, to the Imaum of Muscat, dated the 9 November, 1810,* f. 5641.

and meant that every doubtful element was immediately translated into the weighty accusation of espionage.

These regions were permeated with an atmosphere of misunderstanding, distortion and exaggeration that would intensify in the years to come, transforming the western Indian Ocean into a "receptacle of secrets and full of spies".[69] The presence of two Italians at the Omani court in Muscat, suspected of spying by the British and with wavering fortunes and mishaps, although an anecdotal episode, represented certainly more than just a symbol of the epoch and of the suspicious atmosphere. It help us to have a better grasp on the degree and extent to which Sa'īd bin Sulṭān Āl Bū Sa'īdī, local situations in relation to Anglo-French rivalry and European competition for exclusivity in Indian Ocean trade were all interrelated throughout the 19th century. It is a fact that the clear sign of loyalty shown by the Omani Sultan to British representatives had been induced by these two men's actions and behaviours.

Moreover, British attention towards Zanzibar as a strategic island for English control of the western Indian Ocean was to be developed also with regards to the dangerous and ambiguous presence of two Italian spies.

---

[69] M.V. Jackson Haight, *European Powers and South-East Africa*, op. cit., p. 159.

CHAPTER FIVE

SLAVE TRADE AND BRITISH ABOLITION POLICY

The end of the Napoleonic wars and eclipse of French imperial power resulted in a new European order that led to tangible changes also in international strategic priorities.

In the western reaches of the Indian Ocean, Britain became the driving force and leader of two principal and closely correlated courses of action: the gradual creation of a well-structured system for exercising political power in sub-Saharan East Africa, and the so-called 'politics of ideals'. This latter, over the course of the 19th century, would come to represent the catalyst of all British policy, within the context of London's determined and relentless struggle to abolish slavery and put a stop to the slave trade conducted in the turbulent waters around the island of Zanzibar.

With regard to the former aspect, British policy turned to the eastern African regions which, as have seen, were destined to fall under the far-reaching and undisputed British mantle after the fall of Napoleon. This with the aim of identifying and formalising contacts with local political points of reference capable of ensuring respect for and observance of the agreements and treaties of 'friendship and trade' stipulated by Great Britain.

The principal aim in this area was to maintain and safeguard the sea-routes which linking East Africa with the main ports of India, to guarantee the continuation of the flourishing trade there conducted and to identify local authorities by means of whom such policy and control could be effected.

Conflict and causes of tension were within the British administration and were especially marked between the Government at home and that of the East India Company in both Bombay and Calcutta. The East India Company, in particular, concerned about the costs of such a strategy, constantly urged for a policy based on the greatest caution and circumspection. On the other hand, there were the reports of various officials assigned to the strategic and commercial bases along the coasts of the western Indian Ocean who, more in touch with local and often personal needs, pushed instead for greater intervention in relation to the local authorities.

London, therefore, was determined to avoid any further interference in regions which it considered to be of vital importance and interest for its own commercial empire. Piracy flourished in the Gulf, apparently aided and abetted by the French. These pirates of the Gulf had found virtually impregnable hideaways in the islands of Ras al-Khaima, from whence they emerged to carry out surprise raids against convoys traversing the Straits of Hormuz, returning afterwards to their safe nests. The damage they inflicted was notable and, notwithstanding repeated direct intervention by the English or the East India Company, this plague seemed indomitable.[1]

Britain's decisive response was aimed at extending British control over the various territories along the eastern shores of the Arabian Peninsula (the so-called 'pirates coast', for example). This, in turn, meant encroachment on that territory which had, in the past, been under the control or direct dominion of the Āl Bū Sa'īdī.

It was at this point that Sa'īd bin Sulṭān Āl Bū Sa'īdī decided to try his luck as a merchant prince of East Africa. Without renouncing his interests on the Arabian Peninsula, thanks to the solid financial backing of the powerful Indian merchants, mainly from the Kutch and the Sind, he invested heavily in the island of Zanzibar. This meant that he could avoid further weakening his troops and fortune in actions on the peninsula against the English and the Arab tribes of the interior. On the contrary, the fact that the Indian regions of Kutch and Sind had still not been placed under the direct control of the East India Company, gave him and his Indian supporters a certain degree of room for manoeuvre.

The rulers of Kutch were well known for their religion tolerance policy, although, during the past centuries many crimes were com-

---

[1] See, among others, C.E. Davies, *Britain, Trade and Piracy: the British Expeditions against Ras al-Khaima of 1809–10 and 1819–20*, in, C.E. Davies (Ed.), *Global Interests in the Arab Gulf*, Exeter, 1992, pp. 29–66. The author puts forward the extremely plausible hypothesis that, apart from the declared policy of eliminating piracy, considered equivalent to a 'crime' (the often violent seizure of merchant ships and reduction of their crews to slavery), the East India Company also secretly desired to destroy the *de facto* power of these pirates, rivals and competitors at one and the same time for the international trade conducted along these sea routes. By the same author, see also *The Blood Red Arab Flag. An Investigation into Qasimi Piracy 1797–1820*, Exeter, 1997. The bibliography on this topic is, of course, extensive but of particular note I wish to mention the documents held in the Bombay Archives, copies also at the University of Exeter (Secret and Political). P. Risso presents an interesting perspective in *Cross-Cultural Perceptions of Piracy: Maritime Violence in the Western Indian Ocean and Persian Gulf Region during a Long Eighteenth Century*, "Journal of World History", vol. 12, n. 2, 2001, pp. 293–319.

mitted against Kutch population in the name of Islam. The presence of a glass factory and of good breed horses led Maharao Deshalji II (1819–1860) to maritime long-distance trade with Zanzibar and, most of all, with the Sultan of Oman. And an important motivation for good relationships between the two sovereign was to be found in these common interests and aims within the still 'free from Britain control' strategic ports of the western Indian Ocean.[2]

Till the year 710 A.D. the inhabitants of Sind were Hindu; after the Arab conquest many Hindu converted to Islam and some of them became Sheikh. As Sind was rich in horses, carriages, chariots, jewellery, food and grain, trade routes to south-central Asia conducted by Sind traders, *vanya*, were both by land and by sea. Therefore, some Sindi merchants were to be found trading during the 18th century with the Khan of Kalat in Baluchistan, and with Oman.[3] During the 19th century the British explorer and adventurer Richard Burton wrote about the Baluch in Sind:

> The Belochi is far superior to the common Sindhi in appearance and morals. He is of fairer complexion, more robust frame and hardier constitution. At the same time he is violent, treacherous and revengeful, addicted to every description of debauchery, dirty in person, rough and rude in manners.[4]

As proof of the intense contacts between Sind and the Arabian Peninsula, Burton also gave a description of African slaves:

---

[2] Due to the extensive literature on the history of Sind and Kutch, see, among the many, C. Markovits, *The Global World of the Indian Merchant 1750–1947*, Cambridge, 2000; among the classics, see R.F. Burton, *Sindh and the Races that inhabit the Valley of the Indus*, London, 1851, repr. Karachi, 1988; H. Pottinger, *Travel in Beloochistan and Sinde*, op. cit., *passim*; A.F. Scott, *Scinde in the Forties*, London, 1912; L.F. Rushbrook Williams, *The Black Hills. Kutch in History and Legend*, no place, 1958; C.H. Allen, *The Indian Merchant Community of Muscat*, "Bulletin of the School of Oriental and African Studies", London, vol. 44, 1981, pp. 39–53; I. Banga, *Karachi and its Hinterland under Colonial Rule*, in, I. Banga (Ed.), *Ports and their Hinterlands in India, 1700–1950*, Dehli, 1992; M.Y. Mughal, *Studies in Sind*, Jamsoro, 1989; L. Subramanian, who kindly suggested me these references, *Indigenous Capital and Imperial Expansion in western India Bombay, Surat and the west Coast*, Dehli, 1996; H. Khuhro (Ed.), *Sind through the Centuries*. Proceedings of an International Seminar held in Karachi in Spring 1975 by the Department of Culture, Government of Sind, Karachi, 1981; N.M. Billimoria (compiled by), *Bibliography of Publications relating to Sind & Baluchistan*, Lahore, 1930; see also Alexander Walker comments on Indian colonies in East Africa, in his Papers in The National Library of Scotland, Edimburgh.

[3] See P.J. Marshall (Ed.), *The Eighteenth Century*, The Oxford History of the British Empire, Oxford, vol. II, 1998; A. Porter (Ed.), *The Nineteenth Century*, The Oxford History of the British Empire, Oxford, vol. III, 1999.

[4] R.F. Burton, *Sindh and the Races that inhabit the Valley of the Indus*, op. cit., pp. 239 on.

> The African slaves in Sindh were imported from Muscat and other harbours on the eastern coast of Arabia... from six to seven hundreds Zangibari and other blacks were imported annually from Africa. Their value was from forty to one hundred and fifty rupees. Girls were more valuable than boys and were imported in great numbers.[5]

It was evident that a precious commercial alliance between Sind and Oman was very much exploited on the political level by all parties involved as long as the East India Company left them carrying on their trade and power relationships.

The commercial rise of Zanzibar came about, therefore, under the very eyes of the British, these latter being too preoccupied with conquering bases for their own security in the western Indian Ocean, with French movements and with their struggle to abolish the slave trade. By exploiting this British distraction, and obviously motivated by reasons of pure personal survival, the Omani sovereign and capable Indian merchants gradually moved their capital, ships, investments, people and even personal effects towards a safe harbour, favourable climate and refuge from threats that by now arrived from all directions, a flourishing market for all kinds of goods sought after throughout the Indian Ocean and beyond, towards, that is, a concrete answer to all their desires: the African island of Zanzibar.

The years between the taking of the Mascarene Islands, Mauritius and Bourbon, and the signing in 1822 of the first treaty against the slave trade between Captain Fairfax Moresby (1786–1877) and Sa'īd bin Sulṭān Āl Bū Sa'īdī, thus witnessed the rise, in many ways unexpected by British diplomacy, of Zanzibar, "one of the most important emporiums of the entire African continent".[6]

The second aspect is that of the 'politics of ideals' which saw Great Britain playing a major and crucial role in the struggle against the slave trade, including that in eastern Africa, a struggle which would continue throughout the 19th century.[7] Britain set out on her

---

[5] Ibidem, p. 253.

[6] N.R. Bennett, *A History of the Arab State of Zanzibar*, "Studies in East African History", London, 1987, p. 35.

[7] As is well-known, the Congress of Vienna, 8 February 1815, concluded with a solemn, though hotly debated, declaration on the abolition of slavery. On 24 November 1822 a similar declaration was signed in Verona in the *Procès Verbal de la Conférence relative à l'àbolition dal a Traite des Nègres*, by Metternich, Wellington, Nesselrode, Tatischeff, and other representatives of the European chanceries. P.P. XXII 1821, *Papers relating to the Abolition of the Slave Trade*, f. 669.

policy of 'splendid isolation' which would make her the undisputed ruler of the waves and distance her from European affairs except to the extent that a weather-eye was kept on the balance of power so as to avoid any resurgence of revolutionary ambition. In this context, the fight against the slave trade represented a prestigious political instrument, but also an effective and ambiguous weapon to be wielded with dexterity and cunning. The centuries old trade had made the slave traders immensely wealthy and was then, more than ever, one of the main sources of income in East Africa. At the start of the 19th century the volume of trade had reached staggering proportions and involved not only the Indian Ocean and the Mediterranean basin but stretched as far as the new transoceanic continents.

The British lion, however, could not stand by and observe in silence this endless and unchallenged flow of 'savage herds' through the area under its control.

Although a quite passive attitude towards the horrors of slavery and piracy in the eastern seas was widespread in England, a tangible propaganda policy was set in motion by certain outstanding members of the political panorama of the times such as William Wilberforce (1759–1833),[8] member of Parliament, and Thomas Clarkson. This policy, both philanthropic and humanitarian in nature, was conducted in line with the most rigid principles of Evangelism.

Returning for a moment to 1785, we see that Clarkson, 'the most cultured and untiring of promoters', had dedicated his entire life to campaigning against the slave trade. The growing influence of a strong abolitionist lobby, supported by the intellectual elite of the time—Jane Austen, Samuel Taylor Coleridge, William Wordsworth, Zachary Macaulay, along with many others—aroused emotions and succeeded in awakening the entire nation's opinion to the noble cause of eradicating such a horrendous form of commerce. Thus, thanks to pressure brought to bear on the Court of Directors of the East India Company, the slave trade was finally declared illegal.[9] In

---

[8] T. Buxton, *William Wilberforce. The Story of a Great Crusade*, London, 1933.

[9] The initial results led the Anglo-Indian Government in Bombay to prohibit, in 1805, the importation and exportation of slaves to or from any of the ports under its jurisdiction. In 1807 the commanders of ships not belonging to the East India Company had to declare that they were carrying no slaves aboard, or pay a fine of 500 rupees. From the 1 March 1808 no slave was accepted any longer in the

1811, and in support of Wilberforce, the fearful Henry Brougham formulated and obtained Parliamentary approval for the Felony Act (penal code), considered one of the most efficacious and severe legislative acts in this battle for the abolition of slavery. Moreover, on the 21 January 1815, Lord Castlereagh convinced the representatives of the European chanceries to sign a Convention for the abolition of the slave trade. It was, therefore, necessary to bring pressure to bear on those countries which practiced slavery, suppress the trade on the open seas and prevent communities on the spot from rounding up and exporting human beings from the African interior. The British were the first abolitionists of what publications of the time termed an infamous trade in human flesh.

5.1   *Slaves*

We must remember that the Arab world's perception of slavery as an economic and power policy was entirely different from that of the Christian West which had undersigned the Holy Alliance and strove for abolition. In Islamic society, unlike many others, slavery was not prohibited. It even finds precise dispositions in its support in the Koran: the equality of all men before God implies clear duties also in regard to slaves, but not the suppression of slavery itself, even though it is severely forbidden to reduce another Muslim to the state of slavery. In terms of rights, no political or religious function may be performed by a slave, but owners may delegate to slaves any responsibility or task related to the exercise of their authority. Thus, the slaves of important individuals enjoyed a privileged status and could often attain higher positions of power than free men, the cases of slaves themselves becoming princes not being entirely exceptional, either. In the context of Islam, slavery is a highly-structured concept, regulated down to the smaller detail by the civil and criminal codes. As a result, it is difficult to pass judgement on the moral or physical condition of slaves in the Islamic African world as compared to those in other societies. Conditions obviously varied, and

---

ports or territories under Anglo-Indian Government jurisdiction and, in 1811, the Government of Bengal in Calcutta added a six month prison sentence to the fine. R.W. Beachey, *The Slave Trade of Eastern Africa*, London, 1976, p. 40.

there were certainly those who attempted to escape, but there is no doubt that this institution lay at the very foundation of the entire Islamic society of the cosmopolitan commercial empire founded on the seas by Sa'īd bin Sulṭān Āl Bū Sa'īdī. Moreover, as we have noted, it was inevitable that there would have to be a clash with the Christian west, as represented by Great Britain, over this question.[10]

From the religious point of view slave are considered persons, but being subject to their masters they are not fully responsible, they are at the same time a thing. According to Schacht,[11] slavery can originate through birth or through captivity, if a non-Muslim who is protected neither by treaty nor by a safe conduct falls into the hands of the Muslims. Slaves can get married: the male slave may marry up to two female slaves; the female slave may also marry a free man who is not her owner, and the male slave a free woman who is not his owner. The marriage of the slave requires the permission of the owner; he can also give the slave in marriage against his or her will. The permission implies that the master becomes responsible with the person (rakaba) of the slave for the pecuniary obligations which derive from the marriage, nuptial gifts and maintenance. Minor slaves are not to be separated from their near relatives, and in particular their parents, in sale. The children of a female slave follow the status of their mother, except that the children of the concubine, whom the owner has recognised as his own (umm walad), and this was the case of the numerous sons of the Omani Sultan, is free with all the rights of children from a marriage with a free woman. And this rule has had the most profound influence on the development of Islamic society. The Islamic law of slavery is patriarchal and belongs more to the law of family than to the law of property. Apart from domestic slaves, Islamic law takes notice of trading slaves who possess a

---

[10] On history of slavery in Islamic African societies, amongst the many, see P. Lovejoy, *The Ideology of Slavery in Africa*, Beverly Hills, 1981; P. Lovejoy, *Transformations in Slavery: A History of Slavery in Africa*, "African Studies Series", 36, Cambridge, 1983; P. Lovejoy, *Africans in Bondage: Studies in slavery and the slave trade in honour of Philip D. Curtin*, African Studies Program, Madison, 1986; F. Cooper, *Plantation Slavery on the East Coast of Africa*, Portsmouth, I ed. 1977, II ed. 1997; F. Cooper, *From Slaves to Squatters: Plantation Labor and Agriculture in Zanzibar and Coastal Kenya, 1890–1925*, New Haven, 1980; R. Pouwels and N. Levtzion (Eds.), *The History of Islam in Africa*, Ohio, 2000.

[11] J. Schacht, *An Introduction to Islamic Law*, I ed. Oxford, 1964, II ed. Hong Kong, 1993, p. 127.

considerable liberty of action, but hardly of working slaves kept for
exploiting agricultural and industrial enterprises.

On Swahili coast slavery was mainly characterised as an open and
very much absorptive system, although during the 19th century the
majority of slaves from the interior were destined to cultivations, and
consequently totally excluded from any chance of paternalistic gen-
erosity from their masters. The search for a better life on Zanzibar
and on the Swahili coast was tempted by slaves in many ways: those
who were outside the master's household worked in the master's
mashamba and were expected to taking care of their subsistence cultivating a small plot of the *shamba*; the more privileged cultivated by
themselves a small piece of land, paying an annual or monthly trib-
ute to their master.[12] *Vibaruna* were hired slaves, mainly in urban
centres; they were extremely poor, but in some cases joined Hadrami
Arab's caravans and succeeded in modifying their humiliating conditions of life. The trading slaves, *mafundi*, craftsmen, reached a decent
level of dignity, but they remained under strict control of their master, and 'illegal' or personal initiatives were severely punished.

In Africa slaves were thought as less than human and, even when
they embraced Islam—Sunni and never Ibadi as only the Arabs of
Oman—were thought less than Muslim.

The burning question of slavery went hand in hand with another
and no less relevant factor.[13] In the sub-Saharan East African regions,
and in the eastern Mediterranean, there was no local 'peasant class'
that could be employed on the new cultivations which European
demand had induced rich landowners to introduce and which were
proving to be both extremely successful and profitable (sugarcane,
rice, copal, vanilla, pepper, cardamom, nutmeg and—especially on
Zanzibar, as we shall see—cloves). Consequently, the use of slaves
for tilling the land and other heavy labour on the plantations had
become a question of routine; in other words, when England undertook her crusade against slavery, it was precisely this most miserable
section of society which constituted the economic foundations of the
entire region.

---

[12] J. Glassman, *Feats and Riot*, op. cit., pp. 79–114.
[13] On the lively debate on the question of slavery, amongst the many, see G. Heuman, *Slavery, The Slave Trade, and Abolition*, in R.W. Winks (Ed.), *Historiography*, The
Oxford History of the British Empire, Oxford, vol. V, 1999, pp. 315–326.

The island of Zanzibar was administered by governors representing Sa'īd bin Sulṭān Āl Bū Sa'īdī and exercised all power on his
behalf. The military support which furnished these representatives
with absolute authority over the island and its affairs, consisted of
special troops of proven trustworthiness, that is to say, the Baluch
corps closely tied to the Āl Bū Sa'īdī by fundamentally economic
agreements. The local governors also had the support of the local,
autochthonous Swahili aristocracy, mainly merchants. These came
under the *mwinyi mkuu*, subdivided into *diwan, jumbe, wazee*; and were
tied to the Omani elite by mutual interests in the exploitation of the
resources offered by the island and the eastern shores of Africa.[14]
This mercantile empire, with Sa'īd bin Sulṭān Āl Bū Sa'īdī, moved
its economic and political centre of gravity to Zanzibar, making control of the neighbouring islands and the nearby African coast one
of the cornerstones of its vast system of interests. So much so that,
many years later, the English explorer Richard Burton, would claim
that: "If you play the flute in Zanzibar it will sound as far as the
Great Lakes".[15] Without a shadow of a doubt, European rivalry in
the Persian Gulf and the western waters of the Indian Ocean from
the start of the 19th century on, combined with related upheavals
in power and strategy, had a decisive impact also on the deviation
of the maritime routes followed by this immense commercial traffic.

Clearly, however, the ability of Sa'īd bin Sulṭān Āl Bū Sa'īdī in
exploiting such political contingencies was also to carry a certain
weight.

Within this framework of trade, commerce, bargaining, conflict
and struggle for the control of trade in this or that valuable merchandise, the island of Zanzibar inserted itself with the dynamism
of its officials, merchants, cunning adventurers and slaves. Turning
once again to the question of slavery, we must remember how the
very backbone of Zanzibar's economy at this sensitive stage in its
rise was formed precisely by slaves, the key element in both the local
economy and the immense wealth of its merchants.

These, therefore, were the foundations on which Sa'īd bin Sulṭān
Āl Bū Sa'īdī and the Indian mercantile communities built their great

---

[14] J. Glassman, *The Bondsman's new clothes: the contradictory consciousness of slave resistance on the Swahili Coast*, "Journal of African History", 32, London, 1991, pp. 277-312.

[15] A claim that has been interpreted in many conflicting ways.

commercial emporium in the face of inevitable conflict with the English in the Persian Gulf over the question of piracy.

The contrast is self-evident between the two, profoundly different ways of perceiving objectives and strategies. On the one hand, we have an Arab merchant prince and his traditional court of advisers, warriors, merchants and slaves and, on the other, we have Great Britain which, greatly influenced by marked public pressure, decides to launch a crusade against the slave trade and traders. In other words, an undertaking which has the aim of tearing up from the roots the real economic foundations of the entire western Indian Ocean region and of revolutionising both the traditional mechanisms of local power and traditional culture itself. We thus have a conflict between the force of superior technology and military power of the Europeans and the cunning and ambivalence of the merchant prince of Muscat and Zanzibar, Sa'īd bin Sulṭān Āl Bū Sa'īdī, conscious though he was of his own military weakness.

In sub-Saharan East Africa during the 19th century, it was believed that slavery, if we go beyond the mere capture of human beings, was caused by the tribes of the interior accumulating debts to the slaving merchants of the coast, as well as by the recurrent periods of drought suffered along the Mrima coast, sometimes along that part facing the islands of Zanzibar and Pemba. In alternating phases, therefore, the populations decided to travel to Zanzibar and there sell themselves into slavery.[16]

The slave trade practiced along the East African shores had certain principal characteristics: the slaves did not come from areas of Swahili cultural influence, and were called *mshenzi* (pl. *washenzi*), that is to say, barbarians, uncivilised. They were not Muslims, as were all free Swahili within the domains of the Omani Arabs, and were the property of their owners, slavery being regulated by the principles of Koranic law.

The slaves formed a separate caste. There were *watumwa wajinga*, not yet assimilated into the coastal populations, the *wakulia*, transported as children to Zanzibar, and, in this category, also the *wazalia* (pl. of *mzalia*), those generations born on the coast and fully acculturated into coastal Islamic culture.

---

[16] G.A. Akinola, *Slavery and Slave Revolts in the Sultanate of Zanzibar in the Nineteenth Century*, op. cit., pp. 215–228.

Those enjoying more privileged conditions were, naturally, the domestic slaves. Their relationship with their owners was more that of a member of the family than one of submission and they were called *udugu yangu*, my brother, and the women *suria*, concubines of their owners or nannies. As they were often entrusted with manual labour, household slaves thus became *msimamizi*, guardians, *nokoa*, *kadamu*, first or second head slaves in the spice and coconut plantations on Zanzibar and along the coasts. Others had the task of leading caravans towards the interior. The slave of the *mashamba*—from the French *champ*, or field, that is the plantations[17]—hoed the fields, sieved copal and carried the merchandise to the ports. They could also be assigned a piece of land with which to support themselves, working there on Thursdays and Fridays, the two days of rest. They were also permitted, on payment of a tax, to get married.[18]

The demand for slaves came, primarily, from the various parts of the Arabia Peninsula, where the cultivation of date palms called for a continuous supply of labour, but also from India, where they were employed in local oases and on sugarcane and tea plantations from Central Asia, where cotton was beginning to be grown, as well as from various regions of the Ottoman Empire and from the American continent. African slaves were also used as domestic help or in craftwork in rich families and at the Arab courts. The demand was especially high for young women and girls to serve in the home. Slaves destined for the courts were given special training in entertaining important guests with their singing and dancing. Another speciality was that of the eunuchs, held in particular esteem especially in the Ottoman Empire. These were mutilated without any regard being shown for hygiene, a fact reflected in the survival rate for those transported from Africa of only one in ten. According to Islamic law, mutilation is forbidden inside the dār al-Islām, therefore, only

---

[17] A. Lodhi, *Oriental Influences in Swahili*, op. cit., pp. 46–47.

[18] See, among others, W.G. Clarence-Smith, *The Economics of the Indian Ocean Slave Trade in the Nineteenth Century: An Overview*, in W.G. Clarence-Smith (Ed.), *The Economics of the Indian Ocean Slave Trade in the Nineteenth Century*, London, 1938; E.B. Martin and T.C.I. Ryan, *A Quantitative Assessment of the Arab Slave Trade of East Africa, 1770–1896*, "Kenya Historical Review", Nairobi, 1977; E.A. Alpers, *Ivory and Slaves in East Central Africa*, Berkeley, 1967; E.A. Alpers, *The East African Slave Trade*, "Historical Association of Tanzania", n. 3, Nairobi, 1975; R. Gray and D. Birmingham, *Pre-Colonial African Trade: Essays on Trade in Central and Eastern Africa before 1900*, London, 1970; P. Manning, *Slavery and African Life: Occidental, Oriental and African Slave Traders*, "African Studies Series", Cambridge, 1990.

slaves were mutilated, with some exemptions in Central Asia and in
Persia. The eunuchs were highly priced, three times more than a
slave, and reached high ranks within Islamic societies. The eunuchs
were harīm guardians, as well as guardians of everything sacre, like
the Holy Places, such as Mecca. They retained great prestige and
richness; black castrated slaves were powerful figures in the Ottoman
Empire and eunuchs were highly respected within the whole of dār
al-Islām being very close to Muslim sovereigns.[19]

Great Britain was the first nation to undertake an international
campaign with humanitarian goals. There remained, however, a
weighty and complex knot to unravel. How could they combat slavery and, at the same time, ally themselves with the most famous and
powerful protectors of the slave traders, such as Sa'īd bin Sulṭān Āl
Bū Sa'īdī who, in their turn, obtained their greatest profits precisely
from this trade in human flesh?

It was around this crucial question that relations between the
Omani Arab Sultan, the East India Company and Britain would
revolve, a problem which animated lively political debate also within
the various forces in play.

The slave trade, therefore, represented a highly destabilising elements for British policy, not only on the political but also on a social
and economic level. To this was added the imposing humanitarian
pressure brought to bear by public opinion in Britain which forced
the Government to take decisive action with the specific aim of
putting an end to such trade.[20]

During the 19th century, the growing effectiveness of British measures aimed at abolition caused a reduction in the availability of
African slaves. This lack was, however, partly compensated for by
Asiatic slaves, as shown by the commerce in Asian people from the
coast of Baluchistan destined to be sold in the squares of Arabia
during the first decades of the 20th century.[21]

---

[19] G. Vercellin, *Tra veli e turbanti. Rituali sociali e vita privata nei mondi dell'Islam*,
Venezia, 2000, pp. 186–191.

[20] See the extensive archival documentation contained in *Thomas Clarkson Papers*
and *Liverpool Papers*, The British Library, London. See T.C. Mccaskie, *Cultural
Encounters: Britain and Africa in the Nineteenth Century*, in, A. Porter (Ed.), *The Oxford
History of the British Empire*, vol. 3, Oxford, 1999, pp. 665–689.

[21] H.S.A.—A.G.G. Office—Essential Records, Baluchistan Archives, *Complaint about
existence of Slavery in Baluchistan, from Capt. P. Cox, Consul and Political Agent, Maskat to
Lieut. Col. C.A. Kemball, Agg. Political Resident in the Persian Gulf, 17th September, 1901*,
Political, 5–2/57. B. Nicolini and R. Redaelli, *Quetta: history and Archives. Note of a*

5.2   *Ivory and Spices*

At this point it is useful to indicate another, important factor which played a part in the impressive economic-commercial growth of Zanzibar, as well as the labyrinth of suspicion, diffidence, envy, misunderstanding and open conflict between Britain and Sa'īd bin Sulṭān Āl Bū Sa'īdī of Oman. And here we come to that delicate and precious material which had been exported throughout the Orient since time immemorial: ivory.[22]

Since the 2nd century B.C., ivory had been exported from eastern Africa towards the Mediterranean. From the 7th century A.D., India and China emerged as the main markets for African ivory. Superior to Asian ivory in quality, consistency and colour, African ivory had followed the maritime routes of the Indian Ocean until the end of the 18th century, departing from Mozambique. New fiscal burdens and taxes, however, imposed by the Portuguese at the start of the 19th century and termed 'suicidal' by Sheriff,[23] together with the mercantile ascendancy of France and Great Britain in the Indian Ocean, caused a shift in the ivory trade. The ports of Mozambique having been abandoned, the dealing and sale of this precious material would henceforth be conducted on the island of Zanzibar.

Starting from the second decade of the 19th century, Europe entered the ivory market with its considerable demands. The splendid, shining African ivory, pure white and strong but at the same time easily worked, was increasingly sought after in the west for luxury items such as elegant elements of personal toilette, billiard balls, piano keys, elaborate jewels, fans, cutlery and clothing accessories. In that particular atmosphere of a *fin de siècle* Europe increasingly fascinated by all things Chinese or exotic, ivory was a must. This is made crystal clear by the fact that British imports of ivory rose from 280 tons in 1840 to 800 in 1875.

The economy of the East African interior thus witnessed an immense growth in the demand for *pagazi*, free men recruited from among the African tribes allied between each other (mainly Yao and Nyam-

---

Survey of the Archives of Quetta, Extract from "Nuova Rivista Storica", Year LXXVIII, Fasc. II, 1994, pp. 401–414.

[22] M. Ylvisaker, *The Ivory Trade in the Lamu Area 1600–1870*, in, J. De V. Allen and T.H. Wilson (Eds.), *From Zinj to Zanzibar*, op. cit., *passim*.

[23] A. Sheriff, *Slaves, Spices & Ivory in Zanzibar*, op. cit., p. 81.

wezi), and for slave porters.[24] Women with small children were obliged to abandon their offspring in order to continue transporting elephant tusks.

A complex exchange network soon developed between the interior and the coast, leading to the introduction of rice cultivation in the interior in those areas under Arab dominion such as Tabora, Nungwe, in modern-day northern Congo, and in nearby Kasongo.

Later, thanks to the entrepreneurial ability of Tippu Tip, the greatest and most powerful slave trader of the 19th century,[25] the borders of what had been identified by the English as the Ottoman Empire, pushed further to the north-west into modern-day Rwanda and Burundi. By now, "their movement was like a snowball".[26]

Another wealthy protagonist in this chapter of Zanzibar's history, Jairam Sewji, also profited greatly from this opening up to western markets. A member of the Topan family, he was the richest and most influential merchant in Zanzibar and personally financed almost all of the caravan traffic, accepting responsibility for all the risks and eventual losses this entailed. Throughout the first half of the 19th century, Jairam Topan represented the financial and political kingpin of all activity occurring on Zanzibar (around the year 1840, for example, he had four hundred slaves in his personal service). As such, it was with him that Europeans and Arabs had to deal. A somewhat singular political-financial phenomenon thus came into being, in the figure of Jairam Topan who concentrated Arab, Asian and European interests in his own hands, conducting as though with a baton the ancient, admirable and sophisticated system of commercial currents, connections and links of the Indian Ocean.

A further factor, and no less important than ivory, was the extraordinary and revolutionary expansion of clove cultivation on the island of Zanzibar. The creation of a new niche for agricultural

---

[24] S. Rockel, 'A Nation of Porters': the Nyamwezy and the Labour Market in Nineteenth-Century Tanzania, "Journal of African History", n. 41, Cambridge, 2000, pp. 173–195.

[25] At the end of the 19th century, Hamed bin Muhammad Al Murjebi, nicknamed Tippu Tip, owned 7 mashamba and 10,000 slaves in Africa, a capital worth approximately 50,000 Maria Theresa thalers in total. L. Farrant, Tippu Tip and the East African Slave Trade, London, 1975. Tippu Tip's family has not died out, the last descendant of this great 19th century slave and ivory trader was a doctor in Muscat, Oman. Interview kindly granted by Mrs. Sheila Unwin, 18/10/1993.

[26] J.C. Wilkinson, The Imamate Tradition of Oman, op. cit., p. 60.

exploitation on Zanzibar and Pemba was destined to transform the twin islands into a true commercial empire. According to English publications of the time, at the end of the 18th century the introduction of cloves (*Eugenya caryophyllata*, of the *Myrtacae*, Myrtle family) altered completely perceptions of the economic and commercial potential not, take note, in the eyes of the Europeans but in those of Sa'īd bin Sulṭān Āl Bū Sa'īdī and his Indian *protégés*.

Since the 2nd century B.C. envoys from Java at the Han court of China had sucked cloves to sweeten their heavy garlic breath during audiences with the emperor. Clove plants, originating in the Moluccas, were first exploited by the Dutch who grasped the commercial value of this precious, perfumed spice which also possessed medicinal properties. Around the year 1770, the French merchant, Pierre Poivre, succeeded in obtaining a few seeds with which to start a cultivation on the Mascarene Islands. It was, therefore, the French who, at the start of the 19th century, introduced cloves onto the island of Zanzibar.

These initial attempts proved successful, the environment being perfectly suited to this cultivation which eventually led to Zanzibar being the primary producer of cloves in the world.

From English accounts, it appears that Sa'īd bin Sulṭān Āl Bū Sa'īdī decided to invest his wealth and energy in a project of this kind. Such a move required both courage and faith, as the plants take from seven to eight years to reach maturity and produce the first blooms, and ten years for the first crop. As budding does not occur at regular periods and the buds themselves must be removed before flowering, harvesting occurs in three phases, between August and December. This requires numerous and skilled labour, especially as the plantations also need to be weeded in continuation.[27]

We must also bear in mind the fact that the cultivation of cloves was very similar to that of dates practiced in Arabia and understood to perfection by the Arabs, who proceeded to acquire land on Zanzibar, mainly by expropriation to the cost of the Swahili. The management of land on Zanzibar was organised in three different categories: *wanda*, natural scrubland; *kiambo*, areas suitable for building

---

[27] The cultivation of cloves on Pemba was less successful than on Zanzibar due to a cyclone which destroyed most of the plants in the first decades of the 19th century. N.R. Bennett, *A History of the Arab State of Zanzibar*, op. cit., pp. 28–29.

upon; *msitu*, rural areas and lands surrounding villages. The legalised expropriation practiced by the Arabs and a somewhat questionable interpretation of the juridical institution of usufruct often led to Swahili lands effectively being confiscated.

The *mashamba* of the Sultan of Zanzibar, initially concentrated around Mntoni and Kizimbani, gradually grew to include Bumwini, Bububu and Chiwini. In 1835, Sa'īd bin Sulṭān Āl Bū Sa'īdī possessed as many as forty-five *mashamba* on the island.

Clove 'mania', with its 1000% profit on initial expenditure, produced a real Arab landowning aristocracy, continually financed by the Indian mercantile communities, that slowly replaced the old Swahili aristocracy. This did not, however, cause any kind of rupture, thanks to the dexterity of the Indian exponents who gradually involved the local African elite by delegating to them certain tasks and responsibilities, thus making them active participants in this major Indian Ocean business.

On the coasts of the continent, on the contrary, society experienced significant changes due to the massive influx of slaves from the interior and of Arabs and Asians from abroad (Tabora—a key site on the commercial route towards the heart of the continent—practically became an Arab town). Thus, profound differences developed between the cultural identities of the islands, on the one hand, and the continent on the other, where, from the third decade of the 19th century onwards, the opening up of caravan routes wrought a true revolution in economic, social and cultural terms.

This agricultural turning-point rapidly undermined the traditional order, and the plantations and slaves needed to cultivate them led to the phenomenon known as 'clove fever'.

Naturally, hand in hand with the growth of the plantations went an ever-increasing demand for slaves. In 1811, of the 15,000 slaves that arrived on Zanzibar, 7,000 were destined for labour on the *mashamba*.[28] By 1822 the plants had grown to a height of roughly four and a half metres.

This 'clove fever', therefore, pushed the annual number of new slaves up from 6,000 at the start of the century to 20,000 in the second half, and it was the clove plantations which would prove vital to Zanzibar's economic growth. Profits, in fact, rose phenomenally

---

[28] M.R. Bhacker, *Trade and Empire in Muscat and Zanzibar*, op. cit., p. 128.

from 4,600 Maria Theresa thalers in 1834 to 25,000 in 1840. For
Sa'īd bin Sulṭān Āl Bū Sa'īdī, it was a triumph.

Britain viewed the cultivation and exportation of tropical agricultural produce with an extremely favourable eye insofar as this could
represent for oriental leaders a valid economic alternative to the slave
trade. The increasing number of clove plantations on Zanzibar, however, also necessitated a notable increase in the labour force. High
mortality rates on the *mashamba* meant that almost the entire work-
force had to be replaced every four years which, as we have seen,
created enormous problems and far-reaching changes within East
African society. The confiscation of the more fertile Swahili lands,
the overwhelming influx of slaves and limited numbers of the Hadimu
and Tumbatu tribes present on the island resulted in these latter
being relegated to the very margins of society. In addition, the arrival
of Arabs and Asians drawn by this new and profitable market further exacerbated the situation in the eyes of the English (in 1819
there were 214 Indians resident on the island).

5.3   *The Swahili Coast and the Hinterland*

Maritime city-state of the Swahili coast, according to J. Glassman,
had always been sustained by intimate interaction with the non-
Muslims of their rural hinterlands, and this contributed also to the
consolidation of the coastal identity.[29]

During the first half of the 19th century the demand for ivory
came mostly from India. The Omani Arabs exploited the old slave
trade routes to the interior bringing new people to the coast of East
Africa with Elephant tusks. The Mrima was the major source of
ivory's export for Zanzibar economy. The imports of cloths from
India were given by the Arabs as presents to main African chiefs of
the interior and this represented a clear sign of prestige and superiority within their tribes, although agriculture remained for long
times the primary source of the Swahili coast, long before the boom-
ing introduction of commerce. Salted and smoked fish became an
important item of trade: Zanzibar and Pemba islands soon developed the production of fish to provide the porters to the interior

---

[29] J. Glassman, *Feasts and Riot*, op. cit., p. 33 on.

and for the very profitable exchange with ivory. Also copal resin's demand grew during this period and was produced in Bagamoyo area and bought by the Indian traders, as well as mangrove poles to be taken to Arabia and to the Gulf.

There were three major sets of slave and ivory trade routes to the interior: 1) the 'southern' route from southern ports such as Kilwa to Lake Nyasa and the highlands of the south western interior where the Nyamwezi carried tusks and other goods; 2) the 'central' ivory route from Bagamoyo in west and northwest directions, where the caravan trade became progressively monopolised by the Omani Arabs and by the Indian merchants; 3) the 'northern' route, the Masai route from Mombasa and Malindi towards Kilimanjaro where the Mijikenda were ivory hunters together with the Kamba. The Saadani caravan route did not developed an Arab merchant community, while Pangani route led to the foundation of Ujiji around 1840 and passed through the Bondei hills and along the foot of Usambara and Pare mountains, well watered and preferred by travellers from other towns of the northern Mrima; large quantities of ivory, *pembe*, of soft and high quality, came from Pare and the Rift valley, and this route became the second in importance after Bagamoyo. Taveta trading station never became dominated by coastal Muslims, as it was too dangerous.

Nyamwezi caravan labour was cheaper than slaves porters, and was seen as a way to proving manhood as initiation for young men. Caravans arrived usually in September and porters announced their approach by blowing horns and beating drums.

Another important item destined to change deeply the hinterland power balances was represented by firearms: during the first half of the 19th century matchlocks began to appear in Omani hands whom imported them from the Ottoman Empire and from Europe. The Shirazi, the Swahili important families, gradually lost their power and were putted apart by the Āl Bū Sa'īdī within the growing trade of Zanzibar, although they retained control of the northern caravan trade but the great wealth soon passed into Arabs and Indian hands. As the 'central' route was the most controlled by Arabs, Tabora, near the heart of Unyamwezi, as we have seen above, became an 'Arab' town together with Ujiji. Here Baluch soldiers settled, intermarried, and soon became powerful figures. The impact of Āl Bū Sa'īdī power in Zanzibar on the African hinterland was therefore destined to influencing the lives of East African men and women; considerable modifications underwent in traditional elites patterns of power relationships where client-patronage perspectives never were to be the same, and where new actors were destined to emerging on the new western Indian Ocean scenario in its connections with East African hinterland. To this regard, ivory trade became a mean of travel, adventure and wealth offering a way to modifying the status within the coastal communities. Everybody could share this ambitions but at the same time new tensions were introduced between Swahili rich families, struggling to preserving their precarious domination, and the demand of the 'parvenus' on whose support they relied.[30]

5.4   British View of Sa'īd bin Sulṭān Āl Bū Sa'īdī

On slave trade British abolition policy, following the passing of the Felony Act in 1811, the Anglo-Indian Presidency in Bombay informed the oriental princes concerned of the provisions therein and of London's new political approach. One of those thus informed was Sa'īd bin Sulṭān Āl Bū Sa'īdī who received a personal communication dated 7 February 1812 which is of particular importance:

> Letter to the Imaum, on the subject of the abolition of the Slave Trade and forwarding him translate of the regulations published by the Supreme Government in that effort dated 7th Feb., 1812. . . . It is perhaps already known to your Highness that the Governor of this Presidency taking into consideration the hardship which numerous of your fellow creatures laboured under, from the apprehensive conduct of their masters, was, as an act of humanity induced the same years ago *to prohibit the traffic of the slaves, within the limits of its authority*; and the Supreme Government of British India, having under similar motives, the like measure for the Residency of Bengal, I am directed by the Hon.ble the Governor in Council, in view to the intimate understanding which so happily subsists between the two States, transmit for your information the accompanying copy of the Persian Translation of a regulation formerly promulgated to that effort by the same authority and to request that you will give publicity to the purpose of it, throughout your dominions, in order that your Subjects, who are so much in the habit of frequenting the Port of Calcutta, may not by its infringement, incur the penalties of that ordinance. For the rest I hope you will continue to afford me the gratification of hearing of your welfare.[31]

---

[30] Ibid., p. 78.
[31] The opening and closing phrases have been omitted here. I.O.R. P/383/32, *Bombay Records, Bombay Political and Secret Consultations, 1812.*

Although Great Britain in 1815, represented by Lord Castlereagh (1769–1822) had convinced the European powers to sign the agreement for abolition of the slave trade, the Arabs felt themselves in no way bound to respect its terms, and least of all Sa'īd bin Sulṭān Āl Bū Sa'īdī.

While Britain continued on its anti-slavery crusade, motivated by the more pragmatic purpose of weakening the growing mercantile fortune of the Omani Arabs and other oriental leaders—without foreseeing the enormous wealth that would result from the agricultural conversion introduced by Sa'īd bin Sulṭān Āl Bū Sa'īdī on Zanzibar—France, showing fewer scruples, took advantage of the situation to recapture some of its positions.

To the English, Sa'īd bin Sulṭān Āl Bū Sa'īdī never let a chance slip by to indulge in double-crossing. On the one hand he reassured the English, and on the other courted the French with a view to their possibly supporting him against enemy Arab tribes on the islands of Mafia and Kilwa and in Mombasa.

The combination of these ideal conditions for the slave trade, furnished by the Arabs in East Africa, was exploited to the full by French merchants. Under the Treaty of Paris in 1815, French had regained sovereignty over the island of Bourbon.[32] The French explorer, Guillain, commented that: "rapports intimes qui continuaient d'exister entre l'Arabie et la côte orientale d'Afrique, où nous avons le commerce des esclaves avait lieu de temp immémorial".[33]

A synergy thus developed between Sa'īd bin Sulṭān Āl Bū Sa'īdī and France of common interest in finding new ports and commercial bases. However, after taking the potential purchase of Zanzibar and Pemba into consideration, Paris instead turned its attention towards Madagascar. Given the by now unrivalled supremacy of the Royal Navy, backed also by the Bombay Marine in the western stretches of the Indian Ocean, and the defeats inflicted on the pirates of the Persian Gulf, France did not really have any other choice.[34]

---

[32] The Treaty of Paris, 20 November 1815, provided for the restitution of the island of Bourbon. Complete text in G.F. De Martens, *Nouveau Recueil de Traités de l'Europe, Traité de Paix du 20 Nov. 1815 avec les Conventions Speciales*, Tome II, 1814–15, Gottinge, 1818, pp. 682 on.

[33] M. Guillain, *Documents sur l'Histoire, La Geographie et le Commerce de l'Afrique Orientale*, op. cit., vol. I, p. 162.

[34] On 23 March 1819 the Government of Bourbon stipulated a secret Treaty with the Sultan of Kilwa, under the terms of which French would provide military

In 1817, Lord Hastings (1754–1826), the Governor General of Bengal from 1813 to 1823, proposed strengthening Sa'īd bin Sulṭān Āl Bū Sa'īdī and supporting his power policy in the western Indian Ocean.

The choice made by the Anglo-Indian Government was without doubt influenced by the difficulties caused in that period by the continual raids of pirates in oriental waters, by the commercial and political instability afflicting the entire region and, lastly, by the presence of the French who continued to represent a threat to Great Britain.

From a study of English documents it can clearly be seen how the fickleness and political digressions of Sa'īd bin Sulṭān Āl Bū Sa'īdī were cause for alarm among the British. They were perceived as constituting yet another element of insecurity in a region which was by this time the object of great interest and importance. Since a determined line had to be adopted, Hastings' decision represented a firm stance in favour of Āl Bū Sa'īdī Sultan as a political point of reference for Britain, also in relation to those regions of East Africa in which the Omani Arab dynasty exercised an indirect form of control.

Following Hastings' move, the second official step by the English towards Sa'īd bin Sulṭān Āl Bū Sa'īdī was taken, as we shall see, in 1822.

---

support to the Sultan in exchange for support in retaking Pemba, Zanzibar and the island of Mafia from Sa'īd bin Sulṭān Āl Bū Sa'īdī, for which the French would recognise the authority of the Sultan of Kilwa over the island of Pemba. This treaty was to remain only in French hands to prevent the Sultan from showing it to the English, but it never, in fact, came into effect. The *Ministère de la Maison du Roi* feared British naval superiority and, as a result of further political complications in Europe, the French decided not to place their relations with the increasingly important Sa'īd bin Sulṭān Āl Bū Sa'īdī at stake.

CHAPTER SIX

THE MORESBY TREATY (4/22 SEPTEMBER 1822)

On the 21 March, 1821 the Duke of Gloucester, President of the African Institution, sent a Memorandum to the Court of Directors of the East India Company in which he outlined the extreme urgency of persuasive and mediating intervention with the Sultan of Muscat so as to achieve the total abolition of slavery. Sa'īd bin Sulṭān Āl Bū Sa'īdī responded by communicating the British desires to his representatives and prohibiting the sale of slaves to Christian nations. He could not, however, in any way forbid the exportation of slaves towards Muslim countries.

On 14 April, 1821, Captain Fairfax Moresby[1] was entrusted by the Governor of Mauritius, Robert Farquhar, with the task of keeping an eye on the slave trade conducted by the French between the islands of Zanzibar and Bourbon. Moresby sent word to Port Louis that the French were guilty of more atrocious crimes in the vicinity of Zanzibar, transporting thence negroes and killing those who rebelled, noting also that from two to four hundred slaves had been transported from Zanzibar to Bourbon.[2]

On the tenth of May, 1821 Farquhar wrote to Sa'īd bin Sulṭān Āl Bū Sa'īdī, pointing out that French vessels had set sail from Zanzibar with fully four hundred slaves aboard, bound for Bourbon.

According to A. Sheriff, Farquhar's reports, like those made by Moresby, were, in effect, exaggerated so as to grasp the attention and, consequently, provoke intervention by the Anglo-Indian Government. The losses suffered by Sa'īd bin Sulṭān Āl Bū Sa'īdī as a result of

---

[1] Fairfax Moresby was *Senior Officer* in Mauritius; encouraged by Farquhar, Moresby threw himself into the battle to end piracy and the slave trade in the Indian Ocean. In 1837, physically weakened by the tropical climate, he travelled towards the Mediterranean and, in 1862, was promoted Admiral. G.S. Graham, *Great Britain in the Indian Ocean*, op. cit., p. 198.

[2] The slaves were destined for Mauritius and the flourishing sugarcane cultivations. Thanks to its volcanic origin and tropical climate, Mauritius was, and remains today, the perfect place for growing sugarcane. B.M. Add. 41265, *Clarkson Papers, Letter from Capt. Senior Officer F. Moresby to Gov. Comm. in Chief of Mauritius, Farquhar, 4th April, 1821*, f. 11.

the abolition of the slave trade were also, however, most probably exaggerated to the same extent.[3]

On 1 October of the same year, Farquhar informed the Marquis of Hastings in Calcutta, whose intervention, despite all the past accords, was essential in order to convince Sa'īd bin Sulṭān Āl Bū Sa'īdī to sign a new agreement, commit himself to influencing the slave traders and, above all, to: "gain the cooperation of the Native Chiefs in forcing France also to abandon the slave traffic".[4]

In the autumn of 1821, following extensive correspondence between Farquhar in Mauritius and Montstuart Elphinstone (1819–1827) who had taken over from Napear as Governor of Bombay, the draft of a treaty was drawn up which should have obliged Sa'īd bin Sulṭān Āl Bū Sa'īdī to bend to the British will. This was the result of a policy based on blackmail, threats, flattery, magnificent gifts and grandiose but empty promises made by England to the Omani Sultan.

In the December of that year, the *Imaum* (as the British called Sa'īd bin Sulṭān Āl Bū Sa'īdī) unwillingly agreed to receive a representative of the powerful East India Company, and the congratulations of Farquhar and Elphinstone on his having adopted the policy of a 'truly illuminated sovereign'.[5]

Hastings then gave his approval for the first step in what was to prove a long and hard-fought battle for Britain, officially aimed at the abolition of the slave trade in East Africa.

Still in the same year, the local governors of the principal villages on Pemba, the *madiwani*, who found themselves still under the dictates of the Mazrū'ī in Mombasa, pleaded for help from Sa'īd bin Sulṭān Āl Bū Sa'īdī to overthrow the Mazrui governor of the island. In 1822 the Omani Arabs conquered Pemba with the assistance of their Baluch mercenary troops.

The 27 August 1822, Moresby disembarked from his ship, the *Meani*, at Muscat and, evoking Britain's eternal glory and her privileged relationship of friendship, commerce and alliance with Sa'īd bin Sulṭān Āl Bū Sa'īdī, persuaded this latter to sign a treaty formulated in six articles, the implications of which were of great relevance to both of the parties involved.

---

[3] A. Sheriff, *Slaves, Spices & Ivory in Zanzibar*, op. cit., p. 47.

[4] B.M. Add. 41265, *Clarkson Papers, To Marquis of Hastings, Gov. Gen. of India, 1st October, 1821, from Gov. Comm. in Chief of Mauritius Farquhar*, f. 20.

[5] R.W. Beachey, *The Slave Trade of Eastern Africa*, op. cit., p. 43.

For Sa'īd bin Sulṭān Āl Bū Sa'īdī: "the slave trade was a social and economic necessity which had to be tolerated",[6] and his losses would have been enormous (roughly 40–50,000 Maria Theresa thalers per annum). On the other hand, the political survival of the Sultan in Arabia and Africa was in British hands and the continuation of trade with the Indian ports of the Company was an acceptable compensation.

The first article of the Moresby Treaty of 1822[7] forbade the selling of slave to *Christians* of all nationalities, and provided for a corridor in the western Indian Ocean, along which British ships would patrol. This Moresby line began at Cape Delgado in the south, close to the border with Mozambique, ran along the entire East African coastline and then turned towards western India roughly one hundred miles south of the island of Socotra, finally reaching the Indian port of Diu. Any violations of the Moresby Treaty within this stretch of ocean would lead to the immediate confiscation of the ship and exactly the same sentence for its commander as that foreseen for acts of piracy: "death without benefit of clergy".[8]

Another article of the treaty, however, was to be equally significant in the history of sub-Saharan East Africa. This established the terms of what Britain was prepared to offer in exchange for Sa'īd bin Sulṭān Āl Bū Sa'īdī's collaboration in the fight against the slave trade.

The additional requisition supplementary to the six articles of the Moresby Treaty formally recognised Sa'īd bin Sulṭān Āl Bū Sa'īdī's complete sovereignty and authority over the waters of the eastern shores of Africa: "It is necessary to define a straight line . . . drawn from Cape Delkada and passing sixty miles from Socotra on to Dieu".[9]

---

[6] J.M. Gray, *History of Zanzibar*, op. cit., p. 226.

[7] The original text bears the date 8 September 1822. I.O.R. V/23/217/24, *Treaties and Engagements concluded between Her Britannic Majesty and His Highness the Imaum of Muskat and between the Hon.ble East India Company and His Highness, 1799 to 1846*, pp. 247–259; the second version, instead, shows the date it was signed, 4 September. P.P. *Slave Trade Series*, 361, vol. XXV, *Correspondence with Said bin Sultan concerning the Moresby Treaty of 1822*, p. 66 on; R.W. Beachey, *Anti-Slavery and Anti-Slave Trade Decrees and Treaties: Their Aftermath*, in, *A Collection of Documents on the The Slave Trade in Eastern Africa*, London, 1976, pp. 103–107.

[8] A sentence reconfirmed in the Consolidating Act of 1824.

[9] *Particulars of Additional Requisition, Moresby Treaty*, in R.W. Beachey, *A Collection of Documents on the Slave Trade of Eastern Africa*, op. cit., p. 106.

This was, in fact, the first formal recognition, of the utmost importance, conceded by Great Britain of Sa'īd bin Sulṭān Āl Bū Sa'īdī's
maritime mercantile empire, or rather, an initial step in this direction. The ambiguities contained in the treaty, however, were self-
evident, and between the preparation of the first Arabic draft and
the official translation made in Bombay, serious contradictions emerged:

a) the English text foresaw that the punitive measures would come
   into force four months following the signing of the treaty, that
   is to say, with effect from January 1823, a clause which had been
   omitted entirely from the Arabic version;
b) according to the English text, responsibility for applying sanc-
   tions and sentences to captured individuals should have been
   assigned to Sa'īd bin Sulṭān Āl Bū Sa'īdī, since the waters of
   the East African coast came under his sovereignty as specified in
   article 3 of the Treaty. The Arab text, instead, delegated this
   thankless task to ships flying the British flag.

With this treaty, the East India Company made its 'territorial' recognition of Sa'īd bin Sulṭān Āl Bū Sa'īdī's domains appear to be some
great concession granted in exchange for concrete action aimed at
interrupting the slave trade and putting pressure to bear on local
leaders nominally under his authority.

In reality, the British were conceding nothing, since this policy
had been in practice for some time, at least since the first years of
the 19th century. On the contrary, a precise task was delegated to
Sa'īd bin Sulṭān Āl Bū Sa'īdī, a task close to the heart of the gov-
erning body of the Company and the British Parliament, a topic to
which public opinion had long since been aroused.

And this was an initial, classic example of the weight that public
opinion was acquiring in Britain, also in political terms, a weight
that was to have great influence on Government steps and on real
policy decisions in the field of foreign affairs.

As regards Sa'īd bin Sulṭān Āl Bū Sa'īdī, it was clear that he had
to sign the Moresby Treaty and not improbable that his interlude
with the French in 1819 had made him more malleable in relation
to the painful question of slavery and the slave trade. The far from
neglible advantage for Sa'īd bin Sulṭān Āl Bū Sa'īdī lay in formal
recognition of the extent of his territorial African domains which,
until 1822, had remained undefined in western eyes.

The most significant and new element was that 'His' African empire received the official *placet* of the British Lion and his authority would thus be increased also in the eyes of his enemies on the islands and along the East African shores.

As far as slaves and the lucrative slave trade were concerned: "the boundary line from Cape Delgado to the Persian Coast left the main channels of Arab commerce *intact*".[10]

This treaty, in fact, provided clear proof that Britain's objective was, in reality, that of damaging the French slave trade in the western Indian Ocean and preventing slaves from reaching the Anglo-Indian ports. The treaty did not, however, produce any practical outcome, the slave trade continuing to flourish on the merchant ships flying the red flag of Oman.

Britain, however, moved by the humanitarian and philanthropic fervour of Clarkson and Wilberforce, did not let herself be discouraged. On the contrary, the Moresby Treaty of 1822 was considered to be the first tangible proof that 'things got gradually better and better'. On 1 January 1823 Farquhar defined the Moresby Treaty as the: "successful result of those measures of impressing upon the *Imaum* the solid advantages which he must expect to derive from the continuance of the friendship and protection of Great Britain".[11]

At the start of 1829 Sa'īd bin Sulṭān Āl Bū Sa'īdī decided to move his court from Muscat to Zanzibar where he had a sumptuous palace built at Mntoni, roughly five kilometres from the town. To this significant decision G.P. Badger explained that the Āl Bū Sa'īdī Sultan had become aware of his increased power, enough to convincing him to leaving Muscat for Zanzibar.[12] S.B. Miles gives us a very troublesome picture of this oriental prince much divided between the two ports, but he stressed on the strong will to settling to Zanzibar due also to the British support.[13] C. Nicholls, in more recent times, sustained that the reason of the Sultan's move to Africa

---

[10] G.S. Graham, *Great Britain in the Indian Ocean*, op. cit., p. 200.

[11] P.P. Slave Trade Series, Vol. XXV, *Correspondence with Said bin Sultan concerning the Moresby Treaty, Correspondence Relating to Mauritius*, n. 1, *Copy of Sir R. Farquhar's Despatch dated Mauritius, 1 January 1823; respecting the close of the Slave Traffic by the Imaum of Muscat; addressed to Earl Bathurst. Already laid before Parliament 11 July 1823*, n. 556.

[12] S.I. Razik, *History of Imams and Seyyids of Oman*, translated by G.P. Badger, London, 1871, repr. 1986, pp. 350–351.

[13] S.B. Miles, *The Countries and Tribes of the Persian Gulf*, op. cit., pp. 332–334.

was the expansion of British activities on the Swahili coast because
it was the principal source for the Indian Ocean slave trade[14]. A.
Sheriff stated that the growing cloves cultivation incomes on the
African island, largely for export, was the major answer to the British
slave trade abolitionist policies, and convinced the Omani Sultan of
the positive effects of living permanently in Zanzibar and dedicat-
ing himself to the clove trade, abandoning progressively the slave
trade.[15] This last point has been long debated, and we believe the
Arab Sultan never expected to be 'forced' to such an extent by the
British. M.R. Bhacker gives us a clear explanation quoting many
references and considering all factors involved in the Āl Bū Sa'īdī
Sultan decision to move from Muscat to Zanzibar, if it was a real
decision, and this need for certainties is clearly very much linked to
western perspective.[16]

We also believe Sa'īd bin Sulṭān Āl Bū Sa'īdī decided to transfer the court permanently to Zanzibar because he realised that the
African island was a better place where to live and because his personal exercise of power in Zanzibar would have increased his wealth,
prestige and, most of all, his 'control' and predominance over his
numerous enemies both in Arabia and in Africa, with better results
than from Muscat. The strength was coming from his relationships
both with the Indian merchants and with the Baluch soldiers, an
indispensable tool to his moves within the western Indian Ocean
seas and coasts.

We also believe that this extraordinary decision was the final step
in a chain of events caused by a number of factors all of equal
weight: the Moresby Treaty of 1822 with the Anglo-Indian Government, the progressive political and commercial waning of the Āl Bū
Sa'īdī in the ports of the Persian Gulf, the Owen affair in Mombasa
and the defeat inflicted by Sa'īd bin Sulṭān Āl Bū Sa'īdī on the
Mazrū'ī rebels along the coast and, last but not least, the new and
imposing commercial expansion witnessed by Zanzibar, thanks to its
newly-formed commercial ties with the United States of America.

With regard to the first two points, the Moresby Treaty had re-
affirmed Sa'īd bin Sulṭān Āl Bū Sa'īdī's authority along the eastern
shores from Cape Delgado to Cape Guardafui, including their waters

---

[14] C. Nicholls, *The Swahili Coast*, op. cit., p. 139.
[15] A. Sheriff, *Slaves, Spices and Ivory in Zanzibar*, op. cit., p. 118 on.
[16] M.R. Bhacker, *Trade and Empire in Muscat and Zanzibar*, op. cit., pp. 118–122.

and respective islands. The struggle continued in this region, how-ever, for maritime dominion and control of the great profits deriv-ing from the various forms of trade there conducted.

The indomitable and warlike Mazrui were violent opponents of the Al Bu Sa'īd. Towards the end of 1823, they had appealed for help to the English captain of the *Leven*, William Owens, who had the task of drawing up nautical charts and gathering hydrographic information concerning the shores of eastern Africa. In February 1824, the intrepid Captain Owen, more than a little indignant in the face of the uncontrolled proliferation of the slave trade in Mombasa, and moved by pressing and convincing appeals for political-military help from the Mazrū'ī, decided to found a British 'protectorate' in Mombasa.[17]

This was an entirely personal decision, taken without any orders from the East India Company and, doubtless, dictated by excessive zeal in applying the evangelical political principles which so favoured British rule over the seas. Also behind Owen's initiative were cer-tain ideals of pacification and resolution of the local inter-ethnic rival-ries existing in areas of strategic importance to Britain.

The Union Jack flew for two years from the highest tower of Fort Jesus in Mombasa, gravely offending both Montstuart Elphinstone (1799–1859), Governor of Bombay from 1827 to 1830 and, even more so, Sa'īd bin Sulṭān Āl Bū Sa'īdī.[18]

On 26 July 1826 Bombay ordered Owen to abandon his 'African reign' without delay, reminding the adventurous Captain that the British government had never acknowledged his undertaking and declaring: 'the necessity to withdraw the Establishment'.[19]

At this point the French could not resist exploiting Owen's excess of zeal, which had provoked the English reaction and Sa'īd bin Sulṭān Āl Bū Sa'īdī's anger, disappointment and resentment, with

---

[17] The events of Owen's short-lived protectorate at Mombasa are described by J. Gray, *The British in Mombasa, 1824–1826*, London, 1957; see also W.F.W. Owen, *Narrative of Voyages to Explore the Shores of Africa, Arabia and Madagascar*, 2 vols., London, 1833; W.F.W. Owen, *The Hydrographic Surveys of Admiral W.F.W. Owen on the Coast of Africa and the Great Lakes of Canada, His Fight against the African Slave Trade, His Life in Campobello Island, 1774–1857*, no date, no place, l, repr. Rotterdam, 1979.

[18] P.R.O. Adm. 52/3940, *Journal of Lieut. Emery, who was in Mombasa from 1824 to 1826*, p. 52 on.

[19] P.R.O. Ibidem, *A Journal of the British Establishment in Mombasa from the 28th day of August 1824 to the 10th day of July, 1825, by Commander Owen, by J.B. Emery*.

the aim of strenuously renewing commercial relations between Zanzibar and Bourbon.

Filled with a fervent desire for revenge for the treacherous behaviour of the British, Sa'īd bin Sulṭān Āl Bū Sa'īdī decided to greatly reduce the percentage he took on the sale of cloves to the French, from 14% as established in 1822, to 4% in 1827.

At the same time, however, the embittered Omani sovereign made all haste to bring further pressure to bear on the English, in yet another round of that exhausting game which European powers were unwillingly obliged to play by the certain space for manoeuvre which Sa'īd bin Sulṭān Āl Bū Sa'īdī still enjoyed, although he would not do so for long. The Omani ruler, in fact, exploited those very same political and diplomatic pressures that he had had to suffer under himself, insisting that the British make their position in relation to him clear, in line with the agreements entered into only a few years earlier.

Now lacking Owen's support, the Mazrū'ī offered the port of Mombasa to France, well aware of France's hunt for strategic and commercial ports in these seas. France refused the Arabs' offer of Mombasa, for obvious reasons: the indispensable French commercial alliance with Zanzibar and such a territorial acquisition, in the absence of careful diplomatic preparations, would have exposed the French to an unquestionably violent British reaction. Lastly, the stakes were too high for a Paris by now exhausted by the European wars and still far from finding internal political stability.

After 1826 the Omani Sultan clearly understood that he could not depend upon any coherent or efficacious military support from the English and, at this point, decided that the moment had arrived to act.

Between 1826 and 1830, Sa'īd bin Sulṭān Āl Bū Sa'īdī employed all the forces at his disposal on two fronts: in Arabia and in Africa. Between 1827 and 1828 he suffered resounding defeats at both Basra and in Bahrein.[20] Then, in December 1829, as soon as the monsoon winds were in his favour, he launched an attack against the Mazrū'ī in Mombasa but here, again, the Omani Arabs failed in their attempts.

---

[20] M.R. Bhacker, *Trade and Empire in Muscat and Zanzibar*, op. cit., pp. 96–100.

The Mazrū'ī continued firmly entrenched in their stronghold at Fort Jesus and when, in 1833, the forces of Sa'īd bin Sulṭān Āl Bū Sa'īdī launched another attack, they once more had to withdraw.

Sa'īd bin Sulṭān Āl Bū Sa'īdī did, however, manage to enjoy a brief respite from this series of humiliations when internal power struggles between the Mazrū'ī chiefs led to their no longer presenting a united front against the Āl Bū Sa'īdī and created a power vacuum in Mombasa. Conditions were finally in the Āl Bū Sa'īdī's favour for a decisive action. With the assistance of the Baluch mercenaries commanded by Arab, Persian and Pathan officers, in 1837 the Mazrū'ī chiefs were left to die in the prisons of Muscat and the rule of these Arab rebels over Mombasa, which had last for one hundred years, came to an end.[21]

For the English, this victory placed Sa'īd bin Sulṭān Āl Bū Sa'īdī in the position of true lord of the East African coasts, both in terms of rights (provided by the Moresby Treaty) and in tangible reality (the defeat of the Mazrū'ī).

Thanks to the complete dominion now held over Fort Jesus, the largest fortification in East Africa, and over Mombasa, where the Baluch soldiers were posted, mercantile traffic also now came under his control.

6.1 United States of America and Zanzibar

Trade links with the United States of America represented the deciding factor in Zanzibar's economic-commercial rise and the tropical island's increasing appeal to the Sultan of the Āl Bū Sa'īdī.[22] The East India Company's monopoly over the Indian Ocean had virtually ceased with the Declaration of Independence of the 13 American

---

[21] Relations between the Āl Bū Sa'īdī and the Mazrū'ī in East Africa were, in fact, far more complicated and involved.

[22] The history of relations between the United States of America and Zanzibar during the 19th century has been widely dealt; see, among others, N.R. Bennett, *Americans in Zanzibar: 1825–1845*, repr. in "The Essex Institute—*Historical Collections*", vol. XCV, 1959, pp. 239–262; N.R. Bennett, *Americans in Zanzibar: 1845–1865*, "Tanzania Notes and Records", 1961; N.R. Bennett, *France and Zanzibar, 1844 to the 1860's*, "The International Journal of Africa", Historical Studies, vol. 4, 1973, vol. 7, 1974; N.R. Bennett, *A History of the Arab State of Zanzibar*, op. cit.; N.R. Bennett and G.E. Brooks Jr., *New England Merchants in Africa. A History through Documents, 1802–1865*, Boston, 1965, and relative bibliographies.

colonies in 1776 and the creation of the Marine Society in Salem, New England in 1782. The Napoleonic blockade and the Anglo-American war of 1812 had interrupted American trade links with the Indian Ocean but, on 20 July 1825, the American merchant Lovett landed on Zanzibar. He was followed, in 1827, by Roberts who threatened Sa'īd bin Sulṭān Āl Bū Sa'īdī with a cessation of all trade with Africa unless the sovereign agreed to sign a treaty with the United States of America guaranteeing the same commercial conditions already conceded to the British.

American whalers sailed to Zanzibar carrying muskets, dollars[23] and cotton cloth, far superior to that furnished by the English, and bought ivory, tortoiseshell, copal and rhinoceros horns from the Indian merchants there.

On 21 September 1833, Sa'īd bin Sulṭān Āl Bū Sa'īdī signed a treaty of 'amity and commerce' with the United States, according the new American state the privileges of 'most favoured nation'.[24] This implied the right to trade in ivory and copal resin, the products most in demand by the merchants of New England, in those ports officially under the dominion of the Omani Sultan. Whilst the English were obliged to pay between 50 and 60 Maria Theresa thalers for copal, the Americans could purchase this same substance for a mere 16–20 thalers.

The commercial advantages enjoyed by Zanzibar and its court of merchants following the signing of this treaty with the Americans, however, never satisfied Sa'īd bin Sulṭān Āl Bū Sa'īdī to the full.

The United States were extremely remote and, at the Āl Bū Sa'īdī court, there was no clear perception of precisely what this nation was or how great a potential an alliance of this kind could represent. Moreover, the cautious terms in which President Andrew Jackson (1829–1937) ratified the treaty on 30 June 1834, warning American merchants not to involve the nation in dangerous distant waters, prevented Āl Bū Sa'īdī from acquiring that return in weapons, ammunition and artillery that he had so ardently hoped for, mainly so as

---

[23] Until very recent times, some of the women of Zanzibar wore a nose-ring with an American quarter of dollar hanging from it as a pendant.

[24] *Treaty of Amity and Commerce: The United States and Muscat, 21 September, 1833.* U.S. Treaty Series, n. 247, repr. in J.C. Hurewitz, *Diplomacy in the Near and Middle East*, op. cit., vol. I, p. 108. It is significant that, from 1833 on, Sa'īd bin Sulṭān Āl Bū Sa'īdī was called Sultan by westerners, and also on Zanzibar.

to be able to annihilate the Mazrū'ī. This explains the English reaction to this new western actor on the Indian Ocean stage, and the sudden change in policy in London. It also explains why Sa'īd bin Sulṭān Āl Bū Sa'īdī, confronted with new approaches by the English, was so ready to disown the Americans in favour, once again, of the British.

On 31 January 1834, in fact, Sa'īd bin Sulṭān Āl Bū Sa'īdī was prepared literally to tear up the treaty with the Americans before the eyes of the English Captain Hart, sent on a mission to Zanzibar from Bombay.[25] Hart, however, felt that the revocation of this agreement with the Salem merchants would have forced the Anglo-Indian government into defending Sa'īd bin Sulṭān Āl Bū Sa'īdī against the American protests and reprisals which would inevitably follow such a gesture.

This shrewd English official therefore decided to 'forgive' Sa'īd bin Sulṭān Āl Bū Sa'īdī, making him promise that, in future, he would consult the English *before* entering into diplomatic or commercial relations with other nations.

Relieved and satisfied by Hart's solution, Sa'īd bin Sulṭān Āl Bū Sa'īdī in exchange asked for a representative of the Company to be assigned to him, to give him daily advice on the best policies to adopt.

The *Charter Act* of 1833 abolished the East India Company's trading privileges (with the exception of those relating to salt and opium), thus ending its monopoly in the Indian Ocean. A free market system began to take shape, and the small trading company of Newman Hunt and Christopher was able to set up an agent on Zanzibar, Captain Norsworthy, in commercial competition with the Americans.

A new and important figure was to emerge, however, in these tropical seas. On 17 March 1837, Richard Waters was appointed American Consul to Zanzibar and began a great business with Jairam Topan, the powerful Indian merchant.

In those years, with Anglo-Russian tensions beginning in Central Asia and Persia, it was held indispensable for London to adopt a

---

[25] I.O.R. F/4/1475, *Bombay Political Department, Board's Collection 57973, Capt. Hart's Mission to the Imaum of Muscat, Letter from Capt. Hart to the Hon.ble the Court of Directors for Affairs of the Hon.ble the East India Company, dated 30th Sept., 1834*, n. 26, folios 1–11. This also includes a copy of the treaty between Sa'īd bin Sulṭān Āl Bū Sa'īdī and the Americans.

new political and strategic approach that, naturally, also included the Indian Ocean. Within the context of this new scenario, the East India Company's loss of commercial and political power forced London to review its traditional strategy. Thus, from 1839 on, with Lord Palmerston at the Foreign Office (1784–1865), the diplomatic-naval structure of British security in the Indian ocean moved towards its final completion.

The conquest of Aden by the British in 1839, preceded by the taking of the island of Socotra in 1834, were seen as absolutely necessary interventions for English policy and strategy against the wider background of international rivalries. And, for the English, Sa'īd bin Sulṭān Āl Bū Sa'īdī himself was yet another player in the Great Game.

With this in mind, the Anglo-Indian Government made two diplomatic moves. On 17 December 1839, the British Resident in the Persian Gulf, Lieutenant S. Hennel, got Sa'īd bin Sulṭān Āl Bū Sa'īdī in Muscat to sign three articles which were to complete the Moresby Treaty of 1822.[26] Article 1 redefined the Moresby line followed by patrols battling against the slave trade, which now ran from Cape Delgado to the port of Pasni in Makran, centre for the slave trade sending African slaves into Asia and, together with the port of Gwadar, an enclave of the Āl Bū Sa'īdī.

Article 2 foresaw the confiscation, within this new maritime line, of all ships carrying slaves, whilst the third article prohibited the sale of free Somali women, in marked contrast with the Koranic law on slavery, likening such activity to an act of piracy and, therefore, punishable under the provisions of the 1811 Felony Act.

The second step in this new British strategy in relation to Sa'īd bin Sulṭān Āl Bū Sa'īdī came only a few months later. On 31 May 1839, Captain Robert Cogan, envoy of the Governor of Bombay, Lord Auckland (1786–1849), for the newly crowned Queen Victoria, signed a commercial treaty of 17 articles with the Sultan of Zanzibar.[27]

---

[26] Repr. of the Treaty in R.W. Beachey, *A Collection of Documents on the Slave Trade of Eastern Africa*, op. cit., *Translation of Additional Articles regarding the Suppression of the Foreign Slave Trade*, 1839, pp. 107–108.

[27] The original text sent to Bombay in I.O.R. R/15/1/82, *Political Department, Treaty of Commerce between Her Majesty, the Queen of the United Kingdom of Great and Ireland, and Highness, Sultan Seid Syeed Bin Sultan, Imam of Muscat, 24 Sept., 1839*. Copy held in London in F.O. 54/8, *Extract from the Convention of Commerce between H.M. the Queen and H.H. the Imaum of Muscat, May 31st, 1839*. Repr. in P.P., vol. XXXI, *The*

Article 1 accorded Great Britain the privileges of most favoured nation, like those previously granted to the United States of America. Furthermore, Britain would enjoy those same trading conditions granted the Americans: 5% duty *ad valorem*.

Article 13, naturally reiterated the perpetual abolition of the slave trade between Omani Arab dominions and all Christian nations. Under this treaty, also, a British Consul was finally nominated and assigned to the residence of the Sultan as advisor in political affairs.

At this time, France demanded more than ever before from Sa'īd bin Sulṭān Āl Bū Sa'īdī those same concessions granted to the British and Americans. In June 1840, in fact, the explorer Guillain landed on the island with Noel, the French Consul. The Sultan himself, however, had arranged to be in Muscat and the Frenchmen were both sent back to Bourbon by one of the Sultan's sons, Hilal bin Sa'īd Āl Bū Sa'īdī, with the excuse that he could not take responsibility for such a decision.

It was clear that Sa'īd bin Sulṭān Āl Bū Sa'īdī no longer had any choice but to bow down to the will of the British. He knew, or rather, Britain did not fail to remind him, that his fate depended on his cooperation with a nation whose imperial policy guaranteed his recent territorial acquisitions from seizure by other European rivals.

In 1841 the sudden French occupation of the port of Nossi Bé on Madagascar and, the following year, of Mayotte in the Comoros obliged Sa'īd bin Sulṭān Āl Bū Sa'īdī to come completely under the control of the British.

It is also true, however, that whilst, one the one hand, the European powers interfered increasingly in Sa'īd bin Sulṭān Āl Bū Sa'īdī's political decisions, with requests, reprisals, reciprocal suspicion and commercial and strategic demands, on the other, the African territories along with a Zanzibar at the height of her glory, enabled the merchant prince to exploit the most complex legerdemain so as to free himself for one last brief period from relentless western pressure.

6.2   *Sa'īd bin Sulṭān Āl Bū Sa'īdī and Atkins Hamerton*

The pre-eminent economic-commercial role played by the Omani Arabs, in cooperation with the Indian merchants, in relation to the slave trade and the signing of the treaty with the Americans in 1833 can be viewed as major and crucial elements in the decisive impulse given to British strategy in the Indian Ocean, also in the light of the upheavals occurring in Asia, Europe and on the wider international stage.

The key factors in the new strategic approach adopted by London, Calcutta and Bombay was precisely the need to establish a juridical-international order for British subjects on Zanzibar so as to achieve abolition of the slave trade. In 1837, Sa'īd bin Sulṭān Āl Bū Sa'īdī requested that an English advisor be assigned for his personal assistance and, given the volume of Zanzibar's trade in the western Indian Ocean, together with growing competition from New England— "after the 1833 Treaty with the Americans British Policy took on a new lease of life"[28]—and France and the security of a Sultan who was ever more powerful on the commercial level, the parsimonious and reluctant Court of Directors of the East India Company finally agreed.

On 4 May 1841, Captain Atkins Hamerton (1804–1856) of the 15th Native Infantry of the Calcutta Government was nominated British Consul and Political Agent to Zanzibar.[29]

On the basis of an agreement between the East India Company and the Foreign Office, Captain Hamerton was given the task of overseeing the commercial interests of the Company, a task that was now urgent given the inventive and profitable understanding between the wealthy Indian merchant, Jairam Topan, and the American consul, Edmund Roberts. He was also to communicate directly with the Secretary of State for Foreign Affairs in London, as well as with the Government in Bombay, referring to them: "any intelligence of a political nature which it may be interesting to H.M.G. to be made acquainted with".[30]

In this respect, Bhacker claims that the British aim was that of controlling not Zanzibar, but Muscat, the proof offered by this Omani Arab scholar being the Bombay Government's appointment of

---

Zanzibar Papers, n. 68, pp. 9–16. The treaty was, therefore, to come into effect fifteen months after it had been signed.

[28] G. Graham, *Great Britain in the Indian Ocean*, op. cit., p. 209.

[29] R.H. Crofton, *The Old Consulate at Zanzibar*, London, 1935, *passim*.

[30] See the vast quantity of Hamerton's documents F.O. 54/4 P.R.O. 1841–42; F.O. 54/5 P.R.O. 1843–44; F.O. 54/6 P.R.O. 1844–45; F.O. 54/7 P.R.O. 1845–46; F.O. 54/10 P.R.O. 1846–48; F.O. 54/12 P.R.O. 1848–50; F.O. 54/13 P.R.O. 1850–54.

Hamerton to Muscat, able to leave for Zanzibar *only* if Sa'īd bin Sulṭān Āl Bū Sa'īdī took the sudden and unforeseeable decision to establish his court in East Africa.[31] Therefore, an element of notable surprise as compared to the established structure of British policy.

It is quite true that the presence of Hamerton on Zanzibar reinforced the position of the sole European point of reference for the Sultan should his authority ever be in danger, and a close friendship grew up between Sa'īd bin Sulṭān Āl Bū Sa'īdī and Atkins Hamerton, the only European representative to speak Arabic, which put the other consuls present on the island in the shade. In 1845, Broquant was accepted as French consul at the court of Sa'īd bin Sulṭān Āl Bū Sa'īdī, but he had little influence over the Omani prince, by then entirely beguiled by the eccentric personality of Hamerton. In 1847 Broquant fell ill and died, provoking suspicion amongst the French that he had been assassinated.[32] The new French consul, Belligny, was not appointed until 1849 and left the island in 1855, to be replaced by Cochet.

With full Omani powers established on Zanzibar, the leaders of the Hadimu and the Tumbatu swore allegiance to the Sultan and, with the spread of the Omani Arab possessions, the Tumbatu moved towards the village of Dunga, in the more sheltered and protected interior. The western part of Zanzibar, north of the port of the same name, was instead included in the ever-growing territories occupied by the Omani Arabs. Sa'īd bin Sulṭān Āl Bū Sa'īdī favoured the occupation and exploitation of the forests and more fertile areas of the islands, distributed amongst his followers to be used for cultivating cloves and coconuts, activities which, as we have seen, were extremely labour intensive.

Under constant pressure from Hamerton to abolish slavery throughout his dominions, Sa'īd bin Sulṭān Āl Bū Sa'īdī, by now truly exasperated, ordered his subjects to pray more in the mosques, and made every effort to convince the English official of the good inherent in this ancient custom which he presented as being anything but damaging, on the contrary, as essential to the collective well-being of local society.

---

[31] M.R. Bhacker, *Trade and Empire in Muscat and Zanzibar*, op. cit., *passim*.

[32] N.R. Bennett, *France and Zanzibar, 1844 to the 1860s*, "The International Journal of African Historical Studies", vol. 6, n. 4, 1973, pp. 602–632.

In 1842 Sa'īd bin Sulṭān Āl Bū Sa'īdī decided to send an envoy to London to discuss concessions over Bahrein and the islands of the Persian Gulf in exchange for observance of the clauses on abolition of the slave trade. He obviously also sent splendid gifts to Queen Victoria: "two pearl necklaces, two emeralds, an ornament made like a crown, ten cashmeer shawls, one box containing four bottles of roses, four horses".[33]

The British lion, however, remained unmoved: the slave trade was to be abolished at all costs.

Political events took on their own momentum. On 20 November 1844, the Sultan of Zanzibar signed a treaty of amity and commerce with France.[34] On the basis of Article 17 of this treaty, the French obtained the concession to build *magazins d'approvisionements*, warehouses for their goods on Zanzibar. The British, instead, took this to mean arsenals for storing weapons and a full-blown international diplomatic incident developed.

Britain wanted to put an end to this toing and froing between threats, broken promises, envy, resentment and conflict and, on the 2 October 1845, Sa'īd bin Sulṭān Āl Bū Sa'īdī signed a treaty with Great Britain for the abolition of the slave trade, to enter into effect on the 1 January 1847. This also foresaw the seizure and confiscation of any ship belonging to the Sultan found to be transporting slaves, with the exception of any in the East African ports of Lamu, Kilwa, Pemba, Zanzibar and Mafia. Another far from negligible detail was that, in the future, British subjects would *also* be prohibited from trading in slaves and this, obviously, included the Indian merchants.

Thus the fundamental question arose of the juridical status of the Asian communities resident in Africa, who refused to agree to such orders. Furthermore, Hamerton promised 2,000 pounds to Sa'īd bin Sulṭān Āl Bū Sa'īdī in exchange for his seal bearing two crossed swords on the treaty, but Palmerston did not honour this agreement. And, yet again, the articles of the treaty were expressed quite differently in the Arabic and English versions. This discrepancy would enable

---

[33] F.O. 54/4, *Hamerton to Lord Palmerston, 11 February, 1842*, f. 144.
[34] F.O. 54/5 *From Capt. Hamerton to the Earl of Aberdeen 14 Feb., 1843*, f. 141. In this document Hamerton clarified the position of the French, eager to trade in copal and ivory along the eastern shores of Africa, as was permitted to the Americans and the British. He therefore informed London of the signing of a commercial treaty between France and Saiyid Sa'īd bin Sulṭān Āl Bū Sa'īdī.

Lord Palmerston to send a dispatch in which he specified the fact
that the slave trade was prohibited *throughout* East Africa.

The profit margin was, however, too great. A slave bought on
Zanzibar for 5–10 thalers could be sold in Muscat for 25 and, at
Bushire or Bassora, for 40. The reality of the situation was such that
Hamerton's treaty was totally ineffective.

On 19 October 1856, Sa'īd bin Sulṭān Āl Bū Sa'īdī died on a
ship that was taking him from Muscat towards his favourite island,
Zanzibar. His death was followed, on 5 July 1857, by that of Atkins
Hamerton himself in Zanzibar.

The Āl Bū Sa'īdī's dominions in Muscat and on Zanzibar were
divided under the terms of the settlement of 13 May, 1861 (with
Zanzibar having to pay 40,000 Maria Theresa thalers to Muscat
annually) and formalised by the Canning Award, confirmed by the
Anglo-French Agreement of 1862. With this division, the possessions
were assigned to the sons of Sa'īd bin Sulṭān Āl Bū Sa'īdī, Mādjid
bin Sa'īd Āl Bū Sa'īdī (r. 1856–70), of an Ethiopian mother, on
Zanzibar and Ṭçuwaynī bin Sa'īd Āl Bū Sa'īdī (r. 1856–66), of
Georgian mother, in Muscat.[35] Thus the commercial empire of the
Omani Arabs in the Arabian and East African ports of the Indian
Ocean bowed down before the overwhelming supremacy of the
British.

The gradual and progressive process of eroding Omani Arab power
in East Africa had begun, and British predominance was to increase
still further. The impression and mark left by this charismatic oriental sovereign would, however, be fundamental to the history of
the island of Zanzibar, and to the whole history of the three terminals of the western Indian Ocean.

---

[35] For further details on internal political developments see, among others, M.R.
Bhacker, *Trade and Empire in Muscat and Zanzibar*, op. cit., pp. 179–193 and bibliographical references.

CONCLUSIONS

In this study, attention has been concentrated on extending our knowledge and providing a re-reading and reinterpretation of some of the principal printed and manuscript sources in western languages, which saw the figure of Sa'īd bin Sulṭān Āl Bū Sa'īdī (1806–1856) at the centre of a three-terminals cultural corridor between Makran, Oman and Zanzibar, and of regional and international interests in the western Indian Ocean.

Innumerable historical-political affairs wheeled about this Arab-Omani sovereign during his long lifetime. These included the presence and splendour of a powerful commercial thalassocracy (the famed merchant-states) along the coast of East Africa and South-West Asia, the slave trade with its main offshoots and its transformation during the 19th century. We then have the spread of the ivory trade and the cultivation of spices, especially cloves and the gradual economic and commercial growth of Zanzibar, the land and sea ways along the famous route to British India. Lastly, the organisation of hierarchies of power within regional contexts and relations with the officials of the East India Company in both Calcutta and Bombay, but also with the Foreign Office, as well as links with French officials in the islands of the Indian Ocean and the role played by Napoleon's threatening presence in Cairo.

These are all elements which together create a picture of the highly synchretic nature of this extensive area, where the mingling of peoples, goods and cultures gave life to a homogenous coastal civilisation that without doubt felt the effects of a European presence but nonetheless maintained intact its own appeal.

The 19th century was extremely dynamic and revolutionary, marked by rapid change, and witnessed radical transformations in African and Asian social structures. It was during this century that the irresistible driving force, drawn by the 'blank spaces' on the face of the globe, turned towards the three shores of the western Indian Ocean.

The history and geo-strategic importance of the western Indian Ocean and, in particular, of the Makran region, of the coastal town of Muscat in Oman, and of the island of Zanzibar during the first half of the 19th century, a period of extraordinary developments in the economic-commercial, political, diplomatic and international spheres—offer, as we have said, fascinating points on which to pause and reflect.

The policies adopted by the European powers of the time in relation to the principal ports along the shores of the western Indian Ocean inevitably involved also the local powers and authorities. The scenario which developed was often characterised by three key factors: misunderstanding, over-statement and incomprehension, elements through which relations between Britain and members of the Arab-Omani elite should be interpreted.

Also taken into consideration are certain English documents which reveal little-known aspects to us and which indicate the main policy lines adopted within the workings of British power. From these it can clearly be seen that the political-strategic alliance between Sa'īd bin Sulṭān Āl Bū Sa'īdī and representatives of the British Government in Bombay, Calcutta, London and, after 1841, Zanzibar, were characterised precisely by endless misunderstandings and conflicts of interest.

As a result of the French threat during the Napoleonic era, the British needed to guarantee the security of the *life-line* to India and the principal mercantile routes along the shores of the western Indian Ocean. It was, therefore, in the face of the spreading cloak of British expansionism over these tropical seas that the economic and commercial rise of Zanzibar took shape. The main factors in this ascent consisted of the start of clove cultivations and trade in both slaves and ivory, with all their concomitant implications and repercussions on both a regional and international level.

The growing wealth of an Indian mercantile elite in Zanzibar, closely related to Sa'īd bin Sulṭān Āl Bū Sa'īdī and, at the same time, in touch with the populations of the African interior, as well as with the most important trading centres of western India and Arabia, reveals an interesting aspect of the structural typology of the Indian Ocean. The military class of Baluch warriors represented another fundamental element in the composition of this elite. Famed for the marital skills and courage, the Baluch, called *bulushi* in East Africa, performed the role of personal bodyguard to the Omani Arab dynasties, who thus reinforced their traditional links with these tribes of central-southern Asia long considered the more reliable than Arab mercenaries.

Links between Oman and the Asian region of Baluchistan, as well as between western Indian merchant communities, were both close and numerous. It was there that the Arab princes recruited their soldiery, as well as conducting intensive trade in goods and also slaves destined for the Ottoman and Central Asian markets.

At the peak of Zanzibar's commercial power, it was Britain's firm purpose to abolish the slave trade. And it was to this end that the consolidation of British power on Zanzibar, aided by the presence of the British Consul and Political Agent of the Government of Bombay, Atkins Hamerton, would be directed from 1841 on. However, in the first half of the 19th century, the succession of treaties aimed at eliminating this trade and, at the same time, maintaining Britain's precious alliance with Sa'īd bin Sulṭān Āl Bū Sa'īdī, had very little impact on the slave trade which was at its highest point in the years 1845–47.

A certain degree of modernity must be accorded Sa'īd bin Sulṭān Āl Bū Sa'īdī between the three coasts of Asia, Arabia and Africa, along which the Western presence had the effect of making him the first, authentic Sultan of Zanzibar, and, most of all, protagonist of the history of these three fascinating littorals in the western Indian Ocean.

APPENDIX—COINS IN USE

Since very ancient times, the western Indian ocean has been characterised by an afflux of precious metals which came partly from the interior of the East African continent south of the Saharan desert, then exported through the long-distance trade and monetary, maritime as well as land, routes. Within this vast economic area, the coinage of silver and golden coins eased the growing of mints, stimulating also the rhythms of urban development of new mercantile centres along the East African littorals; these centres gave life to the more splendid riches of financial and political powers during the time object of this study.

It results therefore, of great interest, based on manuscript and printed sources available, a brief examination of the main coins in use during the first half of the 19th century.

1) The cauris (*cypraee*) were small shells used for small exchanges in the East Indies, at the Maldives, and throughout Asia. Their value varied from place to place; during the decade 1780–1790 the exchange rate was five thousand cauris for one Indian rupee, which then was quoted about two English shillings. Starting from 1890, the German commercial company of the Hertz, introduced cauris in Zanzibar and in West Africa as well.

2) The *cruzado* was a Silver coin and its value was very fluctuating, in 1777: 3.75 *cruzados* = 1 *piastre*; in 1813: 2.60 *cruzados* = 1 *piastre*.

3) The *piastre* or mexican, spanish *dollars*, were changed in Zanzibar with a discount from 1 to 6%.

4) The *Maria Theresa thaler*, known also as *crown*, *black dollar*, *kursh*, *rial*, was in use in the Indian Ocean till 1860 when it was substituted by the American dollar. During the first half of the 19th century, 1 taler = 2.10–2.23 rupies, while 1 English pound = 4.75 thalers.

5) The *rupee*, current coin in use in India, was introduced in East Africa by the East India Company. It was unified only in 1836 but its value was very much fluctuating; from 1803 to 1813: 1

Spanish dollar = 2.38/2.14 rupees; from 1841 to 1846: 1 Spanish dollar = 2.10/2.18 rupees.[1]

6) The *pice* were small copper coins which were used together with the Maria Teresa thalers and came from Bombay.

As emerges from an interesting Archive manuscript found in the India Office Library and Records, London,[2] starting from the end of the 18th century the complex question of the double presence of silver and golden coinage in the Indian Ocean, with obviously different values, caused many problems to the British. To this regard, on 10th May 1803 Jonathan Henry Lovett, British Resident in Bushire, in Arabia, from April 1803 to January 1808, decided to compiling a list of coins divided in silver and golden, and trying to fixing the respective and corresponding exchange values to the English pounds. The manuscript, as written by Lovett, is here reproduced as follows:

Silver

1 The Mohamedy or Mamoody	1
2 The Kroosh or Piastre	5.77
3 The Bombay Rupee	7.33
4 The German Crown	15.82
5 The Spanish Dollar	15.82

Gold

1 The Persian Toman	57.75
2 The Mujjer? (or Duch ducat)	33.68
3 The Venetian	37.12
4 The Mehboob	16.50

---

[1] A. Sheriff, *Currency and Weights*, in, *Slaves, Spices & Ivory in Zanzibar*, op. cit., p. 15.

[2] I.O.R./R/15/1/6, *Political Residency, Bushire, Bushire Diary, 6th January, 29th December, 1803, Diary of the Proceedings of the Resident at the Honble Company's Factory of Bushire for the Year of Our Lord 1803*, f. 97. See H. Furber, *John Company at Work*, Cambridge, 1948, pp. 349–350.

SOURCES AND BIBLIOGRAPHY

1. Archive Sources—Manuscripts

British Museum Library, London

Clarkson Papers
Add. 41262–7, Copies of Official Correspondence of Sir Robert Farquhar, Governor of Mauritius, relating to the suppression of the Slave Trade.
Add. 41265, Copy of a letter from Gov. Farquhar to the Imaum of Muscat, 10 May 1821.

Liverpool Papers
Papers relating to the slave trade, 1787–1823 consisting largely of letters to the Ist Earl of Liverpool who was President of the Board of Trade and Foreign Plantation from 1786 to 1804, 434 ff. (Add. 38416).
Add. Ms. 38416 Vol. CCXXVII, Papers relating to the slave trade 1787–1823 presented by the Hon. Henry Berkeley Portman.
Add. Ms. 19391 The Periplus of the Erythrean Sea, Bizantine Manuscript.

Wellesley Papers
Add. MSS, 13, 703, Correspondence relative to Goa, Presented by the Representatives of the Marquess Wellesley.
Add. 13772 Wellesley Papers, Series I, 5 November 1800–18 May 1801.
Add. 13774 Wellesley Papers.
Add. 37291 Wellesley Papers, Series II Vol. XVIII.
Add. 37292 Wellesley Papers, Vol. XIX.

India Office Library and Records, London

Bombay Records—Bombay Political Consultations
P/383/17, Letters from Capt. H. Rudland, Resident and Agent at Mocha, 1810.
P/383/18, Letters from the Imaum of Muscat to J. Duncan, Governor of Bombay, 1810.
P/383/19, Letters from F. Warden, Agent at Mocha, Chief Secretary to Government, 1810.
P/383/20, Letters from Sheriff Hamood bin Moohummud to Capt. Rudland, 1810.
P/383/21, Letters to and from J. Duncan Esq., Governor of Bombay, 1810.
P/383/32, Political and Secret Consultations, 1812.
Z/P/485 Bengal Political Consultation Index Pro Anno 1799.

Muscat Records
R/15/6/6, Political Agency Muscat, and, from 1841, Political Agency Zanzibar.
Residency Records
R/15/1/5, Political Residency at Bushire, Letters inward and outward, 1801–1803.
R/15/1/6, Political Residency, Bushire, Diary of the Proceedings, 1803.
R/15/1/82, Political Department, Secretary to Government to Resident in the Persian Gulf, 1839.

Board of Control Records
F/4/1475, Board's Collections 57973, Capt. Hart's Mission to the Imaum of Muscat, 1834.

Political and Secret Department Records
L/P&S/9/113b, Vol. 125, Abstract of Secret Letters from Political Agents.
Persia Factory Record Series III.
Bombay Secret Letters 1798–1801.

Marine Department Records
L/MAR/C/586 Captain Thomas Smee's Report on Zanzibar, 1811 and Lieut. Hardy, 'Silph'.
I/I/12, French in India 1776–1800.
I/I/13, French in India 1776–1800.
J/1/15, Sir Robert Towsend Farquhar (1776–1830).
Phillimore IV

Public Record Office, Foreign Office, Kew

Muscat
FO/54, Vols. 4, 5, 6, 7, 8, 9, 10, 11, 12, 13, 1834–1905, Correspondence on Zanzibar.

Slave Trade
FO 83/2348, Law Officer's Report Slave Trade, 1839–1840.
FO/84 Slave Trade.

Admiralty Records
Adm./52/3940, Journal of Lt. J.B. Emery, 1824–6.
Adm./62–63, Admiral's Despatches, Cape of Good Hope, 1809–11. Capt. Tomkinson's Report, 1809.

Zanzibar National Archives—Zanzibar—Tanzania

AA Consular and Agency Records—General Correspondence 1837–1890.
AA12/1A, General Correspondence 1841. Miscellaneous inward and outward letters and papers, in English and Arabic, including Hamerton's Report on the Slave Trade, 1841, and on the sale of Indian girls at Zanzibar.
AA/12/1A, General Correspondence.
AA3/1, Bombay Correspondence, 1840–1884. Outward: Political and Secret Depts. (includes letters written by Hamerton before leaving Muscat for Zanzibar), May 1840–1842 Mar.

Archives Nationales, Paris, France

AF III 74–75, Directoire exécutif. relations extérieures, 1792—an VII. Porte Ottomane.
AF IV 1687–1689, Secrétairerie d'Etat Impériale. Porte Ottomane, Egypte, états barbaresques, an VIII-1813.
400 AP 1, Archives Napoléon. Correspondance de Napoléon Bonaparte, 1784–1814.
Archives des Ministère des Affaires Étrangères, Paris, France.
Aff. Etr. Corr. Pol. Perse, vol. 8, f° 66.
Aff. Etr. Corr. Pol. Perse, vol. 8, f° 211–212.

2. *Printed sources*

Baluchistan Archives, Quetta, Baluchistan, Pakistan, H.S.A.—A.G.G. Office—Essential Records.

Bibliographie Critique des principaux travaux parus sur l'histoire du 1600 a 1914, Société d'Histoire Moderne, Paris, 1934–36.

British Parliamentary Papers. *The Zanzibar Papers*, 1841–98, Colonies Africa, n. 68, Shannon, no date.

Butler R., compiled by, *Descriptive Listing of the Extracts from the Bombay Diaries held at the Centre for Arab Gulf Studies*, based on descriptive catalogue of the Secret and Political Departments Series 1755–1820 compiled by V.D. Dighe, Bombay, 1954. University of Exeter, Parts III.

Colonial Reports: Annual, *Zanzibar*, New York, 1986.

Darch C. (Ed.), *Tanzania, World Bibliographical Series*, Oxford, no date.

India Office Library and Records, London.

Official Publications.

V/23/217/24 I.N. 692, Treaties, Engagements concluded between Her Britannic Majesty and His Highness the Imaum of Muskat and between the Hon. East India Company and His Highness, 1799 to 1846.

Selections from the Records of the Bombay Government, No. XXIV, New Series, 1856.

British Parliamentary Papers, London.

    1821 (669) XXII (Mauritius), Papers relating to the Abolition of the Slave Trade.

    1825 Slave Trade Series (361), XXV, Correspondence with Said bin Sultan concerning the Moresby Treaty of 1822.

    1826 (430) Additional Correspondence on the Moresby Treaty.

    1840 (268) LXVII, R. Cogan's Zanzibar Report of 5th December 1839.

    1841 (288) XXXI, Convention of Commerce between Her Majesty and His Highness the Imaum of Muscat, Signed at Zanzibar, May, 31, 1839.

    1843 (485) LIX, Relations with American traders Zanzibar's Authority on the mainland.

    1844 (573) XLVIII, Correspondence from A. Hamerton and others on trading conditions and on American-British rivalry.

    1845 (635) XLIX, Information from A. Hamerton on Zanzibar's population.

    1847 (857) LXVI, Correspondence over the 1845 Treaty with Britain and on British Commerce.

    1849 (1128) LV, An 1848, Letter of Said bin Sultan over the exent of his dominions.

    1851 (1424–I) LVI, pt. 1, Relations with Mozambique and India.

    1853 (920) XXXIX, Said bin Sultan Correspondence of 1850.

    1856 (0.1) LXII, French Interests. Commerce in 1855.

Kurtz L.S. (Ed.), *Historical Dictionary of Tanzania*, African Historical Dictionaries, vol. 15, London, 1978.

Matthews N., Wainwright M.D., Pearson J.D. (Eds.), *A Guide to Manuscripts and Documents in the British Isles relating to Africa*, London, 1971.

Pordes H. (Ed.), *British Museum Subject Index, 1931–35*, vol. II, I–Z, London, 1986.

Tulard J., *Bibliographie critique des Mémoires sur le Consulat et l'Empire*, Genéve-Paris, 1971.

3. *Published Primary Sources*

Agius D.A., *Language of the Dhow in the Arabian Gulf and Oman*, London, 2001.
——, *In the Wake of the Dhow. The Arabian Gulf and Oman*, Reading, 2002.
Aitichson C.U., *A Collection of Treaties. Engagements and Sanads relating to India and Neighbouring Countries*, 11 vols., I° ed. Calcutta, 1892, V ed., Dehli, 1933.
Akinola G.A., *Slavery and Slave revolts in the Sultanate of Zanzibar in the nineteenth century*, "Journal of the Historical Society of Nigeria", vol. 6, n. 2, June, 1972.
Allen C.H., *Sayyids, Shets and Sultans; Politics and Trade in Masqat under the Al Bu Said, 1785-1914*, Ph.D. Thesis, University of Washington, 1978.
——, *The State of Musqat in the Gulf and East Africa 1785-1829*, "International Journal of Middle East Studies", n. 14, Cambridge, 1982.
Allen C.R., *The Indian Merchant Community of Muscat*, "Bulletin of the School of Oriental and African Studies" (SOAS), University of London, vol. 44, n. 1, 1981.
Allen J. de Vere, *The Shirazi Problem in East African Coastal History*, in, J. de Vere Allen and T.H. Wilson (Eds.), *From Zinj to Zanzibar*, "Paideuma", 28, Wiesbaden, 1982.
Alpers E.A., *The East African Slave Trade*, "Historical Association of Tanzania", n. 3, Nairobi, 1967.
——, *Ivory and Slaves in East Central Africa*, Berkeley-Los Angeles, 1975.
——, *"Ordinary Household Chores": Ritual and Power in a 19th Century Swahili Women's Spirit Possesion Cult*, "The International Journal of African Historical Studies", vol. 17, n. 4, 1984.
Anonymus, *The Peryplus of the Erythrean Sea*, The Hakluyt Society, II series, London, 1980.
Axelson E., *Portuguese in South-East Africa, 1600-1700*, Johannesburg, 1960.
Badger G.P. (Ed. and transl.), *History of the Imams and Seyyids of Oman by Salil Ibn Razik*, London, 1971.
Barros De J., *Decadas da Asia*, Coimbra, 1930.
——, *Cronica dos Reyes de Quiloa*, transl. in G.P.S. Freeman Grenville (Ed.), *The East African Coast: Select Documents from the first to the earlier nineteenth century* (repr. from I° ed., London, 1962), Oxford, 1975.
Barth F., *Sohar. Culture and Society in an Omani Town*, Baltimore, 1983.
Beachey R.W., *A Collection of Documents on the Slave Trade of Eastern Africa*, London, 1976.
——, *The Slave Trade of Eastern Africa*, London, 1976.
Becker C.H. and Dunlop D.M., heading: *Bahr al-Zandj*, E.I., Leiden, 1999.
Beckingham C.F., heading: *Bu Sa'id*, E.I., Leiden, 1999.
Bennett N.R., *A History of the Arab State of Zanzibar*, "Studies in East African History", London, 1987.
——, *France and Zanzibar, 1844 to the 1860s*, "The International Journal of African Historical Studies", vol. 6, n. 4, 1973.
——, *The Arab State of Zanzibar. A Bibliography*, Boston, 1984.
Bhacker M.R., *Trade and Empire in Muscat and Zanzibar: Roots of British Domination*, London, 1992.
Bosworth C.E., heading: *Makran*, E.I., Leiden, 1999.
Broome M.R., *The 1780 Restrike Talers of Maria Theresia*, Doris Stockwell Memorial Papers, n. 1, repr. from "Numismatic Chronicle", VII series, vol. XII, London, 1972.
Burton R.F., *Sindh and the Races that inhabit the Valley of the Indus*, London, 1851, repr. Karachi, 1988.
——, *The Lake Regions of Central Equatorial Africa, with notices of the Lunar Mountains and the sources of the White Nile, being the results of an expedition undertaken under the patronage of Her Majesty's Government and The Royal Geographical Society of London in 1857-1859*, "The Journal of The Royal Geographical Society of London", vol. 29, London, 1860.

——, *Zanzibar: City, Island and Coast*, 2 vols., London, 1872.

Casson L., *The Periplus maris Erytraei: text with introduction, translation and commentary*, Princeton, 1989.

Chaudhuri K.N., *Trade and Civilization in the Indian Ocean*, Cambridge, 1985.

——, *Asia before Europe. Economy and Civilization of the Indian Ocean from the rise of Islam to 1750*, Cambridge, 1990.

Chittick N.H., *A New Look at the History of Pate*, "Journal of African History", vol. X, n. 3, London, 1969.

——, *The Coast before the Arrival of the Portuguese*, in, A.B. Ogot (Ed.), *Zamani. A Survey of the East African Coast*, Kenya, 1968, new ed., no place, 1, 1974.

——, *The Peopling of the East African Coast*, in, N. Chittick and R. Rotberg (Eds.), *East Africa and the Orient: cultural syntheses in pre-colonial times*, New York, London, 1975.

Clarence-Smith W.G., *Indian Business Communities in the Western Indian Ocean in the nineteenth century*, African History Seminar, SOAS, University of London, 2 December, 1987.

——, *The Economics of the Indian Ocean and Red Sea Slave Trades in the 19th Century: An Overview*, "Slavery and Abolition", vol. 9, n. 9, London, 1988.

——, *The Economics of the Indian Ocean and Red Sea Slave Trades in the 19th century: An Overview* in, W.G. Clarence-Smith (Ed.), *The Economics of the Indian Ocean Slave Trade in the nineteenth century*, London, 1989.

Cooper F., *Plantation Slavery on the East Coast of Africa*, Portsmouth, I ed. 1977, II ed. 1997.

——, *From Slaves to Squatters: Plantation Labor and Agriculture in Zanzibar and Coastal Kenya, 1890–1925*, New Haven, 1980.

Coupland R., *East Africa and its Invaders. From the earliest times to the death of Seyyd Said in 1856*, Oxford, 1938.

Daftary F., *The Ismailis: their History and Doctrines*, Cambridge, 1990.

Davies C.E., *Britain, Trade and Piracy: the British Expeditions against Ras al-Khaima of 1809–10 and 1819.20*, in, C.E. Davies (Ed.), *Global Interests in the Arab Gulf*, Exeter, 1992.

——, *The Blood Arab Red Flag. An Investigation into Qasimi Piracy 1797–1820*, Exeter, 1997.

De Vere Allen J., *Swahili Origins. Swahili Culture & the Shungwaya Phenomenon*, London, 1993.

Declich L., *The Arabic manuscripts of the Zanzibar National Archives: sources for the study of popular Islam in the island during the 19th century*, International Colloquium: Islam in East Africa: New Sources (Archives, Manuscripts and Written Historical Sources. Oral History. Archaeology), Ed. By B. Scarcia Amoretti, Università "La Sapienza", Roma, 2–4 December, 1999, Rome, 2001.

Duyvendak J.J.L., *China's Discovery of Africa*, London, 1949.

Farsi S.A.S., *Seyyid Said Bin Sultan The Joint Ruler of Oman and Zanzibar (1804–1856)*, New Dehli, 1986.

Filesi T., *Le Relazioni della Cina con l'Africa nel Medio Evo*, Milano, II ed. 1975.

Freeman Grenville G.S.P., *The Medieval History of the Coast of Tanganyka; with special reference to recent archaeological discoveries*, London, 1962.

——, *The French at Kilwa Island: an episode in XVIII century East African History*, Oxford, 1965.

—— (Ed.), *The East African Coast: Select Documents from the first to the earlier nineteenth century* (repr. from I° ed., London, 1962), Oxford, 1975.

——, *The Swahili Coast 2nd to 19th century: Islam, Christianity and Commerce in Eastern Africa*, "Collected Studies Series", London, 1988.

Freitag U. and Clarence-Smith W.G. (Eds.), *Hadrami Traders, Scholars, and Statemens in the Indian Ocean, 1750s–1960s*, Leiden, 1997.

Freitag G.U., *Hadhramaut: a religious centre for the Indian Ocean in the late 19th and early 20th centuries?*, "Studia Islamica", London, 1999.

Frye R.N., heading: *Baluchistan*, E.I., Leiden, 1999.

Geary G., *Through Asiatic Turkey*, London, 1878, in, P. Ward (Ed.), *Travels in Oman*, Cambridge, 1987.

H.A.R. Gibb (Ed.), *I. Battuta, Travels in Asia and Africa 1325–1354*, London, I ed. 1929, new ed. New Delhi, 1992.

Glassman J., *The Bondsman's new clothes: the contradictory consciousness of slave resistance on the Swahili Coast*, "Journal of African History", vol. 32, London, 1991.

——, *Feasts and Riot. Revelry, Rebellion, and Popular Consciousness on the Swahili Coast, 1856–1888*, London, 1995.

Graham G.S., *Great Britain and the Indian Ocean, a study in maritime enterprise, 1810–1850*, Oxford, 1967.

Grant N.P., *Journal of a Route through the western parts of Makran*, "Journal of the Royal Asiatic Society", London, 1839, vol. V, art. XXII.

Gray J.M., *The British in Mombasa 1824–1826*, London, 1957.

——, *History of Zanzibar, from the Middle Age to 1856*, London, 1962.

Guillain M., *Documents sur L'Histoire, La Geographie et Le Commerce de L'Afrique Orientale*, 3 vols., Paris, 1856.

Gundara J., *Fragment of Indian Society in Zanzibar: Conflict and Change in the 19th century*, "Africa Quarterly", vol. XXI, no. 2–4, New Delhi, 1982.

Hamilton G., *Princes of Zinj. The Rulers of Zanzibar*, London, 1957.

Holmes C.F., *Zanzibari Influence at the Southern End of Lake Victoria: The Lake Route*, "African Historical Studies", vol. 4, n. 3, 1971.

Horton M., *Shanga: The Archaeology of a Muslim Trading Community on the Coast of East Africa*, London, 1996.

Horton M. and Middleton J., *The Swahili. The Social Landscape of a Mercantile Society*, London, 2000.

Hughes-Buller R., *Baluchistan District Gazetteer Series*, vol. VII, Makran, Text and Appendices, Bombay, 1906.

——, *The Gazetteer of Baluchistan, (Makran)*, Lahore, 1984.

Hurewitz J.C., *Diplomacy in the Near and Middle East. A Documentary Record*, 2 vols., Toronto, 1956.

Jackson Haight M.V., *European Powers and South-East Africa. A Study of International Relations on the South-East Coast of Africa 1796–1856* (repr. from I° ed. "Imperial Studies Series", Royal Empire Society, n. 18, London, 1942), London, 1966.

Kaye J.W., *The Life and Correspondence of Major General Sir John Malcolm*, 2 vols., London, 1856.

Kelly J.B., *Sultanate and Imamate in Oman*, "Royal Institute of International Affairs", London, 1959.

Kusimba C.M., *The Rise and Fall of Swahili States*, Walnut Creek, CA, 1999.

Lewicki T., heading: *Al-Ibadiyya*, E.I., Leiden, 1999.

Lodhi A., *A Note on the Baloch in East Africa*, in, C. Jahani (Ed.), *Language in Society— Eight Sociolinguistic Essays on Baloch*, Uppsala, 2000.

——, *Oriental Influences in Swahili. A Study in Language and Culture Contacts*, Göteborg, 2000.

Lorimer J.G., *The Gazetteer of the Persian Gulf, Oman and Central Arabia. Historical*, Calcutta, 1915, 2 vols. (repr. from I° ed., vol. 1 (geographical 1908), vol. 2 (historical and genealogical, 1915), no place, 1970.

Macgregor C., *Wanderings in Baluchistan*, London, 1882.

Marshall P.J., *Private British Trade in the Indian Ocean before 1800*, in, O. Prakash (Ed.), *European Commercial Expansion in Early Modern Asia*, vol. 10, Ashgate, 1997.

Mas'udi (Al) A.H., *Muruj al-dhahab wa Ma'adin al Jawar*, Beirut, 1948, in, Meynard C.B. (Ed. and transl.), *Les Praires d'or*, Paris, 1861.

——, *Muruj adh-Dhahab, Muruj al-Dahab wa Ma'adin al-Jawhar, The Golden Pastures*, in, H.N. Chittick (Ed.), *The Peopling of the East African Coast*, in, N. Chittick and R. Rotberg (Eds.), *East Africa and the Orient: cultural syntheses in pre-colonial times*, New York, London, 1975.

Maurizi V., *History of Seyd Said Sultan of Muscat*, Cambridge, New York-London, 1984.

Mcpherson K., *The Indian Ocean. A History of People and the Sea*, Oxford, 1993, repr. Oxford, 1998.

Middleton J., *The World of the Swahili. An African Mercantile Civilization*, Yale, 1992.

Miles S.B., *Notes on the Tribes of Oman*, 27 May, 1881, in, I.S.I. Sirhan, *Annals of Oman to 1828*, Cambridge, 1984.

——, *The Countries and Tribes of the Persian Gulf*, 2 vols. (introd. by J.B. Kelly), I° ed., London, 1919, II° ed., London, 1966.

Nicholls C.S., *The Swahili Coast, Politics, Diplomacy and Trade on the East African Littoral 1798–1856*, London, n. 2, 1971.

Nicolini B., *Little known aspects of the history of Muscat and Zanzibar during the first half of the nineteenth century*, Proceedings of the Seminar for Arabian Studies, vol. 27, London, 1997.

Nurse D. and Hinnenbush T.J., *Swahili and Sabaki: A Linguistic History*, Berkeley, 1993.

Nurse D. and Spear T., *The Swahili: Reconstructing the History and Language of an African Society 800–1500*, Philadelphia, 1985.

Oliver R.A. and Fage J.D. (Eds.), *The Cambridge History of Africa*, Cambridge, 1975–1986.

Oman G., *Personal Names in the Regional Areas of the Sultanate of Oman. Materials for the Study of Arabic Anthroponymy*, "Annali", Istituto Orientale di Napoli, vol. 42, Napoli, 1982.

Omanney F.D., *Isle of Cloves. A view from Zanzibar*, London, 1957.

Owen, W.F.W. *Narrative of Voyages to Explore the Shores of Africa, Arabia and Madagascar*, 2 vols., London, 1833.

——, *The Hydrographic Surveys of Admiral W.F.W. Owen on the Coast of Africa and the Great Lakes of Canada, His Fight against the African Slave Trade, His Life in Campobello Island*, New Brunswick, 1774–1857, Rotterdam, no date, repr., no place, 1979.

Parkin D. and Barnes R. (Eds.), *Ships and the Development of Maritime Technology in the Indian Ocean*, London, 2002.

Pearson M.N. (Ed.), *Spices in the Indian Ocean World. An Expanding World: The European Impact on World History 1450–1800*, vol. 11, Aldershot, 1996.

——, *Port, Cities and Intruders: The Swahili Coast, India and Portugal in the Early Modern Era*, Baltimore, 1998.

Piacentini Fiorani V. and Redaelli R. (Eds.), *Baluchistan: Terra Incognita. A new methodological approach combining archaeological, historical, anthropological and architectural studies*, Oxford, 2003.

Plures, *Wilding Swahili Culture. A Bibliography of the History and Peoples of the Swahili speaking world from earliest times to the beginning to the 20th century*, Nairobi, 1976.

Polo M., *I viaggi in Asia, in Africa, nel mare delle Indie scritti nel secolo XIII da Marco Polo Veneziano. Testo in lingua detto il Milione*, Venezia, 2 vols, 1829.

Pouwels R., *Horn and Crescent. Cultural Change and Traditional Islam in the East African Coast A.D. 800–1900*, Cambridge, 1987.

——, *Eastern Africa and the Indian Ocean to 1800, Reviewing Relations in Historical Perspective*, "International Journal of African Historical Studies", vol. 35, 2002, nos. 2–3.

Pouwels R. and Levtzion N. (Eds.), *The History of Islam in Africa*, Ohio, 2000.

Prins A.H.J., *The Mtepe of Lamu, Mombasa and the Zanzibar Sea*, in, J. de Vere Allen and T.H. Wilson (Eds.), *From Zinj to Zanzibar*, "Paideuma", n. 28, Wiesbaden, 1982.

Qasimi (Al) S.M., *Les Relations entre l'Oman et la France (1715–1905)*, Paris, 1995.

Redaelli R., *The Father's Bow. The Khanate of Kalat and British India (19th–20th century)*, Firenze, 1997.

——. (Ed.), *Il Baluchistan: una "terra incognita" al crocevia dell'Asia*, "Storia Urbana", year XXII, n. 84, Milano, 1998.

Rentz G., heading: *Banu Kharus*, E.I., Leiden, 1999.

Risso P., *Merchants & Faith. Muslim Commerce and Culture in the Indian Ocean*, Boulder, 1995.

——, *Cross-Cultural Perceptions of Piracy: Maritime Violence in the Western Indian Ocean and Persian Gulf Region during a Long Eighteenth Century*, "Journal of World History", vol. 12, n. 2, 2001.

Rockel S.J., *'A Nation of Porters': The Nyamwezi and the Labour Market in Nineteenth-Century Tanzania*, "The Journal of African History", vol. 41, n. 2, 2000.

Ross E.C. (transl. and annotated), *Annals of Oman, by Sirhan ibn Sa'id ibn Sirhan of the Benu Ali Tribe of Oman*, Calcutta, 1874.

Ruete Said R., *Said Bin Sultan (1791–1856). Ruler of Oman and Zanzibar, His Place in the History of Arabia and East Africa*, London, 1929.

——, *The Al-Bu Said Dynasty in Arabia and East Africa*, "Journal of the Royal Asiatic and Central Asian Society", vol. 16, London, 1929.

Serjeant R.B., *The Hadrami Network, Society and Trade in South Arabia*, in, G.R. Smith (Ed.), Aldershot, 1996.

Schacht J., *Introduction to Islamic Law*, I ed. Oxford, 1964, new ed. Hong Kong, 1993.

Shen J., *New Thoughts on the use of Chinese Documents in the Reconstruction of Early Swahili History*, "History in Africa", n. 22, 1995.

Shepherd G., *The Making of the Swahili. A View from the Southern End of the East African Coast*, in, J. de Vere Allen and T.H. Wilson (Eds.), *From Zinj to Zanzibar*, "Paideuma", n. 28, Wiesbaden, 1982.

Sheriff A.M.H., *The Rise of a Commercial Empire: an Aspect of the Economic History of Zanzibar 1770–1873*, Unpublished Phd. Art Th., Univ. of London, London, 1971.

——, *Slaves, Spices & Ivory in Zanzibar: Integration of an East African Commercial Empire into the World Economy, 1770–1873*, London, 1987.

Sheriff A.M.H., and Tominaga C., *The Ambiguity of Shirazi Ethnicity in the History and Politics of Zanzibar*, "Christianity and Culture", n. 24, Sendai, 1990.

Sheriff A.M.H., *Mosques, Merchants and Landowners in Zanzibar Stone Town*, "Azania", vol. 27, 1992.

Singer S., *An Investigation of Land Tenure in Zanzibar, Shamba Land*, "Anthropos", n. 91, 1996.

Smith G.R., heading: *Ya'rubī*, E.I., XI:291b, Leiden, 1999.

Soghayroun I., *Some Aspects of Omani Cultural Influences in East Africa under the Busaidi Rulers of Zanzibar*, paper presented to the International Conference: *The North-western Indian Ocean as Cultural Corridor*, Stockholm University, 17–19 January, 1997.

——, *The history of the Mazrui in East Africa by Shaikh al-Amin ibn 'Ali al-Mazrui. Arab and Swahili culture in historical perspective*, unpublished paper presented at the International Colloquium: Islam in East Africa: New Sources (Archives, Manuscripts and Written Historical Sources. Oral History. Archaeology), Ed. by B. Scarcia Amoretti, Università "La Sapienza", Roma, 2–4 December, 1999, Rome, 2001.

Spear T., *The Shirazi in Swahili traditions, culture and history*, "History in Africa", vol. 11, 1984.

——, *Early Swahili History Reconsidered*, "International Journal of African Historical Studies", vol. 33, n. 2, 2002.

Strandes J., *Die Portugiesenzeit von Deuscht und Englisch Ost-Afrika*, Berlin, 1899, in, J.F. Wallwork P. (Ed.), *The Portuguese Period in East Africa*, Nairobi, 1961.

Strong A.S. (comm.), *Chronicles of Kilwa*, "The Journal of The Royal Asiatic Society", vol. 27, London, 1895.

Tominaga C., *British Colonial Policy and Agricultural Credit in Zanzibar, 1890–1963*, in, G. Austin and K. Sugihara (Eds.), *Local Suppliers of Credit in the Third World, 1750–1960*, London, 1993.
Trimingham S., *The Arab Geographers and the East African Coast*, in, H.N. Chittick and R.I. Rotberg (Eds.), *East Africa and the Orient*, London, 1975.
Tuson P., *Zanzibar Sources in the India Office Records*, London, 1985.
Ward P., *Travels in Oman. On the Track of the Early Explorers*, Cambridge, 1987.
Werner A., *A Swahili History of Pate*, "Journal of the African Society", vol. 14, London, 1915.
——, *The Swahili Population*, in, *The Encyclopaedia of Islam*, 4 vols., vol. IV, London, 1927.
Wheatley P., *Analecta Sino-Africana Recensa*, in, N. Chittick and R. Rotberg (Eds.), *East Africa and the Orient*, New York, London, 1975.
Wilkinson J.C., *The Imamate Tradition of Oman*, Cambridge, 1987.
——, heading: *Maskat*, E.I., Leiden, 1999.
Wilks M., *Historical Sketches of the South India in an attempt to trace the history of Mysoor*, 3 vols., London, I° ed., 1810, II° ed., no place, 1817.
Ylvisaker M., *The Ivory Trade in the Lamu Area, 1600–1870*, in, J. de Vere Allen and T.H. Wilson (Eds.), *From Zinj to Zanzibar*, "Paideuma", n. 28, Wiesbaden, 1982.
Yule H., *The Book of Sir Marco Polo*, London, 1871, (Italian ed.: G. Berchet (transl.), *Marco Polo e il suo libro*, 2 vols., Venice, 1871).

4. Secondary Sources

Allan J., *The Trade in Steel between the Indian Subcontinent and Iran*, paper presented at the International Conference: *Trade and Transformation in the Indian Ocean*, SOAS, University of London, The Ashmolean Museum, Oxford, 30 November, 1996.
Allen C.H., *The Indian Merchant Community of Muscat*, "Bulletin of the School of Oriental and African Studies", London, vol. 44, 1981.
Anonymous, *Notes for Officers Appointed to Zanzibar, disposed of by the Commonwealth Institute*, London, III° ed., 1926.
Arborio Mella F., *L'Impero Persiano da Ciro il Grande alla Conquista Araba*, Milano, 1979–80.
Axelson E., *Portuguese in South-East Africa 1488–1600*, Johannesburg, 1973.
Balfour-Paul J., *Indigo in the Arab World*, Exeter, 1997.
Bang A.K., *Sufis and Scholars of the Sea. The Sufi and family networks of Ahmad ibn Sumayt and the tariqa Alawiyya in East Africa c. 1860–1925*, PhD Thesis Degree of Dr. Art., University of Bergen, 2000.
Banga I., *Karachi and its Hinterland under Colonial Rule*, in, I. Banga (Ed.), *Ports and their Hinterlands in India, 1700–1950*, Dehli, 1992.
Barendse R., *The Arabian Seas: The Indian Ocean World of the Seventeenth Century*, New York, 2001.
Barros De J., *Da Asia*, Lisboa, 1777–8.
Baumann O., *Der Insel Pemba und Ihre Kleineren Nachbar Inseln*, Leipzig, 1899.
Bellew H., *From the Indus to the Tigris*, Karachi, 1977 (repr. I° ed., 1874).
Bemis S.F., *The Diplomacy of the American Revolution*, New York, 1935.
Bennett N.R. and Brooks G.E. Jr., *New England Merchants in Africa. A History through Documents, 1802–1865*, Boston, 1965.
Bennett N.R., *Americans in Zanzibar: 1825–1845*, repr. "The Essex Institute—Historical Collections", 1959.
——, *Americans in Zanzibar: 1845–1865*, "Tanzania Notes and Records", 1961.
——, *Mirambo of Tanzania, ca. 1840–1884*, New York, 1971.
——, *France and Zanzibar, 1844 to the 1860's*, "The International Journal of Africa", Historical Studies, vol. 4, 1973, vol. 7, 1974.

Bernardi B., *Antropologia sociale e culturale*, Bologna, 1971.

Bernardino S.G.F., *Itinerário da India por terra até à Ilha de Chipre*, Lisboa, 1953.

Bertoncini E., *A Tentative Frequency List of Swahili Words*, "Annali", Istituto Orientale di Napoli, n. 33, Napoli, 1973.

Besenval R. and Sanlaville P., *Cartography of Ancient Settlements in Central Southern Pakistan Makran: New Data*, "Mesopotamia", Florence, 1990.

Bidwell R., *Bibliographical Notes on European Accounts of Muscat 1500–1900*, "Arabian Studies", London, vol. 4, 1978.

N.M. Billimoria (compiled by), *Bibliography of Publications relating to Sind & Baluchistan*, Lahore, 1930.

Bivar D., *Gli Achemenidi e i Macedoni: stabilità e turbolenza*, in, G. Hambly (Ed.), *Asia Centrale*, Storia Universale Feltrinelli, 16, (orig. ed.: *Fischer Weltgeschichte Zentralasien* 16, Frankfurt a.M., 1966), I, Milano, 1970.

Blackurst H. (Ed.), *Africa Bibliography*, Edimburgh, 1990.

Blanchy S., *Karana et Banians. Les Communautés commerçantes d'origine indienne à Madagascar*, Paris, 1995.

Boulnois L., *La Via della Seta* (orig. ed.: *La route de la soie*, Genève, 1992), Milano, 1993.

Boxberger L., *On the Edge of the Empire: Hadhramawt, Emigration, and the Indian Ocean, 1880s–1930s*, Suny Series in Near Eastern Studies, Albany, 2002.

Boxer C.R., *Portuguese Conquest and Commerce in Southern Asia 1500–1750*, London, 1961, repr. Aldershot, 1990.

——, *Race Relations in the Portuguese Colonial Empire 1415–1825*, Oxford, 1963.

Buxton T., *William Wilberforce. The Story of a Great Crusade*, London, 1933.

Chakrabarti D.K., *The Indus Civilization and the Arabian Gulf. An Indian Point of View*, in, C.S. Phillips, D.T. Potts, S. Searight (Eds.), *Arabia and its Neighbours. Essays on prehistorical and historical developments presented in honour of Beatrice de Cardi*, Brepols, 1988.

Chabal P., *Africa: Modernity without development?*, ISIM Newsletter, n. 5, Leiden, 2000.

Chandler D.G., *Le Campagne di Napoleone* (orig. ed.: *The Campaigns of Napoleon*, London, 1966), Milano, 1968.

Chapman G.P. and Baker K.M. (Eds.), *The Changing Geography of Africa and The Middle East*, London, New York, 1992.

Cipolla C.M., *Vele e cannoni. Alle origini della supremazia tecnologica dell'Europa (XIV–XVII secolo)* (orig. ed.: *Guns and Sails in the early phase of European expansion 1400–1700*, London, 1965), Bologna, 1983.

Clarence-Smith W.G., *The Economic Role of the Arab Community in Maluku, 1816 to 1940*, "Indonesia and the Malay World", vol. 26, n. 74, 1998.

Colletta P. *Storia del Reame di Napoli*, Milano, 1989.

Corbin H., *Storia della Filosofia Islamica* (orig. ed.: *Histoire de la philosophie islamique*, Paris, 1964), Milano, 1991.

Cordano F. (Ed.), *Antichi viaggi per mare: peripli greci e fenici*, Pordenone, 1992.

Crofton R.H., *The Old Consulate at Zanzibar*, London, 1935.

Curtius Quintus Rufus, *Alessandro Magno*, Q. Curtii, Rufi de rebus gestis Alexandri Magni libri decem, Parisiis, 1757.

Curzon G.N., *Persia and the Persian Question*, London, 1892, 2 vols.

Davidson B., *La Civiltà Africana* (orig. ed.: *The Africans. An Entry to Cultural History*, 1969), Torino, 1995.

Davis J., *L'Italia nella diplomazia delle grandi potenze*, paper presented at the LVIII Congress of the Istituto per la Storia del Risorgimento Italiano, Milano, 2–5 October, 1996.

Devisse J., *Les Africain, la mer et les historien*, "Cahiers d'Etudes Africain", vol. 29, Paris, 1989.

Diamond J., *Armi acciaio e malattie. Breve storia del mondo negli ultimi tredicimila anni* (orig.

ed.: *Guns, Germs and Steel. The Fates of Human Societies*, New York London, 1997), Torino, 1998.

Dunn Ross E., *The Adventures of Ibn Battuta. A Muslim Traveller of the 14th Century*, no place, 1993.

Elgood R., *Firearms of the Islamic World*, London, 1995.

Eryes G.B., *Elphinstone nel Cabul, nell'Afghanistan*, in, G.B. Sonzogno (Ed.), *Compendio di Viaggi Moderni dal 1780 ai Nostri Giorni*, Venezia, 1830.

Evans D.L., *On the Designs of Russia*, London, 1828.

——, *On the Practicability of an Invasion of British India and the Commercial and Financial Prospects and Resources of the Empire*, London, 1829.

Fabietti U., *Power Relations in Southern Baluchistan: A Comparison of three Ethnographic Cases*, "Ethnology", XXXII, 1992.

Farrant L., *Tippu Tip and the East African Slave Trade*, London, 1975.

Farwell B., *Burton, a Biography of Sir Richard Francis Burton* (repr. from I° ed. 1963), London, 1990.

Fiorani Piacentini V., *Aspetti originali della politica napoleonica in Persia nel quadro del duello anglo-francese*, "Storia e Politica", Milano, 1968.

——, *L'Emporio e il regno di Hormoz (VII fine XV secolo d.C.). Vicende storiche. Problemi ed Aspetti di una Civiltà Costiera del Golfo Persico*, "Memorie dell'Istituto Lombardo", Accademia di Scienze e Lettere, vol. XXXV (1), Milano, 1975.

——, *International Indian Ocean Routes and Gwadar Kuh-batil Settlement in Makran*, "Pakistani Archaeology", 1988.

——, *Merchants —Merchandise and Military Power in the Persian Gulf (Suriyan —Shahriya —Siraf)*, "Memorie", Atti della Accademia Nazionale dei Lincei, Roma, 1992.

——, *Traces of Early Muslim Presence in Makran*, "Islamic Studies", vol. 35, n. 2, Islamabad, 1996.

Forrest D., *Tiger of Mysore. The Life and Death of Tipu Sultan*, London, 1970.

Furber H., *Imperi Rivali nei Mercati d'Oriente. 1600–1800* (orig. ed.: *Rival Empires of Trade in the Orient, 1600–1800*, Minneapolis, 1976), Bologna, 1986.

——, *John Company at Work*, Cambridge, 1948.

——, *The Overland Route to India in the Seventeenth and Eighteenth Centuries*, "Journal of Indian History", vol. 29, London, 1951.

Gardane A. De, *Mission du Général Gardane en Perse sous le premier empire*, Paris, 1865.

Gibb H.A. (Ed.), *Battuta I., Travels in Asia and Africa 1325–1354*, London, 1939.

Gibb H.A.R. and Kramers J.H., *Shorter Encyclopaedia of Islam*, Leiden, 1995.

Gilbert E., *Coastal East Africa and the Western Indian Ocean Long-Distance Trade, Empire, Migration, and Regional Unity, 1750–1970*, "The History Teacher", vol. 36, n. 1, Nov., 2002, www.historycooperative.org.journals.

Giglio C. (Ed.), *Storia Universale dei Popoli* (orig. ed.: Oliver R. & Attmore A., *Africa since 1800*, London, I° ed., 1967, II° ed., 1980), Torino, 1980.

Gray R. and Birmingham D., *Pre-Colonial African Trade: Essays on Trade in Central and Eastern Africa before 1900*, London, 1970.

Habib I. (Ed.), *Confronting Colonialism. Resistance and Modernization under Haider Ali and Tipu Sultan*, London, 2002.

Haellquist K.R. (Ed.), *Asian Trade Routes, Studies on Asian Topics*, n. 13, London, 1991.

Hatch J.C., *Tanzania. A Profile*, London, 1972.

Hawley D., *Some Surprising Aspects of Omani History*, "Journal of Asian Affairs", vol. 13, n. 1, London, 1982.

Hawley R., *The British Embassy in Muscat. A Short History*, Muttrah, 1980.

Heuman G., *Slavery, The Slave Trade, and Abolition*, in R.W. Winks (Ed.), *Historiography*, The Oxford History of the British Empire, Oxford, vol. V, 1999.

Hiskett M., *The Course of Islam in Africa*, Edimburgh, 1994.

Hitchcock M., *Research Report on Indonesian and Tanzanian Maritime Links*, IC., n. 59–60, November 1992/March 1993.

Holland Rose W.J., Newton A.P., Denion E.O. (Eds.), *The Cambridge History of the British Empire*, Cambridge, 1941.

Holdich T., *The Gates of India, being an Historical Narrative*, London, I ed. 1910, repr. Quetta, 1977.

Holmes C.F., *Zanzibari Influence at the Southern End of Lake Victoria: The Lake Route*, "African Historical Studies", vol. 4, n. 3, 1971.

Hopkirk P., *The Great Game. On the Secret Service in High Asia*, Oxford, 1991.

Hoskins H.L., *British Routes to India*, New York, 1928.

Hourani G.F., *Arab Seafaring in the Indian Ocean in Ancient and Early Medieval Times*, Princeton, 1951 (new ed. Princeton, 1995).

Hrbek I., *Towards a Periodisation of African History*, in, T.O. Ranger (Ed.), *Emerging Themes of African History*, Nairobi, 1968.

Huttenback R.A., *British Relations with Sind, 1799–1843, An Anatomy of Imperialism*, Berkeley, Los Angeles, 1962.

Ingham K., *A History of East Africa*, London, 1962.

Ingrams W.H., *Arabia and the Isles*, London, 1966.

Jabarti (Al) Abd Al Rahman, *Napoleon in Egypt* (transl. by S. Moreh), London, 1995.

Jain V.K., *Trade and Traders in Western India (AD 100–1300)*, New Dehli, 1990.

Johnson P., *The Birth of Modern*, no place, 1991.

Khuhro H., (Ed.), *Sind through the Centuries*. Proceedings of an International Seminar held in Karachi in Spring 1975 by the Department of Culture, Government of Sind, Karachi, 1981.

Ki-Zerbo J., *Storia dell'Africa Nera. Un continente tra la preistoria e il futuro* (orig. ed.: *Histoire de l'Afrique Noire. D'Hier à Demain*, Paris, 1972), Torino, 1977.

—— (Ed.), *Methodology and African Prehistory*, Unesco General History of Africa, 8 vols., vol. I, I° ed., Paris, 1987.

Kirkman J.S., *The History of East Africa up to 1700*, in, Kirkman J.S. (Ed.), *Prelude to East African History*, London, Nairobi, 1966.

Koponen J., *People and Production in Late Precolonial Tanzania. History and Structures*, Helsinki, 1988.

Lapidus I.M., *Storia delle Società Islamiche. La Diffusione dell'Islam* (orig. ed.: *A History of Islamic Societies, Islam in East Africa and the Rise of European Colonial Empire*, Cambridge, 1988), 3 vols., Torino, 1994.

Lattimore O., *La Frontiera. Popoli e Imperialismi alla frontiera tra Cina e Russia* (orig. ed.: *Studies in Frontier History*, Paris, 1962), Torino, 1970.

Leech R., *Notes taken on a Tour through parts of Baluchistan in 1838 and 1839 by Hajee Abdun Nabee, of Kabul. Arranged and translated by Major Robert Leech*, "Journal of the Asiatic Society of Bengal", n. CLIII–CLIV, London, 1844.

Leed E.J., *Per mare e per Terra. Viaggi, missioni, spedizioni alla scoperta del mondo* (orig. ed.: *Shores of Discovery. How Expeditionaries have constructed the World*, New York, 1995), Bologna, 1996.

Lenz W., *Voyages of Admiral Zheng He before Columbus*, in, K.S. Mathew (Ed.), *Ship-building and Navigation in the Indian Ocean region AD 1400–1800*, New Dehli, 1997.

Ligios G., *Sovranità, Autorità e Potere nella Pubblicistica Classica*, in, V. Fiorani Piacentini (Ed.), *Il Pensiero Militare nel Mondo Musulmano*, 3 vols., vol. III, Roma, 1992.

Limbert M., *The place of the rural in contemporary Oman*, Seminario di Antropologia del Medio Oriente e del Mondo Musulmano, Milano, 31 March, 2000.

Lobo L., *They came to Africa. 200 Years of the Asian Presence in Tanzania*, Dar-es-Salaam, Tanzania, 2000.

Lofchie M.F., *Zanzibar: Background to Revolution*, Princeton-London-Nairobi, 1965.

Lombard M., *Splendore e Apogeo dell'Islam VIII–XI secolo* (orig. ed.: *L'Islam dans sa première grandeur (VIII–XI siècle)*, Paris, 1971), Milano, 1980.

Longworth Dames M., *The Baloch Race. A Historical and Ethnological Sketch*, London, 1904.

Lovejoy P., *The Ideology of Slavery in Africa*, Beverly Hills, 1981.
——, *Transformations in Slavery: A History of Slavery in Africa*, "African Studies Series", 36, Cambridge, 1983.
——, *Africans in Bondage: Studies in slavery and the slave trade in honour of Philip D. Curtin*, African Studies Program, Madison, 1986.
Malcolm J., *Histoire de la Perse*, Paris, 1821.
——, *The Political History of India from 1784 to 1823*, 2 vols., London, 1826.
——, *Sketches of Persia from the Journal of a Traveller in the East*, London, 1828.
Manning P., *Slavery and African life: Occidental, Oriental and African Slave Traders*, "African Studies Series", Cambridge, 1990.
Markovits C., *The Global World of the Indian Merchant 1750–1947*, Cambridge, 2000.
Marsh Z. and Kingsnorth G.W., *A History of East Africa. An Introductory Survey*, London, 1972.
Marshall P.J. (Ed.), *The Eighteenth Century*, The Oxford History of the British Empire, Oxford, vol. II, 1998.
Martens G.F. De, *Nouveau Recueil de Traités de l'Europe*, to. II, 1814–15, Göttingen, 1818.
Martin E.B. and Ryan T.C.I., *A Quantitative Assessment of the Arab Slave Trade of East Africa 1770–1896*, "Kenya Historical Review", Nairobi, 1977.
Martin E.B. and Martin C.P., *Cargoes of the East. The Ports Trade and Culture of the Arabian Seas and Western Indian Ocean*, London, 1978.
Masson C., *Narrative of a Journey to Kalat*, London, 1843, 4 vols., repr. Karachi, 1976.
Mathew G., *The Dating and Significance of the Periplus of the Erithrean Sea*, in, Chittick N. and Rotberg R. (Eds.), *East Africa and the Orient: Cultural Syntheses in Pre-Colonial Times*, New York-London, 1975.
Matveiev V., *The Shaping of Swahili Civilization*, "Unesco Courier", Paris, 1979.
Mc Lynn F., *Stanley. The Making of an African Explorer*, Oxford, 1991.
Mccaskie T.C., *Cultural Encounters: Britain and Africa in the Nineteenth Century*, in, A. Porter (Ed.), *The Oxford History of the British Empire*, vol. 3, Oxford, 1999.
Miles W., *History of Tipu Sultan*, Calcutta, no date.
Morice J.V., *Projet d'un établissement sur la côte orientale d'Afrique*, no place, ca. 1777.
Mosca L., *Opere sul Madagascar e le altre isole del sud-ovest dell'Oceano Indiano nella Biblioteca della Facoltà di Scienze Politiche*, Napoli, 1985.
——, *Africa Orientale, Kenya, Tanzania, Uganda*, Napoli, 1993.
——, *Il più bell'enigma del mondo: il popolamento dell'isola del Madagascar*, Napoli, 1994.
Mughal M.Y., *Studies in Sind*, Jamsoro, 1989.
Müller K.O., *Geographi graeci minores*, Parisiis, 1882.
New C., *Life, Wanderings and Labours in Eastern Africa*, London, 1873, repr., no place, 1971.
Newitt M., *The Comoro Islands, Struggle against Dependency in the Indian Ocean*, London, 1984.
Nicolini, B., *Little Known Aspects of the History of Muskat and Zanzibar during the first half of the 19th Century. Proceedings of the Seminar for Arabian Studies*, 27, London, 1997.
Nicolini B. and Redaelli R., *Quetta: history and Archives. Note of a Survey of the Archives of Quetta*, Extract from "Nuova Rivista Storica", Year LXXVIII, Fasc. II, 1994.
Northcote Parkinson C., *Trade in the Eastern Seas 1793–1813*, London, 1953.
——, *War in the Eastern Seas 1793–1815*, London, 1954.
O'Connor A., *The Changing Geography of Eastern Africa*, in, G.P. Chapman and K.M. Baker (Eds.), *The Changing Geography of Africa and the Middle East*, London, 1992.
Panikkar K., *Asia and Western Dominance*, London, 1953.
Pastner C.&S., *Agriculture Kinship and Politics in Southern Baluchistan*, "Man", 1972.
——, *Adaptation to State-Level Polities by the Southern Baluch*, "Pakistan, The Long View", Durham, 1977.

Pastner S., *Desert and Coast: Population Flux between Pastoral and Maritime Adaptations in the Old World Arid Zone*, "Nomadic People", n. 6, 1980.

——, *Conservatism and Change in a Desert Feudalism: the Case of Southern Baluchistan*, "The Nomadic Alternative", Paris, no date.

——, *Feuding with the Spirit among the Zikri Baluch: the Saint as Champion of the Despised*, "Islam and Tribal Societies", London, 1984.

Philips C.H., *The East India Company 1784–1834*, I° ed., Manchester, 1940, II° ed., no place, 1961.

Phillips C.S., Potts D.T., Searight S. (Eds.), *Arabia and its Neighbours. Essays on pre-historical and historical development presented in honour of Beatrice de Cardi*, Brepols, 1988.

Plures, *Conference on the History of Tanzania*, Dar-es-Salaam, 1967.

Porter A., (Ed.), *The Nineteenth Century, The Oxford History of the British Empire*, vol. III, Oxford, 1999.

Pottinger H., *Travel in Beloochistan and Sinde*, London, 1816.

Prior J., *Voyage on the Frigate "Nisus"*, London, 1819.

Ranger T.O., *Emerging Themes of African History*, Nairobi, 1968.

Rao A.M., *Le strutture militari nel regno di Napoli*, paper presented at the LVIII Congress of the Istituto per la Storia del Risorgimento Italiano, Milano, 2–5 October, 1996.

Rediker M., *Sulle Tracce dei Pirati. La storia affascinante della vita sui mari del '700* (orig. ed.: *Between the Devil and the Deep Blue Sea*, Cambridge, 1987), Casale Monferrato, 1996.

Reichert F.E., *Incontri con la Cina. La scoperta dell'Asia orientale nel Medioev* (orig. ed.: *Begegnungen mit Cina. Die Entdeckung Ostasiens in Mittelalter*, Sigmaringen, 1992), Milano, 1997.

Ritchie G.S., *Persian Gulf Pilot. Comprising the Persian Gulf and its approaches, from Ras al Hadd, in the South-West, to Ras Muari, in the East*, XI ed., London, 1967.

Risso P., *Merchants and Faith. Muslim Commerce and Culture in the Indian Ocean*, Boulder, 1995.

Rivoyre De D., *Mascate. Il Sultanato dell'Oman*, Milano, 1900.

Rossabi M., *Decline of the Central Asian Caravan Trade* in, J.D. Tracy (Ed.), *The Rise of the Merchant Empires. Long-Distance Trade in the Early Modern World 1350–1750*, Cambridge, 1994.

Ruphin Andriananjanirina S., *Zanzibar—1840–1939*, Thèse nouveau doct. en Histoire, Paris VII, Paris, 1993.

Rushbrook Williams L.F., *The Black Hills. Kutch in History and Legend*, no place, 1958.

Sachau E. (Ed.), *Alberuni's India. An Account of the Religion, Philosophy, Literature, Geography, Chronology, Astronomy, Customs, Laws and Astrology of India about A.D. 1030*, 2 vols, I ed. London, 1888, new ed. New Dehli, 1998.

Salim A.I., *The East African Coast and Hinterland, 1800–45*, in, J.F. Aiayi (Ed.), *Africa in the Nineteenth Century until the 1880s*, Unesco General History of Africa, Paris, 1989.

Salzman. P.C., *Adaptation and Political Organization in Iranian Baluchistan*, "Ethnology", X, n. 4, 1971.

——, *Multi-Resource Nomadism in Iranian Baluchistan*, "Perspectives on Nomadism", Leiden, 1972.

Scammel G.V., *The First Imperial Age. European Overseas Expansion c. 1400–1715*, London, 1989, repr. London, 1992.

Scarcia Amoretti B., *Controcorrente? Il caso della comunità khogia di Zanzibar*, "Oriente Moderno", Year XIV (LXXV), nn. 1–6, Roma, 1995.

Schroeder P., *The Transformation of European Politics 1763–1848*, Oxford, 1994.

Scott A.F., *Scinde in the Forties*, London, 1912.

Scott S.F. and Rothaus B. (Eds.), *Historical Dictionary of the French Revolution, 1789–1799*, Connecticut, U.S.A., 1985.

Seton-Watson H., *The Russian Empire 1801–1917*, Oxford, 1967.

Severin T., *The Sindbad Voyage*, London, 1983.

Sheriff A.M.H. and Ferguson E. (Eds.), *Zanzibar under Colonial Rule*, London, 1991.

Sinanti D., *Strategy and Structure. A Case Study in Imperial Policy in British Baluchistan*, PhD Thesis, University of London, London, 1991.

Sinclair W.F. (transl. and annotated), *The Travels of Pedro Teixeira; with his "Kings of Harmuz" and extracts from his "Kings of Persia"*, London, 1902, repr. Nendeln, 1967.

Sobel D., *Longitudine* (orig. ed.: *Longitude*, USA, 1995), Milano, 1997.

Sordi M., *Alessandro Magno tra Storia e Mito*, "Ricerche dell'Istituto di Storia Antica", Milano, 1984.

Spear P., *India. A Modern History*, London, 1961.

Spooner B., *Politics Kinship and Ecology in Southeast Persia*, "Ethnology", VII, n. 2, 1969.

Subramanian L., *Indigenous Capital and Imperial Expansion in western India. Bombay, Surat and the west Coast*, Dehli, 1996.

Sutton J.E.G., *The Settlement of East Africa*, in, A.B. Ogot (Ed.), *Zamani. A Survey of the East African Coast*, I° ed., Kenya, 1968, repr., no place, 1974.

Sykes P.M., *Ten Thousand Miles in Persia*, London, 1902.

——, *A History of Persia*, 2 vols., London, 1930.

Taylor A.J.P., *The Struggle for Mastery in Europe, 1948–1918*, Oxford, 1954.

The Imperial Gazetteer of India, Provincial Series, Baluchistan, Lahore, Pakistan, 1908.

Tate P., *Kalat. A Memoir on the Country and the Family of the Ahmadzai Khans of Kalat, from a Ms. account by the Akhund Muhammad Sindik, with notes and appendices from other manuscripts as well as from printed books*, Calcutta, 1896.

Theal G.M., *Records of South Eastern Africa*, London, 1898.

Tibbets G.R., *Arab Navigation in the Indian Ocean before the coming of the Portuguese. (being a translation of Kitab al-Fawa'id fi usul al-bahr wa'l-qawa'id of Ahmad b. Majid al-Najdi)*, London, 1981.

Torri M., *Trapped Inside the Colonial Order: The Hindu Banker of Surat and their Business World during the Second Half of the Eighteenth Century*, in, G. Borsa (Ed.), *Trade and Politics in the Indian Ocean. Historical and Contemporary Perspective*, New Delhi, 1990.

——, *Storia dell'India*, Roma, 2000.

Tracy J.D. (Ed.), *The Rise of Merchants Empires. Long-Distance Trade in the Early Modern World, 1350–1750*, Cambridge, 1990.

Trevelyan G.M., *History of England*, London, 1960.

Triulzi A. (Ed.), *Storia dell'Africa*, Firenze, 1979.

Ubaydli A., *Democracy in the Islamic World: the Agrarian Economy as a Base for Early Democratic Tendencies in Oman*, Brismes Conference, University of St. Andrews, 8–10 July, 1992.

Unomah A.C. and Webster A.C., *East Africa: The Expansion of Commerce*, in, Flint J. (Ed.), *The Cambridge History of Africa, 1790–1870*, 8 vols., London, 1976, vol. V.

Vansina J., *La Tradizione Orale e la sua Metodologia*, in, J. Ki Zerbo (Ed.), *Storia dell'Africa. La Preistoria dell'Africa* (orig. ed.: *Methodology and African Prehistory. Unesco General History of Africa*, Paris, 1987), Milano, 1989.

Vercellin G., *Tra veli e turbanti. Rituali sociali e vita privata nei mondi dell'Islam*, Venezia, 2000.

Vismara N., *La monetazione di Maria Teresa*, unpublished paper presented at a Conference at the Circolo Culturale Milanese, Milano, May, 2002.

Wallerstein I., *Africa and the World Economy*, in, J.F.A. Aiayi (Ed.), *Africa in the Nineteenth Century until 1880s, Unesco General History of Africa*, 8 vols., vol. VI, Paris, 1989.

Watson I.B., *Fortifications and the 'Idea' of Force in Early English East India Company Relations with India*, in, D.M. Peers (Ed.), *Warfare and Empires. Contact and conflict between European and non-European military and maritime forces and cultures*, vol. 24, Ashgate, 1997.

Westerlund D. and Evers Rosander E. (Eds.), *African Islam and Islam in Africa*, London, 1997.

Wheeler M., *Rome beyond the Imperial Frontiers*, London, 1954.

Wilson T.H., *James Kirkman and East African Archaeology*, in, J. de V. Allen and T.H. Wilson (Eds.), *From Zinj to Zanzibar*, "Paideuma", n. 28, Wiesbaden, 1982.

Witherell J.W. (Ed.), *The U.S. and Africa: Guide to U.S. Official Documents and Govt.-sponsored Publications on Africa, 1785–1975*, Washington, 1978.

Wolpert S., *A New History of India*, Oxford, I° ed., 1977, II° ed., 1982.

Wright M., *East Africa, 1870–1905*, in, R. Oliver and G.N. Sanderson (Eds.), *The Cambridge History of Africa, 1790–1870*, 8 vols., vol. VI, Cambridge, 1985.

GLOSSARY

Ahl al-zang, land of the zang, blacks, 60

amān, protection, 38, 65

banyan, trader, 38, 39

barasti, hut, 23, 25

Beglerbeg, tribal chief, 15

bulushi, Baluch in kiswahili, 150

dār al-Islām, land of Islam, 121, 122

darogha, administrator, 13

dhows, western Indian Ocean boats, 11

diwan, counsellor, advisor, 119

ghee, clarified butter, xix, 9, 20, 46

Gining'i, invisible town in Pemba island, 43

ginn, jinn, or *pepo*, ghosts, 44

hakim, chief, 16

harīm, place where only women live, 122

Ichthyophagoi, fish eaters, 5

jagir, grant, 33

Jam, tribal chief, 13, 14

jam'dar, pl. *majemadari*, head of the gate, 6

jumbe, head farmer, 69, 119

khanjar, typical Arab knife, 24

kiambo, land for cultivation, 69, 125

kiwanda, pl. *viwanda*, land for cultivation, 69

madiwani, local governors, 133

mafundi, craftsmen, 118

mahoga, kind of flour, 51

majengo, urban agglomerate, 69

mashamba, sing. *shamba, champ*, plantation, 69, 70, 118, 121, 126, 127

masika, wind, 27

mshenzi, pl. *washenzi*, uncivilized, barbarians, 120

msimamizi, guardians, 121

msitu, rural areas, 126

muscatel, wine from Muscat, 24

mushrikūn, politheists, 38

mwaka kogwa or *nauruzi*, 62

mwinyi mkuu, local African chief, 119

mwungwana, pl. *waungwana*, urban Muslims, 68

naib, local Arab chief, 17

niabat, Chiefdom, 17

nokoa, kadamu, first or second head slaves, 121

nyka, wild, 26

pagazi, caravan porters, 123

pembe, ivory, 128

qādi, judge, religious leader, 44

qanat/kariz, irrigation system, 19

raḳaba, responsiblity of a slave, 117

roga, wizard, 43

sāhil, sawāhil, belonging to the coast, 56

sahukar, trader, usurer, 36

sanbūq, boat, 11

sardar, tribal chief, 14, 15, 17

sarruf, money taster, 38

shawkāh, the strength, xvii, xxii, 6, 34

sheikh, Arab chief, 113

shihiri, mercenaries, 40

sowar, soldier, 6

suria, concubines, 121

udugu yangu, slave with a specified social status, 121

umm walad, slave girl who has born her master a child, 117

utamaduni, those who lived in stone towns, 68

vaniyo vanij, vanya, merchant, 38, 113

vibaruna, hired slaved, 118

vuli, wind, 27

waganga/wachawi, wizard, 43, 44, 60

wakulia, slaves transported as children, 120

wanda, natural scrubland, 125

waqf, religious endowments, 69

washenzi, pl. of *mshenzi*, pagans, 68

watumwa wajinga, slaves not yet assimilated, 120

wazalia, pl. of *mzalia*, slaves born on the African coast, 120

wazee, Swahili aristocracy subdivision, 119

zangik, black, 58

zanj, black from East Africa, 58, 60

zingi, African black, 58

Zingion, land of the blacks, 59

NOTES ON THE INDEX

1) Methods of transcription and transliteration are same as in the text; 2) when family names could not be found, people's entries have been placed under their first names; 3) the names of authors have only been included when their works are discussed in considerable detail, or when they did play historical roles; 4) all dates are A.D.; 5) military and political titles are reproduced as in the text; 6) when found, complete names have been indicated.

The author is fully aware of the limits of this index and its phonetic-etymologic transcription; nevertheless, it is hoped that specialists will make allowances for the inconsistencies, and that the general readers will not feel too disturbed.

INDEX OF NAMES

INDEX OF PLACES

ABOUT THE AUTHOR

BEATRICE NICOLINI graduated in the Faculty of Political Science, Catholic University of the Sacred Heart, Milan, Italy, where she teaches History and Institutions of Africa. She has a degree in International Relations and Comparative Government from Harvard University and a Ph.D. in History of Africa from Siena University, Italy. Her doctoral research focused on Southwestern Asia, the Persian/Arab Gulf, and sub-Saharan East Africa. The history of the Indian Ocean, together with slave routes and development issues in sub-Saharan East Africa, is the focus of her current research, which she explores through archive and field-work investigations. She has published nearly one hundred texts, most of them peer-reviewed in English and some also translated into Arabic. A contributor to numerous international workshops and conferences, Professor Nicolini often has been the only Italian scholar invited to participate in these meetings.

CPSIA information can be obtained at www.ICGtesting.com
Printed in the USA
BVOW07s1939300713

327272BV00001B/7/P